POSTMODERNISM AND ORGANIZATIONS

edited by

John Hassard and Martin Parker

WITHDRAWN

SAGE Publications
London • Newbury Park • New Delhi

Editorial arrangement and Introduction
© John Hassard and Martin Parker, 1993
Chapter 1 © John Hassard, 1993
Chapter 2 © Paul Jeffcutt, 1993
Chapter 3 © Steve Linstead, 1993
Chapter 4 © Gibson Burrell, 1993
Chapter 5 © Pippa Carter and Norman Jackson, 1993
Chapter 6 © Dag Björkegren, 1993
Chapter 7 © Mats Alvesson, 1993
Chapter 8 © Albert J. Mills, 1993
Chapter 9 © Jeff Hearn and Wendy Parkin, 1993
Chapter 10 © Michael I. Reed, 1993
Chapter 11 © Paul Thompson, 1993
Chapter 12 © Martin Parker, 1993

First published 1993

SAGE Publications Ltd
6 Bonhill Street
London EC2A 4PU

SAGE Publications Inc
2455 Teller Road
Newbury Park, California 91320

SAGE Publications India Pvt Ltd
32, M-Block Market
Greater Kailash – I
New Delhi 110 048

British Library Cataloguing in Publication Data

Postmodernism and Organizations
    I. Hassard, John   II. Parker, Martin
    302.3

ISBN 0–8039–8879–6
ISBN 0–8039–8880–X (pbk)

Library of Congress catalog card number 93–084225

Typeset by Mayhew Typesetting, Rhayader, Powys
Printed in Great Britain by The Cromwell Press Ltd,
Broughton Gifford, Melksham, Wiltshire

Contents

Notes on Contributors

Mats Alvesson is Professor at the Department of Business Administration, University of Gothenburg. He has held previous positions at the Universities of Stockholm, Linkoping and Lund. He has written a number of books, including *Organization Theory and Technocratic Consciousness* (de Gruyter, 1987), *Corporate Culture and Organizational Symbolism* (de Gruyter, 1992, with P.O. Berg), *Critical Management Studies* (Sage, 1992, edited with H. Willmott), *Cultural Perspectives on Organizations* (CUP, 1993) and *Communication, Power and Organisation* (Routledge, in press). His journal articles have appeared in *Academy of Management Review, Acta Sociologica, International Studies of Management and Organizations, Journal of Management Studies, Organization Studies* and the *Scandinavian Journal of Management*.

Dag Björkegren is Associate Professor of Organization and Management Theory at the Stockholm School of Economics. He received his PhD from that institution in 1986 and has been a visiting scholar at Harvard and New York Universities. His research interests include managerial and organizational cognition, postmodernism and organizations, and cultural studies and organizations. He is currently researching the management of art-related businesses such as film and television companies. His most recent book is *Arts Management* (Carlsson, 1992, in Swedish).

Gibson Burrell fortunately has a sister who readily confirms that he was born in the early hours of 31 January 1948 some 2 kilometres north of the Tyne bridge. She also tells him that he comes from an unbroken line of ag. labs. and insists she went to school with Bobby Charlton. Some families have all the luck, like.

Pippa Carter is a lecturer in the Department of Management Systems and Sciences at the University of Hull. She previously studied at the University of Lancaster, Manchester Business School and Aston University. Her research interests are in the field of organization theory with particular regard to the ontological and epistemological conditions of organization, the function of management and the nature of work. These research interests are informed by the radical critique of organization theory. Her current research is concerned with the potential contribution of the modernism/postmodernism debate to organization theory.

John Hassard is Professor of Organizational Behaviour at Keele

University, England. He previously taught at the London Business School and Cardiff University. His publications include *Time, Work and Organization* (Routledge, 1989, with others), *The Theory and Philosophy of Organizations* (Routledge, 1990, co-edited), *The Sociology of Time* (Macmillan, 1990, edited) and *Sociology and Organization Theory* (Cambridge, 1993). His research interests lie in organization theory and industrial sociology.

Jeff Hearn is Reader in Sociology and Critical Studies on Men, and co-convenor of the Research Unit of Violence, Abuse and Gender Relations, University of Bradford. His publications include *The Gender of Oppression* (Wheatsheaf, 1987), *'Sex' at 'Work'* (Wheatsheaf, 1987, with W. Parkin), *The Sexuality of Organization* (Sage, 1989, co-edited), *Taking Child Abuse Seriously* (Unwin Hyman, 1990, co-edited), *Men, Masculinities and Social Theory* (Unwin Hyman, 1990, co-edited) and *Men in the Public Eye* (Routledge, 1992). He is currently researching men's violence to women, and organizational responses to such violence, and working on a co-edited collection on Managements and Men.

Norman Jackson is a lecturer in the Management Division of the University of Newcastle-upon-Tyne. After a number of years in engineering management he gained an MA in Organizational Psychology from the University of Lancaster and a PhD from Aston University, having also studied at Manchester Business School. His research contributes to the radical critique of organization theory and he is particularly interested in the possibility of non-surplus repressive organization. He is currently researching the contribution of the modernist/postmodernist debate to this possibility.

Paul Jeffcutt re-entered higher education as an adult educator after a diverse career in manufacturing and service industry. He went on to obtain a Masters Degree and PhD from Manchester University, where his interests developed to focus on organizational culture and symbolism. A formative member (from 1982) of the Standing Conference on Organizational Symbolism, he was appointed to the Chair of this international cross-disciplinary research network in 1992. He currently lectures in the School of Management of Stirling University, having previously held positions at Southampton and Manchester Universities. As his chapter exemplifies, his recent work has been concerned with tensions between modern and postmodern approaches to the understanding of organization, a topic upon which he is currently finalizing a book, *The Culture of Organization: Modern and Postmodern Understandings of Organizations and Social Change* (Sage, forthcoming).

Steve Linstead is currently visiting scholar (1992–93) at Hong Kong University of Science and Technology. From 1989 to 1992 he was Senior

Teaching Fellow in Management Development at Lancaster University developing programmes for major corporate clients. Previous to that he was Head of European Business at Leeds Metropolitan University. His original discipline was English and American literature (Keele, 1970–74; Leeds, 1976) which developed into an interest in organizational development (Sheffield Hallam, 1980) and ideology and ambiguity (Sheffield Hallam, 1984). He has a special interest in international business as well as organizational symbolism and the social anthropology of organization. He is a member of the board of the Standing Conference on Organizational Symbolism and is a former editor of its house journal, *SCOS Notework*.

Albert J. Mills is Associate Professor of Management at St. Mary's University, Nova Scotia. His research interests centre on the impact of organizations on people – focusing on organizational change and human liberation, in particular the liberation of women. These concerns were formulated through involvement in the movements for social change that dominated the 1960s. Mills's early images of organization – images of frustration, of power disparities, of conflict and of sexually segregated work – were experienced through a series of unskilled jobs and given broader meaning through campaigns for peace, environmental survival, social change and women's liberation. He is the co-author of two books, *Organisational Rules* (OUP, 1991, with S. Murgatroyd) and *Reading Organization Theory* (Garamond, in press, with T. Simmons). He is also the co-editor of *Gendering Organisation Theory* (Sage, 1992, with P. Tancred).

Martin Parker is a Lecturer in Sociology at the University of Staffordshire, Stoke-on-Trent. Since 1988 he had been trying to finish a PhD on organizational culture after previously having studied at the Universities of Sussex and London (Goldsmiths College). His research interests are in cultural studies, organization theory and his three children (Ben, Max and Zoe), but he still has dreams about wishing to become a freelance journalist. He is no longer interested in postmodernism but if someone offers him a book contract he may think again.

Wendy Parkin is a half-time Senior Lecturer in Social Work and Applied Social Studies at the University of Huddersfield and also a half-time social worker in a family centre with Kirklees Metropolitan Council. Her research and writing has focused on issues of gender and sexuality within organizations, for example 'Private experiences in the public domain' in J. Hearn et al. (eds), *The Sexuality of Organisation* (Sage, 1989). Her recent writing has focused on emotionality and organization and she is also interested in exploring feminist perspectives on older women in organizations. She has also published on her practice in the field of child protection.

Michael Reed is Senior Lecturer in the Department of Behaviour in Organizations, University of Lancaster. He has published in the fields of organizational analysis and the sociology of management. Recent publications include *Redirections in Organisational Analysis* (Tavistock, 1985), *The Sociology of Management* (Harvester, 1989) and *The Sociology of Organisations: Themes, Perspectives and Prospects* (Harvester, 1992). His current research interests focus on the restructuring of expert work in advanced industrial societies and its implications for work organization and management.

Paul Thompson is Professor in the Business School of the University of Central Lancashire. He has published numerous books and articles; the latest is an edited collection entitled *Labour in Transition: the Labour Process in Eastern Europe and China* (Routledge, 1992, with Chris Smith). His other current research i .. rest is comparative work organization. When not being a business acaɑemic he edits *Renewal: A Journal of Labour Politics*.

Introduction

Martin Parker and John Hassard

The chapters in this book are arranged as a movement from an exposition and celebration of the ideas of postmodernism to a series of critiques. This may not suit some of the authors who are wedded to a more polysemic model of knowledge, but the editors feel that this preserves the modernist ideas of linear argument that academic and publishing conventions usually require. Should readers wish to subvert the editors' intention they should read the book backwards to reverse the flow of argument. That much, at least, we have learned from postmodernism.

This volume was conceived at a conference entitled 'Towards a new theory of organisations', held at the University of Keele in April 1991. Eight of the chapters were presented as papers at that conference but all have been revised, and those by Hassard, Burrell, Hearn and Parkin, and Parker have been written for this volume.

The first chapter by John Hassard forms a general introduction to the issues raised in the book. Hassard begins by outlining the distinction between postmodernism as a periodization of organizational and social forms (postmodernity – an ontology) and postmodernism as a set of problems with the representation of knowledge about organizations (an epistemology). He then distinguishes between two forms of modernism, a totalizing systemic modernism that is so often the Aunt Sally of post-modernists and a critical modernism that is intent on radicalizing the enlightenment project. The writings of Derrida, Lyotard and Baudrillard are then analysed and their consequences for organizational theory are examined in terms of representation, reflexivity, writing, difference/ *differance* and decentring the subject. Rather than commit himself to an absolute position, Hassard argues for a middle ground that recognizes the instability of knowledge but is at the same time engaged in an attempt to say meaningful things about organizations. He concludes by outlining a 'relational' theory of power that leans on this form of 'soft' post-modernism.

The next three chapters provide views of why postmodernism deserves to be taken seriously within organization studies. Paul Jeffcutt's piece provides theoretical and referential weight to a postmodern manifesto by locating the emergence of postmodern understandings within the field of postmodern anthropology and the literature on organizational symbolism. Jeffcutt's argument is that there has been a change of focus from the problem of how the researcher can interpret data to postmodern concerns for representing knowledge. Issues of rhetoric and narrative hence become central as a way of understanding what it is that organization theorists are doing when they write about organizations. Jeffcutt's own writings are clearly central here since his 'I' cannot escape the deconstruction of the authorial 'we'. He finds that few organization theorists have achieved the kind of postmodern ethnography that would move them from modernist forms of representation, and that this is largely due to the commodification of academic knowledge, a point that Burrell expands upon later. His alternative is a form of writing that continually resists the separation of order and disorder, and hence is only an opening for more discourse and never an attempt to have the final word on a particular organizational topic.

The chapter by Steve Linstead builds upon Paul Jeffcutt's chapter in arguing for the possibility of 'deconstructive ethnography'. Linstead suggests that the engagement with the other and the insoluble problems of relativism that this poses for the researcher means that any form of ethnography prefigures the postmodern abandonment of the meta-narrative. However, he insists that an ethnography that takes deconstruction seriously does not have to abandon all standards of logic and truth. Arguing against forms of 'vulgar deconstruction', Linstead suggests that a closer reading of Derrida allows us to see how organizations can be viewed as multi-authored texts that partially inscribe subjectivities upon actors. He then applies these insights to corporate culture and corporate image, suggesting that the simulacra of organizational identity always contains within it its own negation – the other, the suppressed. The aim of deconstructive ethnography is hence to demystify hegemonic thought, but without recourse to some external standard. Rather than asking 'is this true?', Linstead wishes us to ask 'how is this truth effect achieved?'

Gibson Burrell's chapter demonstrates the power of postmodernism and postmodern modes of writing to subvert academic conventions. As with a video that the author developed for the Keele conference, this paper 'pisses on the feet' of modernist conservatism. It sits uneasily within this collection but were it to do otherwise it would be failing in the task it sets itself. Burrell argues that if postmodernism is of any value it is not simply as another theoretical perspective. Along with Jeffcutt he suggests that the modernist university values conformity to core values as a way of establishing the credibility of the goods it trades in. Bureaucratic discipline and the valorization of linear argumentation lead to the restriction of the academy to a modernist marketplace – everything has a price but value is discussed infrequently. Against this logocentric sterility, Burrell proposes the possibility of the sensual postmodern university in which desires are no longer suppressed and new forms of knowledge and representation are encouraged. The ironies of such a suggestion from a Professor of Organizational Behaviour at a modernist university are not lost on Burrell, but then serious playfulness is an essential constituent of his postmodernism.

The next section contains five papers that engage with postmodernism without losing sight of a critique that in some way evades or transcends it. Pippa Carter and Norman Jackson focus on the absence of novel theories of motivation in the organizational context. They argue persuasively that Vroom's expectancy theory can be seen as an example of an 'embryonically postmodern' theory of motivation to work. Unlike previous modernist and managerialist theories, Vroom eschews the possibility of a grand narrative of motivation and, as a result, has produced a theory that cannot be inserted into modernist management practice. Expectancy theory effectively argues that motivation is a matter of subjective definition and cannot be theorized on a law-like basis. As a consequence modernist attempts to manage by rationalized forms of action must be seen as – in a Foucauldian sense – attempts to coerce actors through a discourse of consensus which does not reflect the actual polymorphous perversity of employee desires. Carter and Jackson conclude that management itself may be an intrinsically modernist practice and, as such, unable to cope with issues of subjectivity and plural rationalities.

Dag Björkegren's chapter compares the practices and products of art and organization theory. He argues that the practice of producing objects of beauty for the appreciation of an elite is common to both fields. The criteria by which value and quality are judged are hence the result of socially constructed practices which do not necessarily rely on assessments of usefulness or truth. Björkegren follows Baudrillard in describing this as a form of 'hyper-reality' in which words and images are connected through 'fictional', socially relative, forms of intellectual practice. He concludes by suggesting that the aesthetic value (form) of a given work in organizational science may be a more valuable guide to its usefulness than its supposed relation to truth (content). Echoing Linstead, instead of asking 'is this true?', he asks 'is this beautiful?'

Mats Alvesson's piece on metaphors is similarly influenced by the postmodern 'turn', but with specific reference to language. He begins by arguing that organizations cannot be directly apprehended in some pre-theoretical way and that, instead, the linguistic metaphors we use shape the objects of our enquiry. The advantages of such a recognition are that it, firstly, allows for a recognition of pluralism and difference, and secondly can enable core assumptions about the nature of organization to be more clearly articulated. Alvesson deepens Gareth Morgan's (1986) insights into this area by suggesting that it is not only the root (first order) metaphor that matters, but also its modifier (second order), which sharpens and focuses the enquiry. He concludes by suggesting that metaphors are helpful in generating creative thought, but that a fully blown acceptance of relativism is neither consequential nor helpful. Instead he asserts that debate about the value and effect of metaphorical thought can sensitize organization theorists to new forms of 'moderate rationality'.

The chapter by Albert Mills makes links between modernist and male understandings of rationality. Using a broadly Foucauldian line of inquiry he notes that conceptions of the self developed in organizations are characterized by patriarchal forms of discipline which, he argues, are politically and theoretically disabling. If we follow a loosely postmodern form of analysis, the modernist assumption of the existence of a unique and authentic self gives way to an account of selves constructed in and through discourse. Whilst Mills 'uses' postmodernism, he is clearly reluctant to commit himself to saying that it is a sufficient account in itself, since he suggests that it does not provide the grounds for effective political strategies of resistance, a position which is also adopted in the following chapter.

Jeff Hearn and Wendy Parkin's piece attempts to ask whether postmodernism is an approach that opens spaces for the theorization of oppression in organizations. As with the previous authors, they are somewhat qualified in their enthusiasm. They note that, within a postmodern worldview, organizational inequalities (for example gender, sexuality, ethnicity, disability and age) are often reduced to Derridian difference – a concept which they argue has little political force. However, it is not easy to disavow the possibility of postmodernity being 'useful' when many writers articulate it as a method that can deconstruct the *male*stream of social science. They conclude that power over what counts as theory is, in itself, a form of oppression. As a consequence, any attempts to totalize (postmodern included) should be treated with suspicion if they hide socially constructed relations of power.

The final three chapters develop positions that are more explicitly critical of postmodern formulations. Mike Reed stresses that variations on the discontinuity thesis tend to ignore the extent to which organization theory has strong underlying continuities. Reed asserts that modernity (and modernism) is not dead, or even dying, but is instead becoming more radicalized and global. He suggests that the picture painted of modernism by the adherents of postmodernism is far too totalizing in itself and that modernity contains elements of critique and reflexivity that are too important to deny. Indeed, Reed goes further in suggesting that the postmodern critique may itself, by commission or omission, do much to support authoritarian and imperialistic ideas. In seeking to more beyond, or around, postmodernism to a new sense of intellectual heritage Reed is clearly calling for a kind of 'grounded rationality' that does not claim everything but does not disavow the possibility of knowing something and persuading others of its importance.

Paul Thompson in a sense echoes Reed's argument in dismissing postmodernism as a distraction from key issues in organizational analysis, though he does so from a more clearly socialist standpoint. Thompson focuses initially on an arena that is outlined by John Hassard in Chapter 1, the possibility of a postmodern organization (as opposed to a postmodern epistemology of organization) and clearly has little sympathy for such a periodization. He accuses postmodernists of having fallen victim to technological determinism and of revisiting a discredited version of the convergence thesis with no empirical foundation for so doing. Thompson asserts that capitalist forms of organization are about control and that, although the techniques and language may be changing, postmodernists mistake the surface of organizations for their substance. In epistemological terms Thompson suggests that even postmodernists need some conception of what is 'real' in order to pursue their totalizing theory of modernism. He, then, like Hassard in Chapter 1, pursues the concept of power to illustrate that an analytic notion of 'power everywhere' will simply not cope with the manifest inequalities in the consequences of action. Thompson concludes by asserting the difference between attractive theory for literary criticism and the political responsibilities of organization theorists whose engagement with postmodernism reflects a disengagement with the politics of organizations.

The final chapter, by Martin Parker, continues and elaborates the critical arguments of Reed and Thompson. Parker suggests that the oppositions of modernity–postmodernity and modernism–postmodernism are unhelpful. He argues that the periodization is a distraction from a rigorous analysis of organizational changes within global capitalism, and that the epistemology is both flawed and dangerous in ethical–political terms. Whilst accepting many of the implications of postmodern thinking he argues that postmodern relativism is essentially a way of avoiding responsibility for the implications of organizational analysis. Relying loosely on neo-pragmatist arguments Parker asserts that postmodern theories of organization may be philosophically defensible but they are not useful, merely a way of being more 'heteroglossic' than the next theorist. Parker argues that the very act of writing itself involves a claim that 'the world can be seen like this', and it hence becomes incumbent on theorists to be clear about what aspects of organizations they wish to change and what their intended outcomes might be. He concludes by suggesting that what he terms 'critical modernism' can support such arguments, and that postmodernism is therefore a set of ideas that should enable organization theorists to think more reflexively about their own political and ethical motivations.

Finally, the editors would like to thank Ian Atkin, Louise McArdle and Penny Tyldesley, who all enabled the original conference to run smoothly, and Sue Jones and Rosemary Campbell at Sage for their editorial advice and support. The production of the conference and this book prove at least that social organization is a practical possibility, even if none of the participants are likely to agree on how or why it is done, and each would tell different stories about what actually happened.

1

Postmodernism and Organizational Analysis: an Overview

John Hassard

This chapter introduces elements of a postmodern approach to organizational analysis. We contrast modern and postmodern forms of explanation and explore a family of terms derived from these two concepts. In so doing we discuss whether postmodernism is best described as an 'epoch' or an 'epistemology', a distinction which underpins current debates. Through reference to the works of Jean Baudrillard, Jacques Derrida and Jean-François Lyotard, we produce an inventory of key concepts for postmodern organizational analysis – 'representation', 'reflexivity', 'writing', '*differance*' and 'de-centring the subject'. By explicating the main arguments associated with these concepts – and by developing the middle ground between the epoch and epistemology positions – we lay conceptual foundations for a nascent postmodern theory of organizations.

What is Postmodernism?

In its most stark sense, postmodernism stands for the 'death of reason' (Power, 1990). It offers a frontal assault on methodological unity. Through the postmodern method of 'deconstruction' (Derrida, 1978) a whole range of philosophical pillars are brought down, the most notable of which are the 'unities' of meaning, theory and the self.

Power (1990) suggests that as there is no absolute line to demarcate the modern from the postmodern, the latter comes to signify both the termination of the former and a differentiated continuation of it. This inherent ambiguity is accepted in order to offset the tendency of commentators to make simple categorizations. Power notes, for example, that while modernist trajectories in the visual arts have challenged the concept of autonomous representation, postmodernism appears in contrast to be more radical still. Postmodern visual art seems to represent:

> a continuation of this avant-garde aesthetic without a nostalgia for direct contact with a 'real world' . . . the postmodern aesthetic of the sublime is precisely such a conscious withdrawal from traditional concepts of artistic reality. It seems to make visible the fact that there is something which may be

thought but cannot in principle itself become visible or represented. (Power, 1990: 110)

The first characteristic feature of postmodernism, therefore, is that it rejects the notion that reference is, or can be, a univocal relation between forms of representation (words, images, etc.) and an objective, external world. At the postmodern level of analysis the focus is upon 'the rules grounded in practices which precede subjectivity' (Power, 1990: 111), which is essentially the structuralist attack upon the philosophy of consciousness. There is no real space for the voluntary actor as, instead, the actor's space is found in the notion of action as 'play' rather than as 'agency' (see Lyotard and Thébaud, 1985). For Power, postmodern analysis succeeds in distancing itself from the assumptions of unity implicit in the Enlightenment notion of reason. Unlike modernism, where there is faith in the recovery of a relationship with nature, postmodernism gives rise simultaneously to 'increasing liberation from the natural world and to the splintering of culture into discrete spheres' (Power, 1990: 111). In postmodern thought, therefore, energies are released that demand reunification yet assert its impossibility.

Other writers define the modern or postmodern through contrasting associated sets of antinomies (cf. Featherstone, 1988; Clegg, 1990). Featherstone (1988), for example, expands upon a family of terms derived from these two generic concepts. Specifically he contrasts: 'modernity and postmodernity', 'modernization and postmodernization' and 'modernism and postmodernism'. On deploying these terms, Featherstone notes how the prefix 'post' seems to signify 'that which comes after'. The postmodern appears to represent a break with the modern, which is defined in contrast to it. Like Power, however, he suggests that the situation is more complex than this, for the term postmodernism is also used to denote not so much a rupture with, as a negation of, the modern. While in one sense the postmodern is that which comes after the modern, in another it is an abandonment of the modern, with the emphasis being placed on a relational move away.

A further distinction is that between postmodernism as the signifier of a historical periodization, or as a theoretical perspective. This underpins both Bauman's (1988a, b) demarcation of 'postmodern sociology' and a 'sociology of postmodernity' and Parker's (1992a) splitting of post-modernism ('with a hyphen') from postmodernism ('without a hyphen'). Both writers use their first term to signal a new epoch of sociological inquiry and the second to suggest a new form of epistemology (see Table 1.1).

In the first use, postmodernism as an epoch, the goal is to identify features of the external world that support the hypothesis that society is moving towards a new postmodern era. The practice is based on the realist notion that we simply need to find the right way of describing the world 'out there'. The 'post' prefix is related to a number of other concepts which reflect specific features of post-modern society. While the

Table 1.1   *Postmodernism as epoch and epistemology*

	Perspective	
Level of analysis	Epoch	Epistemology
Discipline	History	Philosophy
Ontology	Realism	Difference
Epistemology	Foundationalism	Anti-foundationalism
Subject-matter	Ethno-industrialism	The text
Method	Empiricism	Serious play
Evidence	Brute facts	Paradoxes

most common of these are post-Fordism, post-capitalism and post-industrialism (Bell, 1974; Piore and Sabel, 1984; Harvey, 1989), Callinicos (1989) notes how that at least 15 other 'post'-prefixed terms share this naming of a new historical period. A theme associated with many of these post-prefixed concepts is that the social and economic structures reproduced since the industrial revolution are now fragmenting into diverse networks held together by information technology and under-pinned by what Lash and Urry (1987) call a 'postmodernist sensibility'. The emphasis is placed upon 'disorganization, untidiness and flexibility'. Writers who ride this bandwagon suggest that these 'New Times' (Hall and Jacques, 1989) require explanation and codification. It is assumed that if we can understand them we may be able to control them.

In contrast to the notion of post-modernism as an historical epoch, postmodernism as an epistemology reflects developments in post-structuralist philosophy. Postmodern epistemology suggests that the world is constituted by our shared language and that we can only 'know the world' through the particular forms of discourse our language creates. It is argued, however, that as our language-games are continually in flux, meaning is constantly slipping beyond our grasp and can thus never be lodged within one term. The task of postmodern writing, therefore, is to recognize this elusive nature of language, but never with the aim of creating a meta-discourse to explain all language forms. We must beware of trying to explain formal structuring, for this is impossible. The 'myth of structure' is just one of the processes through which social action is reproduced. The postmodern theorist should instead seek to uncover 'the messy edges of mythical structure, the places where the [structuring] process becomes confused and defies definition by the discourses that are used within it' (Parker, 1992a: 10).

Modernism: Theory and Analysis

To examine the possibilities for a postmodern paradigm in organizational analysis we must first explore the characteristics of our other generic concept, *modernism*. To achieve this we will define the main theoretical positions within the modernism debate and clarify what is meant by the modernist approach to organization theory.

According to Cooper and Burrell modernism is 'that moment when man invented himself; when he no longer saw himself as a reflection of God and Nature' (1988: 94). Like Power (1990) and Featherstone (1988), Cooper and Burrell trace the origins of the modernist trajectory to the Enlightenment notion of 'reason', which is held to be the highest of human attributes. Similarly they point to the influence of Kant, and centrally his suggestion that we discover reason when we cease to depend on any external authority as the basis of belief. Kant's idea of 'dare to know' (*Aude sapere*) offers a 'critical' posture in which we not only display powers of rational discrimination but also have the courage to express them.

Cooper and Burrell suggest that reason was also appropriated by writers on society. Notable were works by Saint-Simon and Comte on the particular problems of government and administration brought about by increasing industrialization. Indeed, in these writings we find elements of organizational thinking. Cooper and Burrell suggest that at this historical point reason was appropriated by 'an early form of systems thinking which subverts its critical edge to the functional demands of large systems' (1988: 94–5). While Saint-Simon's followers were drawing up a blueprint for the *système de la Mediterranée* (a projected association of peoples of Europe and the Orient through a network of railways, rivers and canals), Comte was, likewise, defining industrial organization as the foundation for community and progress. Modernization became represented by the organization of knowledge as expressed in the development of macro-level technological systems.

We find, therefore, two theories of modernism emerging here. On the one hand we have a *systemic modernism*, which reflects 'the instrumentation of reason envisioned by Saint-Simon and Comte', and, on the other a *critical modernism*, which offers 'a reanimation of Kant's programme of enlightenment' (Cooper and Burrell, 1988: 95). We will examine these in turn.

Systemic Modernism

In contemporary writing it is *systemic* modernism which represents the dominant form of reason (Cooper and Burrell, 1988). This is characterized by the notion of 'instrumental rationality', a significant expression of which is found in Bell's (1974) thesis that modern, or 'post-industrial', society differs from earlier societies in relying on knowledge that is predominantly theoretical. In Bell's notion of the post-industrial epoch we find theoretical knowledge of a kind that is both systematic and technocratic. The main purposes of knowledge are to facilitate social control and to direct innovation and change. Theoretical knowledge offers a rational methodology for administering the large-scale systems which control patterns of activity in the modern world. The technologies developed to accomplish this include cybernetics, game theory and decision theory. The main function of these technologies is to define rational action and the means for achieving it. Rational action is that which will choose the best outcome when confronted with numerous competing alternatives. The main social achievement of systemic modernism, therefore, is to facilitate the control of complex and large-scale operations through a range of highly programmed knowledge technologies.

Critical Modernism

In contrast, critical modernism stands against the programmatic absolutism of systemic modernism. The main contemporary advocate of this position is Habermas (1972, 1974, 1979, 1981, 1987), whose objective is to confront the increasing power of instrumental reason in social life and in so doing to recapture the spirit of enlightened rationalism for late modernism. Habermas seeks to decode the repressive dimensions of instrumental reason and to effect the emancipation of social actors (Connerton, 1980; Power, 1990). For Habermas, discourse is the medium of analysis because language is the medium of reason. Habermas outlines the contradiction between ordinary language, whose foundations lie in the spontaneous actions of the life-world, and the instrumental–calculative language of modern rational systems (Held, 1976). Obscured but still active within ordinary language is a form of natural reason which communicates itself through instinctive wisdom.

The modern fate of this communicative rationality, however, has been its repression by the discourse of systemic modernism (Cooper and Burrell, 1988). Critical reason is urgently required because of this colonization of the life-world by systemic reason. We require Kantian reason to enable us to emancipate social actors from the totalizing control of systemic logic. For Habermas it is through the 'language of the community' that we will rediscover that lost sense of enlightenment that Kant first revealed to us (Power, 1990).

Nevertheless, despite the opposition of systemic and critical forms of modernism – the one championing the mechanization of social order, the other seeking the emancipation of the life-world – they share a commitment to an inherently logical social world constituted by reason (Cooper and Burrell, 1988). In systemic modernism the rational subject is the system itself, which acts according to a cybernetic discourse in which reason is a privileged property distinct from its parts. In critical modernism, on the other hand, it is the knowing subject who, through experiencing a network of meanings, and thus the common sense of ordinary language, reaches the consensus of human understanding. In both positions, therefore, we find the assumption of an underlying unity that provides legitimacy and an authoritative logic. What is criticized, above all, in these two forms of modernism are positions that would fragment the idea of this unity. As Cooper and Burrell state: 'it is such legitimizing meta-positions to which postmodernism objects' (1988: 98).

Modernism and Organizational Analysis

The development of a modernist trajectory in organizational analysis is described by both Gergen (1992) and Clegg (1990). Gergen contrasts an advancing postmodern period for organization studies with a retreating modern one. He suggests that modernism has advanced in concert with faith in the notion of progress and our absorption in the machine metaphor. These various assumptions remain central to Western culture and have left a lasting impression on our theories of organization. Not only have modernist principles granted the professional investigator a privileged position in the domain of organizational inquiry, but they have promised that progress can be attained in our understanding of organizational life. Gergen notes how such views are variously represented in:

> Scientific management theory along with time and motion methodology. General systems theory in its various modifications and extensions, including contemporary contingency theory (e.g. Lawrence and Lorsch). Exchange theorists (e.g. Homans), along with related investigators of equity and bargaining and expectancy value analyses of individual behaviour. Cybernetic theory in which organizations approximate sophisticated mechanical automata. Trait methodology which presumes the stability of individual patterns of behaviour and the possibility of selecting individuals to fit different positions . . . [and] cognitive theories of individual behaviour [in organizations] (see also Ilgen and Klein 1989). (1992: 211–12)

Gergen argues, however, that the paradigm of modernist organization theory may be in decline. While the modernist discourse is far from exhausted, for a great deal of research is still carried out in its name, Gergen feels that it has lost its sense of 'lived validity'. While organization theory has so far drawn its inspiration predominantly from the modernist leitmotif, he suggests that the gains to be acquired from this tradition are diminishing. There is generally a 'yearning for alternatives', the modernist discourse having almost become a 'formalism' or, worse, an 'ideological mystification'. For Gergen, it is this sense of unease which has prompted a growing interest in the 'postmodern turn' in organization studies.

In contrast, Clegg (1990) suggests that, rather than notions from the Enlightenment, it is the concept of structural differentiation which represents the motive force behind the modernist theory of organizations. A key part of the sociological enterprise has been the emphasis on processes of differentiation as a basic element of the modern experience. In particular, the division of labour is one of the core concerns of both classical sociology and political economy. It was, for example, one of the key issues which joined the otherwise disparate works of Adam Smith, Karl Marx and Emile Durkheim.

In tracing this trajectory, Clegg argues that the key modernist thesis on organizations is found in Max Weber's work. Indeed the 'modernness' of modern organizations stems from the way they are appreciated 'within a genre of more of less harmonious variations on the theme of Weber's composition of bureaucracy' (1990: 176). Clegg suggests that Weber's work on bureaucracy ranks alongside, if not above, Smith's pin factory and Marx's conception of the labour process. It is Weber and his followers who personify organizations as one of the greatest achievements of modernity. In Weber's work, organizations become the crucible within which processes of differentiation take place.

Clegg argues, therefore, that modernism is premised on an increasing functional differentiation of social phenomena. Organizations are the frameworks which link these differentiations, and the management of modernity involves practices for integrating the core processes of differentiation. It was Weber's achievement, Clegg suggests, to construct a model which codified and formalized the rules for such administrative differentiation. This model saw the managerial function constructed as distinct from that of ownership. Under modernism, organizational relations were mediated through 'mechanisms of market exchange and state regulation rather than through moral sentiment' (1990: 11).

Postmodernism: Theory and Analysis

As with modernism, we are confronted with a diverse set of positions in writings on postmodernism. We argue, however, that commonalities can be found within sociologically influenced work on postmodernism. To illustrate this, and to help produce a postmodern epistemology for organizational analysis, we explore the ideas of three leading writers: Jean Baudrillard, Jean-François Lyotard and Jacques Derrida.

Jean Baudrillard and 'Simulations'

Jean Baudrillard was perhaps the first to organize into a postmodern social theory the anticipations of postmodern thought by, for example, Barthes (1957), Debord (1970) and Lefebvre (1971) (Kellner, 1988a; Norris, 1990). Although Baudrillard did not adopt the term postmodernism until the 1980s, his work of the late 1960s/early 1970s incorporated many prescient themes, notably in the images of the consumer society, the media and its messages, cybernetic systems, and contemporary art and sign culture (see Baudrillard, 1968, 1970, 1972).

In Baudrillard's work from the mid-1970s onwards, however, an essentially postmodern form of social theory is developed, for example, in *Symbolic Exchange and Death* (1976), *In the Shadow of the Silent Majority* (1983a) and especially *Simulations* (1983b). Baudrillard discusses the end of an era of modernity dominated by production and industrial capitalism and the onset of an epoch of postindustrial postmodernity represented by alternative forms of technology, culture and society

(Kellner, 1987). Unlike in modern industrial society, where production was the cornerstone, in the postmodern society simulations structure and control social affairs. Models and codes precede reality and are reproduced unceasingly in a society where the contrast between the real and the unreal is no longer valid. As Baudrillard says, 'the real is not only what can be reproduced, but that which is already reproduced, the hyper-real' (1983b: 146). In this society, 'simulacra' – that is, copies or representations of objects or events – now constitute 'the real'. Whereas in the modern world we possess meaning in the laws of production, we find in the postmodern world a universe of nihilism where concepts float in a void.

As a postmodern society theory, Baudrillard's work operates on a high plane of abstraction. He suggests a break between the modernist epoch and the postmodern one, and develops a set of propositions to conceptualize this transition. While modernist society was characterized by an explosion in the forces of social differentiation – especially through mechanization, market forces and commodification – Baudrillard argues that postmodern society sees an implosion of nearly all those forms of distinction and opposition maintained by orthodox social theory, especially those of high and low culture and image and reality (Kellner, 1988b). This signals the end of the grand positivist statements of traditional social theory, and thus the end of the finalities of social systems analysis. While modernist social theory is characterized by the increasing social differentiation of structural–functionalism, postmodern social theory will be defined as a process of 'de-differentiation' (Lash, 1988).

Jean-François Lyotard and 'The Postmodern Condition'

The challenge of developing a specifically postmodern social theory is most commonly associated with the work of Jean-François Lyotard and his book *The Postmodern Condition* (1984).

In this book, Lyotard's goal is to describe 'the condition of knowledge in the most highly developed societies' (1984: xxiii). In so doing he decides to use the word postmodern to describe that situation. This term he feels is appropriate to describe, 'the state of our culture following the transformations which, since the end of the nineteenth century, have altered the game rules for science, literature, and the arts' (1984: xxiii).

Lyotard feels that the term 'postmodern' reflects an epistemology which is appropriate to these new conditions of knowledge. The book's main aim, therefore, is to document the differences between the grand narratives of philosophy and social theory and what he terms 'postmodern science', which represents a preferable form of knowledge to traditional modes of philosophical and scientific inquiry. It is in this context that Lyotard defines postmodern discourse as 'the search for instabilities' (1984: 53). New and unpredictable moves are needed for science to make progress, yet these are antithetical to the idea of scientific 'performativity', linked as it is to the notion of a stable enterprise in which inputs and outputs can be regulated and controlled (Power, 1990).

This objective, in turn, resonates with Lyotard's associated definition of modernity, which, unlike Baudrillard's, is primarily a form of knowledge rather than a condition of society. Lyotard argues that modernity reflects that dominant form of science which acquires its legitimacy through reference to a 'meta-discourse', that is, through recourse to grand narratives such as the creation of wealth or the emancipation of the subject. In contrast, postmodernism is about the rejection of totalizing meta-narratives. Postmodern knowledge, to quote a popular passage, 'refines our sensitivity to differences and reinforces our ability to tolerate the incommensurable. Its principle is not the expert's homology, but the inventor's paralogy' (1984: xxv).

Lyotard's epistemology is a language-game approach in which knowledge is based on nothing more than a number of diverse discourses, each with its own rules and structures. In Lyotard's view, each language-game is defined by its own particular knowledge criteria. Importantly, no one discourse is privileged. The postmodern epistemology concerns knowledge of localized understandings and acceptance of a plurality of diverse language forms. Thus postmodernism sees the fragmentation of grand narratives and the discrediting of all meta-narratives.

Indeed, Lyotard rejects what he sees as the totalizing master narratives of modern, orthodox social theory, especially those reductionist narratives derived from Marx and Hegel. The postmodern society is one in which actors struggle with an infinite number of language-games within an environment characterized by diversity and conflict. As Lyotard says in the appendix to the English version of *The Postmodern Condition*, 'Let us wage a war on totality; let us be witness to the unpresentable; let us activate the differences and save the honour of the name' (1984: 82).

Lyotard's work is not, however, concerned exclusively with epistemological issues. A sociological perspective is also developed in which the status of social knowledge changes as societies enter the postindustrial age and culture enters the postmodern age (Featherstone, 1988). Like Baudrillard, Lyotard in many ways associates postmodernity with post-industrialism. He suggests that postmodern society is one of complex and rapid change, as reflected in new advances in science and technology. Above all, it is an information society characterized by an explosion in scientific knowledge. Lyotard clearly sides with the postindustrialists when he defines postmodern society as 'the computerization of society'. He does not, however, like Bell and his followers, suggest that postmodern society is a postcapitalist one. Instead, he suggests that developments in knowledge and technology follow the traditional pattern of the flow of funds in capitalist societies (Kellner, 1988a).

Finally, while Lyotard suggests that it is impossible to suggest a new theoretical paradigm for social theory – for this will inevitably involve the construction of another grand narrative – he does, however, offer a new paradigm for the practice of theory. He calls this 'just gaming' (see Lyotard and Thébaud, 1985), which is an idea developed from his earlier view of social action as a language-game. The inference is that modern science is founded on 'indeterminancy', and thus it poses a 'dialectic of difference' (Cooper and Burrell, 1988). In 'doing' science, we only enter into a number of games with our colleagues. We are in fact involved in a form of 'serious play', which sees us intervene in a variety of language-games, make moves in a number of debates or discussions, and seek to oppose the moves and positions of other players while advancing our own positions. The notion of language-game includes the idea of 'agonistics' or contest, which give rise to social action. Domination is vitalized not through the complete annihilation of one opponent by the other, but by maintaining a state of continuous 'difference'. When struggle goes out of the game it loses its potential to motivate social action (Cooper and Burrell, 1988).

Jacques Derrida and 'Deconstruction'

The notion of 'difference' is more readily associated with the work of Jacques Derrida (1973, 1976, 1978, 1981, 1982). Derrida's postmodernism is founded on a *deconstructive* approach which, on inverting the notion of construction, illustrates how superficial are the normative structures of the social world. Derrida's aim is to show how processes of rationality serve to obscure the logical undecidability which resides at the core of social action (Cooper and Burrell, 1988). For Derrida, normative social structures result from systems which privilege unity and identity over separation and difference. In contemporary society this occurs within a modernist arena in which the contest between reason and unreason takes place. Derrida's project is founded on the postmodern notion that knowledge and discourse have to be 'constructed' from a 'chameleonic' world (Cooper and Burrell, 1988). Social action is encapsulated by a phenomenological ambivalence, which serves as the motive to organize.

Derrida, however, presents a unique interpretation of ambivalence, one which transcends the psychology and sociology of the actor and locates itself instead in the concept of the 'text'. The text refers both to the interplay of discourses – political, social, philosophical, etc. – and the stage upon which the process of deconstruction is enacted (Cooper, 1989). In deconstruction theory, Derrida's goal is to expose the inherent contradictions which reside in any text. He argues that the general yet mistaken assumption is that texts reflect the notion of language as a medium for the communication of thoughts; that is, thoughts hold primacy and language is merely the vehicle of their transmission. Derrida argues that this reflects a mental strategy of 'logocentrism', for it pivots social action upon the notion of an original 'logos' or prefixed meta-physical structure (e.g. mind, soul, reason, etc.) which validates social action. Logocentrism is a structure with a given point of origin that censors the self-errant tendencies of the text; it specifies a central form of organization with an essential metaphysical origin that guarantees stability and surety (Cooper, 1989).

Inherent within this censoring process, therefore, is a tendency for logecentric 'encapsulation', or a process of prefixed boundary main-tenance. To offset this tendency, deconstruction employs the twin movements of 'overturning' and 'metaphorization' (Cooper, 1989). The process of overturning assumes that texts are structured around polar opposites (e.g. good–bad, male–female) in which one term dominates the other. Derrida suggests that to deconstruct the opposition we initially must 'overturn the hierarchy at a given moment' (1981: 41, quoted in Cooper, 1989: 485). He is careful, however, to draw our attention to the trap of simply overturning the superordinate term and replacing it with the subordinate, which in turn becomes the superordinate and is now ready for overturning.

To avoid this, he suggests we activate the second movement of deconstruction, 'metaphorization', which is the distinctive feature of deconstruction as a critical posture. The objective of metaphorization is to prevent the deconstructive process regressing into a simple structure of opposites. Derrida achieves this by demonstrating that there is an essential double-dynamic *within* the opposition. This sees the superordinate term defined only in contrast to the subordinate term, which itself serves to threaten constantly the former's hegemony (Cooper, 1989). The relation-ship between the opposing terms is in fact one of mutual dependence in which each term 'inhabits' the other. Seemingly unique terms submit to a process which sees them combine in a continual exchange of 'undecid-able' characteristics. The process of undecidability underpins the dynamic of metaphorization and becomes a medium for textual transportation in which the speaker or writer is simply carried along (Cooper, 1989).

Towards a Conceptual Framework

Having introduced some basic ideas from leading writers, our aim now is to outline the distinctively postmodern approach to knowledge (see Table 1.2). In so doing we make progress towards a conceptual framework for postmodern organizational analysis. To realize this we begin by exploring five key epistemological notions which underpin the works of Baudrillard, Lyotard and Derrida – 'representation', 'reflexivity', 'writing', '*differance*' and 'de-centring the subject'.

Representation

We have suggested that postmodernism as a theoretical perspective is directed against the idea of a theory-neutral observation language. In particular it is directed against the 'picture theory' of language in which physical properties of the world are considered fixed while language can be adjusted to meet the needs of their description. Among works which have stimulated a protest against the picture theory approach are Wittgenstein's (1953, 1958) analysis of 'language-games', Kuhn's (1962, 1970, 1974) description of 'scientific revolutions', and Pepper's (1972) analysis of 'world hypotheses'. These writers examine the effects of reality rather than the causes. They argue that our knowledge of the world is constructed as a problem of 'representation' rather than one of factual accuracy.

A first theme of the postmodern approach to knowledge, therefore, is the notion of the replacement of the factual by the *representational* (see Gergen, 1992; Linstead and Grafton-Small, 1992). This suggests that attempts to discover the genuine order of things are both naive and mistaken. In particular the modernist objective of determining factual relationships through the empirical method is considered problematic. In the modernist view the empirical method reflects the assumption that language is a slave to observation and reason. The logic is that through rigorous research we will continuously improve language through a more accurate correspondence with nature.

Under a postmodern approach, however, the empirical process is re-defined. The language which is produced by the empirical process does not equate with an increasingly accurate correspondence with reality. Instead, it represents a process of professional self-justification. Research proceeds on the basis of discourses which are already shared within a particular scientific community. The evidence which is produced is inter-preted and justified within a restricted linguistic domain. As the empirical process starts with its theoretical assumptions intact, data produced through experimentation are defined by reference to an existing theoretical spectrum (Gergen, 1992). Findings produced through empirical science reflect pre-existing intellectual categories.

Reflexivity

In a postmodern approach to knowledge we must also possess the ability to be critical or suspicious of our own intellectual assumptions (Lawson, 1985). This is achieved through the notion of *reflexivity* (see Platt, 1989). The rationale for reflexivity is that propositions which remove representa-tion from the grasp of the factual are themselves representations. In other words they treat as real both language and a universe divorced from language. The result is that they beget their own critical analyses.

The reactions of postmodernists to this irony have been varied. Derrida has pursued intentionally ambiguous and self-negating practices in seeking to deconstruct his own propositions. In contrast, Julia Kristeva (1980b) has attempted to develop forms of expression which appear nonsensical within traditional conventions but are, she argues, sensible within a primordial semiotic. Others have proposed the less heady alternative of the intellectual 'playing the fool' (Gergen, 1992). Uniting all these approaches, however, is the view that we should not portray knowledge as a prestigious and objective estate divorced from the mundane activities of everyday life. Instead, the forms of language we call 'knowledge' should be viewed in a more humble way. Knowledge bases are things which are either more or less interesting to us, but no more than that. They are not the stuff of which ultimate commitments are made.

In Lyotard's terms, therefore, we should beware of subscribing to the grand narrative of progress, for the prime purpose of this discourse is to justify our actions. Above all, we should not subscribe to the seriousness of the progress narrative, for its assumption of unitary and linear progression only serves to suppress the possibility of a multitude of alternative voices. We must, though, acknowledge that in everyday affairs our knowledge discourses will be informed by 'serious play'. While we may cease to credit our forms of knowledge with epistemological primacy, we must accept that they are taken seriously on entering society, especially when they may alter patterns of relationships. If theories lend themselves, for example, to repulsive forms of behaviour, we must be able to subject them to criticism. This is reminiscent of Wittgenstein's (1953, 1958) view that while language-games are beyond justification, what we say within them is not.

Writing

A postmodern approach to knowledge is concerned with the way we learn to fix the flow of the world in temporal and spatial terms. For Derrida this is achieved through the notion of '*writing*'. Writing is the means by which social actors define order in their environments. It is a universal technology which is concerned with spacing, listing and contrasting (McArthur, 1986). In this sense, writing relates to the structure of representations more than to the meaning of messages (Cooper, 1989).

Derrida's aim is to overturn a logocentric image of writing which sees language as a sign system for concepts which exist independently in the object world. His concept of writing concerns the physical action of inscribing marks on a surface and not of assuming a logocentric origin beyond those marks. Writing only illustrates how the social actor is materially involved in the world through a process of reflecting. Writing is in fact a paradoxical – or 'undecidable' – form of action, for terms are always inhabited by their opposites. In this view, consciousness comes to us 'on the rebound', as the delayed effect of an involuntary action; it is 'not a direct reflection *on* the outside world but a relationship made with what has already been inscribed' (Cooper, 1989: 485). The corollary is that in the process of deconstruction the structured terms of logocentric writing are separated by showing their intrinsic 'supplementarity'. As Cooper notes:

> the various terms of a text point away from themselves to other terms in a continuous, unstoppable movement so that writing appears to be in the grip of

an autonomous self-propelling force that lies beyond the intentions of the individual actor. (1989: 486)

'Differance'

We have seen how Derrida's notions of deconstruction and writing rely on a denial of conceptual mastery and definition. It is necessary, therefore, for Derrida to develop a strategy of thought which reflects but does not capture this process. He achieves this through the notion of 'differance'. In defining *differance* we see the extension of Derrida's wish to express writing as a self-deferring process of 'difference'.

Cooper (1987) suggests that the concept of difference can be compared with the concept of 'information' in information theory, where it takes the form of a binary structure based on the idea of division. There are two ways of considering division (or difference): by focusing on the two forms that have been separated; or by focusing on the actual process of separating. While the former suggests logocentrism, through emphasizing hierarchical binary oppositions, the latter suggests that division is not simply a static act of separation but can also represent an undifferentiated state where terms are conjoined (Cooper, 1990a). Division thus both separates and joins: the act of separation also creates the image of something that is whole.

The second sense of division reflects Derrida's notion of undecidability, in which terms inhabit each other. To counter the static logocentrism of hierarchical binary oppositions – and to activate the processual sense of difference – Derrida invents the term *differance*; which is derived, in part, from Saussure's (1974) conception of language as a system of differences (Cooper, 1990a). In developing the term *differance* he incorporates two senses of the French verb *différer* – to differ (in space) and to defer (in time) – into one designation which both subverts and produces the illusion of presence and consciousness (Johnson, 1980). To explain the concept, Derrida outlines how our traditional understanding of the sign is that which we substitute for the absent thing we wish to present. The sign represents the present in its absence – it is 'deferred presence'. Derrida argues against the notion of a fully present reality that is directly available to our understanding. Instead he posits a world that is continually deferred both in space and time. Thus: 'the signified concept is never present in and of itself . . . every concept is inscribed in a chain or in a system within which it refers to the other, to the concepts, by means of the systematic play of differences' (Derrida, 1982: 11; quoted in Cooper, 1990a: 178).

Differance, therefore, can never be grasped in the present. It is an ever-active and essentially prior form of play which cannot be located in a particular place; it is perpetual absence, for the differences of *differance* do not have a specific cause; and it is continuous movement, although not the movement of things. For social theory, Derrida feels that the paradox of social action lies in the censoring of the very dynamic, *differance*, that gives the actor power. Characteristic of our conceptions of agency is an inherent tendency to deny the origins of agency. As a result, the agent *necessarily* suppresses the forces of its own 'becoming', which arise from the conflict that is *differance*. Derrida's image of agency is of a field of interactive forces activated by the process of *differance* (Cooper, 1989). To reclaim itself as an active agent, the postmodern subject must, therefore, 'view itself *in the act of distancing . . .* this is exactly the function of deconstruction which shows agency to be an enigmatic process that denies the very thing that gives it life' (Cooper, 1989: 492).

De-centring the Subject

Our final theme develops Derrida's analysis of the deconstruction of presence in terms of its implications for human agency. This is achieved through the notion of *de-centring the subject* as the locus of understanding.

From the logocentric view the human agent represents a holistic and clearly bounded cognitive universe. Human agency is founded on a personal, subjective core of awareness in which actions and emotions are coordinated from a knowing self. The agent acts within the context of its own dynamic presence.

In contrast, we have seen in Derrida's work that presence is always already mediated by absence. We noted earlier how consciousness is never a direct and unmediated experience but rather comes to us in an indirect way. In this view, agency is an artefact and subjectivity is a process of locating identity in the language of the 'other' (Harland, 1987). Agents are constituted through a symbol system which locates them while remaining outside of their awareness (Linstead and Grafton-Small, 1992).

The process which establishes agency, therefore, is one which takes recourse to the concept of the 'other' (Cooper, 1983). The subject is de-centred and thus bereft of the logocentric authority it possessed when self-aware and present. The self-conscious agent of modern psychology becomes an image which is no longer sustainable. Derrida (1978) replaces the grand isolation of the modern subject with the notion of agency as a system of relations between strata. The subject is no longer self-directing but is instead a convenient location for the throughput of discourses. As Linstead and Grafton-Small suggest, subjectivity becomes 'a weave, a texture, fragmented but intertwined rather than hierarchical and integrated, a process and a paradox having neither beginning nor end' (1991: 39).

Postmodern Organizational Analysis

We started this chapter by noting the tendency to define postmodernism as representing either a historical periodization (an epoch) or a theoretical

Table 1.2   *Elements of postmodern knowledge*

Concept	Argument
Representation	'Attempts to discover the genuine order of things must be regarded as naive and mistaken.'
Reflexivity	'We must possess the ability to be critical of our own intellectual assumptions.'
Writing	'The logocentric image of writing (which sees language as a sign system for concepts which exist independently in the object world) must be overturned.'
Differance	'We must develop a strategy which reflects but does not capture the process of deconstruction.'
De-centring the subject	'The grand isolation of the modern subject must be replaced with the notion of agency as a system of relations between strata.'

perspective (an epistemology). We have since listed five key elements of a postmodern approach to knowledge – 'representation', 'reflexivity', 'writing', '*differance*' and 'de-centring the subject'. We now discuss, in a modernist way, how these two lines of analysis offer conceptual tools for assessing contributions to the nascent postmodern approach to organization studies.

On the one hand, the epoch–epistemology distinction offers an ideal-type model for interpreting the basic orientation of the analysis. By using this distinction we can plot the degree to which an investigation is centred upon historical or philosophical concerns. On the other hand, the five knowledge bases offer a guide to the degree of epistemological sophistication present within a study. Whilst not defining intellectual worth, the presence (or absence) of these concepts indicates the extent to which basic principles have been applied.

Finally, we use this framework to show how, in their 'strong' form, both the epoch and the epistemology positions actually inhibit theory-building for postmodern organizational analysis. We argue, instead, that a position which develops the 'middle ground' between these extremes – and which employs the knowledge base to check that postmodern analysis is achieved – offers a more appropriate basis for organization studies.

The Epoch Position and Organization

A work which reflects the 'epoch' orientation is Clegg's (1990) book *Modern Organizations: Organization Studies in the Postmodern World*. In this work Clegg advances the periodization position by citing detailed empirical examples of postmodern organizational forms. Declaring his objectivist intentions from the start, Clegg remarks: 'empirical realities are neither imaginary nor whimsical: they cannot be side-stepped'

(1990: 5). Indeed the tangible description of postmodern organization structures – ones which can be distinguished from the classical modernist form of the bureaucracy – defines this work. Clegg documents the structural properties of postmodern organizations from a review of comparative data. He argues that, unlike the highly differentiated and modernist bureaucracy, the postmodern organization is based on a 'de-differentiated' form.

Specifically the postmodern organization has structural characteristics which reflect the ethno-industrial theories of 'flexible specialization' and 'post-Fordism' (see Piore and Sabel, 1984; Pollert, 1988; Smith, 1989; Hirst and Zeitlin, 1991). Clegg argues that examples of the postmodern form are found in the business enterprises of Japan, Sweden, East Asia and the Third Italy. The suggestion is that these are organizational structures in which we find, *inter alia*, a niche-based marketing strategy, a craft-oriented or multi-skilled workforce and a technical core of flexible manufacturing. Although postmodern organizational forms are as yet relatively ill-defined, Clegg suggests they may encourage, as in Sweden, progressive developments in industrial democracy and the skill levels of labour. He reminds us, however, that the postmodern form, while in certain respects appealing, may also rely upon repressive and elitist industrial practices. Such organizations may be based on a segmented labour force with a clear stratification of privilege, as in Japan.

The Epistemological Position and Organizations

Alternatively, an example of the strong epistemological position is found in the work of Cooper and Burrell (1988: see also Burrell, 1988; Cooper, 1989). Although, like Clegg (1990), Cooper and Burrell address the modernist assumptions which underpin Weber's work on bureaucracy, the implication is that postmodern concepts are appropriate to an 'anti-foundationalist' rather than positivist appreciation of organizational phenomena.

Rather than privilege the functionality associated with increasing levels of differentiation, Cooper and Burrell seek a more abstract understanding of the principles of bureaucratic organization. Their discussion of Weberian modernism centres on the alienating forces of bureaucracy and, in particular, on the notion of bureaucracy as the 'iron cage' which imprisons modern consciousness. Instead of Weber's analysis representing a functional assessment of organizational design, for Cooper and Burrell it is a grand narrative of administrative progress. Although Weber's work emphasizes the processual character of organizational life, modern organizational analysis has seen it de-contextualized and re-written to emphasize static issues of efficiency and administrative control. Such re-writing has emphasized the role of the organizational analyst as a privileged, professional observer who possesses the expertise to construct an authoritative meta-narrative of organizational development. The professional observer is able to control the increasing complexity of organizational life by overlaying a template of functional rationality on emergent and perhaps disorderly patterns of social relations. It is the modernist project which reproduces these models of control and allows predictions about organizational activities to be made by the professional cadre of administrative analysis.

Cooper and Burrell argue that the postmodern project emphasizes the futility of such totalizing tendencies. The idea of a superior, objective standpoint is completely rejected, emphasis being placed on the inherent instability of organization. The discourses of organization are no more than changing moves within a game that is never completed. Cooper and Burrell suggest that under postmodernism we should seek to disrupt continuously our normative structures about the organized world. Above all, we should seek to explode the myth of robust structural relations through establishing the fragile character of organizational life. For Cooper and Burrell a postmodern analysis should focus on 'the production of organization rather than the organization of production' (1988: 106). Under this nominalist strategy we must eschew the idea that organizations are formed and then act themselves to structure relations. We realize, instead, that it is the analysis alone which creates a discourse on organization. The constructs we employ to make sense of organization are moral imperatives which serve to presuppose certain features of organization while excluding the possibility for others. The academic study of organizations is reduced to nothing more than a series of discourses which have no prior claim to an understanding of organizational affairs.

Towards a Conceptual Framework

However, even in an analysis as sophisticated as Cooper and Burrell's, it remains difficult to discern any significant movement beyond a 'perspective' on postmodern organization, especially in the direction of a conceptual 'framework'. Although they offer a deeper level of conceptual reflection than, for example, writers who associate postmodern organization with flexible specialization or post-Fordism, it can be argued that Cooper and Burrell have, nevertheless, avoided being explicit about how concepts are developed or theories built.

Indeed, when faced with the problem of constructing a postmodern conceptual model at the institutional level we have few exemplars to consult (see Kreiner, 1989 on this point). An obvious reason for this difficulty stems from the assumptions of rationality and purpose which underpin the theory building process. Traditional theory construction is founded on belief in the factual nature of a knowable universe. The dominant knowledge bases of social theory are found to rest on logocentric foundations. Given these assumptions it seems that postmodernism must reject the very idea of theory construction at the institutional level. If a factual world is beyond our grasp, what are the grounds for developing such static formulations? Why should we seek to develop formal schemes if the method of deconstruction shows them to be objects for our amusement, elements of 'serious play' at best? Is not theory-building a form of intellectual imperialism, and one which fails to acknowledge the basically uncontrollable nature of meaning?

The main postmodern positions in organizational analysis indeed appear to be successful in inhibiting theory-building, albeit in an unconscious way. On the one hand, the epoch position provides positivist descriptions which are developed with scant reflection on the philosophy of postmodern analysis. On the other hand, the epistemological position explodes the myth of the structural form, but fails to account for the everyday experiences of social actors. As such, neither develops a framework in which formal organization is acknowledged as a phenomenon which is accessible to postmodern deconstruction.

Developing the Middle Ground

For those wanting a more robust framework for postmodern organizational analysis, a way forward is offered by Gergen (1989, 1992), who argues that postmodern statements do not necessarily leave us bereft of the potential for theory-building. Gergen suggests that the discourses which have historically shaped organization theory – romanticism and modernism – are beginning to lose their lustre, especially when compared with the emergent discourse of postmodernism. Although Gergen does not wish to suggest that postmodernism has greater explanatory power than these older discourses, he feels that it is more closely attuned to the spirit of the times.

Gergen argues, in fact, that the hallmark of an organization theory should be whether or not it supports patterns of relationships we feel have positive rather than negative consequences for social life. He feels that 'if the function of theories is *not* derived from their truth value, but from their pragmatic implications, then theoretical voice is restored to significance' (1989: 17). It is suggested that the potential for theory building is in fact greater under postmodernist conditions than under modernist ones. Under modernism, an acceptable theory is constituted by years of 'pure' research by scientists before being 'applied' in the real world by practitioners – that is, by members of a separate culture. Under postmodernism, however, the essence of theory is not its database but its intelligibility.

Indeed it is the successful communication of this intelligibity which provides the grounds for its usefulness. Theory and practice are inseparable: there is 'no language of understanding placed beyond the boundaries of potential' (1989: 17). We should be continuously in the process of absorbing other cultural intelligibilities into our own. Like the postmodern architect, we should feel free to draw from the entire repository of human potentials. As postmodernists we are concerned not only with the social relationships championed or discredited by particular theories, but also with the potential for theories to offer new possibilities for our culture.

In this analysis it can be argued Gergen develops the middle-ground between the 'strong' epoch and epistemology positions. The advantage for us is that this quasi-synthetic position maintains in tension the empirical reality of organizations and the fragile nature of their reproduction. As such it represents a more fertile location for propagating a postmodern approach to organization studies.

Auditing Postmodern Organizational Analysis: the Case of the 'Relational' Theory of Power

By using elements from the knowledge base we can subject existing material in postmodern organizational analysis to a conceptual audit. This process will indicate the extent to which a postmodern interpretation has been achieved in any one piece of analysis. To assess the substance of our preferred middle ground position we can audit Gergen's deconstructionist (or 'relational') theory of organizational power. This will provide a case study of the conceptual framework in action.

Gergen argues that the concept of postmodern writing can offer new options for organization theory. Indeed it directs him to 'go-beyond' speculation about a substantive contribution to postmodern organization theory and to offer one himself, in the form of a 'relational' theory of organizational power. In accepting that a tangible aspect of organization can be addressed from a deconstructionist position, this work achieves a tension between the epoch and epistemological approaches to postmodern analysis. Above all, in being a programmatic evaluation, Gergen's work represents an important step towards a postmodern organization theory.

Although Foucault's work plays its part in orienting Gergen's analysis, the project draws more tangibly upon two concerns in Cooper and Burrell (1988) – the 'indeterminancy of meaning' and the tensions which result between forces for 'organization and disorganization' (see Cooper, 1990a). Gergen wishes to extend these concerns and specifically to erect the 'conceptual scaffolding' for a relational theory. He achieves this by constructing an analysis around the notions of: 'indeterminate rational-ities', 'social supplementarity', 'power as social coordination', 'power as self-destructive', and 'heteroglossia and the recovery of efficiency'. In so doing, however, Gergen also draws inspiration from the ideas of Derrida and Lyotard and, moreover, takes recourse to elements of the framework of postmodern knowledge outlined earlier, especially to the notions of '*differance*', 'reflexivity' and the 'de-centred subject'.

For analysing organizational power, Gergen argues that the postmodern 'drama' begins with the realization that the rational sayings available to the manager are in fact of indeterminate meaning. It is here that the concept of *differance* comes into play for, as Derrida suggests, the meaning of any word is derived from a process of 'deferral' to other words which 'differ' from itself. For Gergen, therefore, the strength of the single concept *differance* is that it reflects both the simultaneous and conflated processes at work in organizational power.

The postmodern plot thickens as it becomes clear that there are multiple meanings for the everyday terms used in organizational power networks. Such terms are polysemous: they have been used in many contexts and thus bear 'the trace', as Derrida says, of many other terms. The position becomes more complicated still when we discover that each term employed for clarifying an original one is itself obscured until the process of *differance* is once again set in motion. We know that these terms subsequently bear the traces of others in an expanding network of significations (see Lash, 1988 on this point). Thus, statements which appear to be but simple pieces of organizational rationality, 'on closer inspection can mean virtually anything' (Gergen, 1989: 20).

This spread of signification is also underpinned by the process of 'ironic self-negation', and thus *reflexivity* is realized. From Derrida we derive the notion that every proposition implies its own contradiction, or in other words that by affirming something we set in motion a chain of significations that confirm its negation. This process finds that each attempt at decoding the original proposition itself becomes another encoding. These encodings are in fact undecidable until constrained by a listener. A speaker may signify, but a supplement, in the form of a listener, is required to determine its meaning. The agent of propositions is therefore a *de-centred subject*. In an organization, ' a manager's words . . . are like authorless texts; once the words are set in motion, the manager ceases to control their meaning. They are possessions of the socius' (Gergen, 1989: 21–2). The rationality of a manager's actions is dependent on the reactions of colleagues and subordinates, for it is they who supply the interpretations of propositions. Managers themselves are never rational. Instead their 'rationality' is a product of collective action.

This postmodern theory of organizational power demonstrates, therefore, that we are empowered only through the actions of others – through 'social supplementarity'. This suggests that textbook theories, which locate power in individual discretion or the structural properties of organization, should be abandoned. Relational theory suggests that managers do not control the fate of their decrees. Instead power is a matter of 'social interdependence'; it is effected through the coordination of actions around specified definitions.

Furthermore, the theory suggests that as sub-units achieve power, so they simultaneously contribute to their own downfall. As a department or function becomes increasingly powerful within itself, so is the organization as a whole devitalized. As the achievement of power at the local level contains within it the negation of power originally sought, so organizations to sustain themselves require means for maintaining a dynamic tension between empowerment and disempowerment. As full consensus within an organization threatens its well-being, then organizational vitality depends on restoring the process of *differance*. This is true not only for relationships within the organization, but also for the relationship between the organization and those elements which comprise its environment.

Thus Gergen's analysis is underpinned by key concepts from the postmodern theory of knowledge – especially 'reflexivity', *'differance'* and the 'de-centring of the subject'. It is also developed from the middle-ground between the 'strong' epoch and epistemology positions. More important still, the analysis is far removed from the modernist one. The grand modernist narrative that suggests we achieve progress through the application of reason and objectivity is rejected. Similarly the image of the ideal organization as a smoothly running machine is viewed as mistaken and dangerous. Instead relational theory suggests that organizational survival depends upon 'the prevalence of creative confusion' (Gergen, 1989: 26).

Conclusions

In this chapter we have examined a new concern for organization theory – *postmodernism*. Initially the analysis saw the concept of postmodernism defined and contrasted with its sister term – *modernism*. We suggested that currently we possess no firm agreed meaning for the concepts of modernism and postmodernism. Instead we find a range of meanings associated with these generic terms.

We attempted to place some structure on the debate by identifying two main orientations within the literature – postmodernism as either a historical periodization or a theoretical position. The former approach suggests that postmodernism is an *epoch* of culture and intellectual life: the latter that it is an *epistemology*. In the former we can explain cultural change by reference to empirical examples. In the latter we counter the totalizing tendencies of empiricism by presenting a conceptual alternative.

To establish a conceptual framework we joined the epoch–epistemology distinction with themes from a 'postmodern approach to knowledge'. This was developed by introducing leading writers on postmodernism and extracting key concepts from their works. Drawing upon Derrida and Lyotard in particular we identified five key themes of postmodern knowledge relevant to social and organization theory – 'representation', 'reflexivity', 'writing', *'differance'* and 'de-centring the subject'.

Finally, these themes and distinctions formed the structure for a discussion of postmodern organization. Contrasting the epoch and epistemology positions we argued that in their present form neither offers an adequate basis for a postmodern organization theory. Instead we suggested that the middle-ground between these extremes represents a more promising location for theory development. This argument was supported by reference to a case study of Gergen's (1989, 1992) 'relational' theory of organizational power. Underpinned by elements of the conceptual framework, this study successfully deconstructed a tangible issue in organizational life.

2

From Interpretation to Representation

Paul Jeffcutt

This chapter is concerned with fundamental transitions that are taking place in organization studies (ie the theory and practice of organization) through tensions between modern and postmodern approaches to knowledge. Its primary objective, however, is not to give a further account of these reorientations in the Human Sciences, but to situate such tensions in terms of the articulation of significant problems within a particular arena of organization studies. Hence the chapter is focused on considering the theorization of culture and symbolism in organizations as a rhetorical and philosophical episode in organization studies. As will be developed throughout the chapter, I argue that contemporary debate concerning culture and symbolism in organizations exposes fundamental tensions between the problematics of interpretation and the problematics of representation in organizational analysis. In this chapter's interrogation of these important tensions, the narrative forms of such organizational interpretation come to be seen as empowering the continuing modernization of organization studies. In contrast, the chapter is concluded by the initial consideration of a theory and practice for postmodern organization studies.

Interpretation and Organization Analysis

As I have argued earlier (see Jeffcutt, 1989, 1991), the developing 'field' of organizational culture and symbolism has typically been stratified in terms of differences between interpretative strategies (for example Smircich, 1983a; Allaire and Firsirotu, 1984; Sypher et al., 1985; Smircich and Calás, 1987; Frost et al., 1991). However, such accounts have also become characterized by: on the one hand, the generation of a dense and at times seemingly trackless forest of attributions and citations from across the 'human sciences' (Marcus and Fischer, 1986); and on the other hand, the elaboration of differentiations of this 'field' that have also been exposed as contradictory, incompatible and inconsistent (see Smircich and Calás, 1987; Jeffcutt, 1989, for detailed and definitive expositions). The resultant methodological unorthodoxy and theoretical irregularity with which the 'field' has become identified (the so-called 'organization culture chaos' – see Turner, B., 1986, 1990), needs not only to be perceived as interesting (that is endearing as well as exasperating), but also as philosophically significant. In my view the complex issues and debates that have structured and delineated this putative 'field' should be approached as articulations that are exposing the problematics of interpretation in organization studies. Accordingly, following Jeffcutt (1989, 1990a, b, 1991), interpretative tensions as expressed in the organizational culture and symbolism literature can be summarized in terms of debates surrounding the following three interlinked themes:

1 culture as a frame or unit of organizational analysis;
2 the dynamics of cultural transition;
3 the orientation of the analyst to these symbolic processes.

In terms of separations traceable throughout the above themes, analysts and their products have typically become positioned in relation to epistemological, methodological and ethical debates in organizational analysis. Accordingly, across the substantial quantity of review and position papers that have both sought to situate and stratify this putative 'field' (see Jeffcutt, 1989, 1991, 1993c) a number of contradictory discourses have become constructed and embellished in order to give coherence to differing positions in the interpretation of organizational culture and symbolism:

1 culture as a corporate (managerial) possession, (aka 'Corporate Culture')
2 culture as a communal (collective) expression, (aka 'Culture in Work').

In organization studies, as we have been observing, considerable attention has already been given to the separation of these contradictory discourses in terms of producers, their positions and the products of interpretation (for example Allaire and Firsirotu, 1984; Sypher et al., 1985). The primary concern of this chapter is, hence, not only to further explore these contradictory discourses in terms of their apparent opposition, but also to investigate the nature of their connection and compatibility. In pursuing this objective, particular attention is given to the work of writers who have undertaken the theorization of organization and interpretation from the perspective of a postmodern approach to knowledge (for example Marcus and Fischer, 1986; Clifford and Marcus, 1986; Clifford, 1988; Rosaldo, 1989; Spencer, 1989; Cooper, 1989, 1990a, 1992; Cooper and Burrell, 1988; Burrell, 1988; Smircich and Calás, 1987; Travers, 1989; Linstead and Grafton-Small, 1989, 1990a, b; Arrington and Francis, 1989; Power, 1990; Daudi, 1990; Jeffcutt, 1991, forthcoming; Gergen, 1992). As we shall be considering, when working from a postmodern approach to knowledge the focus of concern in organization studies becomes switched, from the problematics of interpretation to the problematics of representation. The following discussion will introduce, situate and develop these different foci in organization studies:

As we have considered, the organizational analyst, in constructing an account of culture and symbolism in an organizational setting, is manifesting particular logics or strategies to attain both authenticity and persuasion. As an interpretative project the construction of an authoritative and credible account is a problem that is solved through the employment of an appropriate 'mode of engagement' (see Smircich and Calás, 1987). Here, through the experience and technique of the researcher, meaning is translated from data into a meaningful account. The interpretative process whereby 'reality' is apprehended, transposed and reconstituted is taken to be unproblematic; instead, it is the alternative modes of doing so (and the criteria of their appropriateness) that become the focus of dispute. This approach underpins the popularity of particular differentiations that, as we have seen, have been repeatedly used to stratify this putative 'field' of organization studies, for example culture as something an organization 'is' or 'has' (Smircich, 1983a), and the research- or consultancy-led focus of the 'field's' development (Barley et al., 1988).

In contrast, from a postmodern approach to knowledge, 'reality' is not separated from its reconstitution, and the world we know is the world as represented (see Rabinow, 1986a). However this 'reality' needs to be understood as an inscription of order in relation to the otherness (and disorder) of the 'unreal' (see Cooper, 1983; Cooper and Burrell, 1988). Hence 'reality' or 'truth' becomes an effect and not an absolute position, an outcome of a particular reading of the privileged orderings of a text by an author. Such a focus on the problematics of representation in organizational analysis leads to concern for authorship and the achievement of authority (rather than agency), and for rhetorical style in the staging of meaning effects (rather than 'mode of engagement').

In order to approach the exposure of the problematics of the representation of culture and symbolism in organization studies a number of conscious representational strategies have been adopted. The initial part of this process has been to critically review the organizational culture and symbolism literature from the perspective of a postmodern approach to knowledge. In this project, however, I had of course to acknowledge my own participation (and complicity) in the development of this particular literature, particularly in terms of ethnographic fieldwork, reporting and writing (see Jeffcutt, 1983, 1984, 1986, 1988, 1989, 1990a, b). Hence my own positioning and products have been specifically included in this critical review process, which has come to focus in particular on representational style. At the same time as undertaking this particular review of the organizational culture and symbolism literature, I have also been seeking to contribute to current debates concerning the problematics of representation in organizational analysis. These issues, which will be progressively more fully discussed and developed, can be initially expressed as paradoxes of textuality in both the inscription of order, and in the production and consumption of meanings (see Cooper and Burrell, 1988; Cooper, 1989; Linstead and Grafton-Small, 1989, 1990a, b).

Representational Styles in Organizational Interpretation

The sheer quantity of analyses of culture and symbolism completed in an enormous diversity of organizational settings, accumulated over the past decade (see Turner, B., 1986, 1989, 1990; Jeffcutt, 1989; Gagliardi, 1990; Alvesson and Berg, 1992), provides ample evidence of an emerging genre of writing in organization studies; that of organizational interpretation (for example Jones et al., 1988). The texts of this genre appear to be symptomized by a number of distinctive characteristics:

1 The employment of a range of qualitative research styles (Van Maanen, 1983; Trice, 1985; Turner, B., 1988) in the pursuit of organizational analysis in the diverse settings of the empirical 'field'.
2 The translation of a range of 'key' interpretative texts (such as Geertz, 1973) from the broad field described as the 'human sciences' (Marcus and Fischer, 1986) to the understanding of the theory and practice of organization (see Ouchi and Wilkins, 1985).

We can thus observe that such organizational interpreters have imported and re-described ways of working and writing that were established in other disciplines and in relation to other settings. In this process, analysts of organization (with markedly different degrees of insight and sensitivity) have become linked to practices of interpretation and representation that were initiated and developed over 60 years previously in British social anthropology – for example Malinowski, Radcliffe-Brown et al. (see Geertz 1988; Clifford, 1989), and in the Chicago School of Sociology – for example Park, Burgess et al. (see Adler and Adler, 1987; Van Maanen, 1988). These interpretative practices, though evolving through different arenas of social research ('developing world' rural communities/'developed world' urban communities), have informed traditions of representation which have been formative in the recent proliferation of organizational interpretation.

Yet, as we have also been considering, this recent proliferation and profusion of organizational interpretation appears to have been both confusing and confused. Hence, on the one hand, the genre manifests competition between interpretative strategies expressing 'modes of engagement' that are perceived as contradictory, incompatible and 'all speaking at the same time' (Smircich and Calás, 1987). On the other hand, the genre manifests confusion within interpretative strategies with frequent disjunctures between the approaches adopted for the generation of research data and the abstractions employed in the interpretation and representation of that material (see Jeffcutt, 1990b).

In order to pursue the exploration of these issues, the following section of the chapter summarizes a review of the representational styles (ie narrative voice and form) employed by organizational interpreters as they seek to construct persuasive accounts of both fieldwork, and the 'field' of organizational culture and symbolism (see also Jeffcutt, 1991, 1993c). As we shall observe, sympathetic to the 'classic norms' of interpretative research (see Clifford, 1989; Rosaldo, 1989), the genre of organizational interpretation appears to have been likewise dominated by the representational style of the quest (see Turner, B., 1990). In this representational form a heroic figure (the questor) undertakes an arduous journey towards a compelling but forbidding objective (Culler, 1975; Bordwell, 1985). The quest can thus be understood as a heroic process of passage through which the questor, and his or her world, becomes re-ordered and re-formed. As the following sections elaborate, in the course of this process of passage (the quest), struggles and transformations take place which expose a number of recurring narratives:

Epic (a perilous journey contains a crucial struggle, success in this ordeal results in the exultation of the hero). The epic narrative is centrally concerned with a melodramatic passage that has three distinct stages (see Denzin, 1990). The questor here becomes transformed from a state of seduction to a state of redemption through success in a crucial ordeal (the struggle of corruption). This popular narrative form has expression in two distinctive directions in the literature.

On the one hand, we have 'practitioner tales' of quests that seek to achieve corporate success in the face of threats from both within (inefficiency) and without (competition). Here organizational culture and symbolism becomes the transitional force through which such 'excellence' is achieved. We are hence regaled with travellers' tales from management gurus and visionaries concerning the dramatic objectives of organizational turnaround and regeneration. A typical ordeal would begin with the identification of an organization's attachment to traditional working practices that were outmoded but unchallenged. Such seduction by 'bureaucratic' obstacles and handicaps (for example Peters and Waterman, 1982) both exemplifies and intensifies the nature of the ordeal, whilst raising the corruptive spectre of failure which is usually juxtaposed with glowing configurations of organizational success (for example Deal and Kennedy, 1982; Mitroff and Kilmann, 1985). Redemption occurs through the heroic struggle with these limitations (such as radical restructuring, transformations in employee and managerial effectiveness), and culminates in the organization's assertive rebirth and subsequent burgeoning (see Slatter, 1984). With vision, charisma and belief identified as the special qualities that enable the successful attainment of this quest, many texts are thus concerned with the mystical properties of leadership (such as Garfield, 1986), as well as the implementative strategies of control (such as Hickman and Silva, 1985). The narrator here typically adopts the position of one who has witnessed the attainment of the quest, and hence uses the voice of a prophet or evangelist (see Wright, 1987; Thomas, 1989) in dispensing persuasive strategies to encourage recalcitrant others.

On the other hand, we have 'researcher tales', epic narratives that are both moral (Denzin, 1990) and confessional (Van Maanen, 1988). The isolated questor here embarks on a process of academic passage towards the interpretation of culture and symbolism in a particular setting. Success in the quest is the achievement of a persuasive account, through the ordeal of being physically and theoretically exposed. The qualities that empower success here are those of endurance and academic purity. These epic tales take the form of melodramatic memoirs whereby the questor exposes their passage through the self-same transitional steps of seduction, corruption and redemption. Here authors reveal both their physical and emotional transition (initiation, identification with, and estrangement from natives in the field – for example Van Maanen and Kolb, 1985); as well as their theoretical transition (investment in traditional methods, the failure of those methods, and the recovery of a persuasive form of theorization – for example Agar, 1986). Accordingly, through this exposure of the trials and tribulations of the quest the narrator attains the authority of self-abasement, and is empowered to interpret a culture from the point of view of the 'natives'. These heroic tales are typically told through the voice of a privileged witness or acolyte.

Romantic (obstacles are posed by opponents in a restrictive society, these are overcome enabling passage into a new and integrated state of society). This is perhaps the most pervasive narrative form in the literature on organizational culture and symbolism, having numerous stylistically linked expressions. The objective of a harmonious and integrated society is expressed in a desire for organizational unity, with culture and symbolism as the agency by which obstacles and restrictions are overcome. These divisions are exposed as the products of processes of change (such as organizational growth, technological change; see Morgan, 1988), the forces of which are needing to be controlled and harmonized. These texts typically adopt anthropomorphic modes of expression (for example 'founders', 'legacy', 'life-cycle'; see Dyer, 1985; Lundberg, 1985) in a search to articulate a corporate meta-narrative (such as 'saga', 'myth', 'tradition'; see Pettigrew, 1979; Berg, 1985) that will re-create an organizational state of harmony and unity that has become lost or subverted. In an interesting paradox there are proponents of both managerial and anti-managerial arguments who employ this narrative form. On the one hand, we have texts which privilege management's a-cultural position as orchestrators of meta-narratives; that is as the managers of creative tension in the process of organizational adaptation (see Kanter, 1983; Peters, 1987). On the other hand, we have texts which express a romantic humanism, where the articulation of the cultural products of the organizationally disadvantaged is taken as an effective strategy of empowerment (the assertion and restoration of dignity) in a critique of rational–technical forms of organization (see Ebers, 1985; Jones et al., 1988). These romantic narratives, whether managerialist or contra-managerialist, tend towards the authority of the narrator's presence, though despite this authority of having been there 'natives' tend to be reported in an absent voice.

Tragic (obstacles triumph, opponents gain their revenge, and any reconciliation or reintegration occurs in a sacrificial mode or in another world). This narrative form, the obverse of the romantic, occupies a minor theme in the literature. Organizational failure is most commonly articulated as cultural rigidity or lack of adaptability (see Schein, 1985; Gagliardi, 1986), a senile and degenerative extrapolation of the anthropomorphic logic of the life-cycle theorists. Hence such 'death' becomes a natural process that proceeds to transformation beyond the grave where new organizations are spawned through 'disbanding and reconnecting' (Sutton, 1987). Clearly reintegration is a more attractive mode of expression here, instead of the discomfort of exposing the pain of loss and closure (Asplund, 1983). 'Managerialist' texts typically construct a contingent relationship here between organization, culture, and an inhospitable environment (Schein, 1985). Transitional failure is thus projected as a multi-faceted lack of fit between these factors, providing enormous opportunity for the construction of meta-narratives that express maladaption (Schneider and Shrivastava, 1984) and expose both insurmountable obstacles (Rosen, 1988) and scapegoats (Smith and Simmons, 1983). 'Contra-managerialist' texts typically construct a similarly contingent (but inverted) structure which expresses inequalities between interests (Alvesson, 1984; Deetz, 1985), exposing the inevitable products of disharmony (Kaplan and Zeigler, 1985) and domination (Ray, 1986). Hence there is disequilibrium between organization, culture and environment (Seabrook, 1990) that is only able to be reconciled through systemic transformation (in contrast to managerialist discourses where the 'sacrifice' of individual elements is reconciled with systemic perpetuation, on the grounds of efficiency). Both of these tragic forms (that is whether articulating adaptive or conflictual meta-narratives) commonly adopt a realist mode of expression, with the narrator using the voice of a detached observer.

Ironic (quests prove unsuccessful and society is not transformed, the hero must here learn that there is no escape from the world except through death or madness). This narrative form, the obverse of the epic, again occupies a minor theme in the literature. Indeed, given the heroic nature of organizational 'turnaround', as well as the emotional simplicity of the epic narrative form, there are understandably few accounts of such disaster in the literature. A number of cautionary tales exist that expose fallibility and culpability in the untimely deaths which take place both of organizations and their members (see Turner, 1978). As we have observed, the melodrama of the epic form requires the expression of these transitional stages (of seduction and corruption) as a precursor to the heroic stage of redemption; however, in the ironic narrative form no such escape exists. Here we have instead the ironic deconstruction of the role of the hero in organizational transformation, as a narcissistic desire for immortality (Walter, 1983; Schwartz, 1990) that expresses the search for a vain and unrealizable escape from the inevitability of our own temporality and mortality (Sievers, 1987). The ironic form typically adopts the authority of exposure/self-disclosure, with the narrator frequently using the voice of an expert witness.

The Problematics of Representation in Organizational Analysis

In the above analysis of the production of interpretative texts we have been focusing on the representational strategies of authorial voice and narrative form. When approached from this perspective the commonalities that connect apparent oppositions in the organizational culture and symbolism literature become more evident. Indeed, the contradictory separations between interpretative strategies can here be approached in terms of representational connection and compatibility. Hence, as we have been observing, the organization culture and symbolism literature is distinguished by heroic quests for closure; being dominated by authors adopting representational styles that privilege epic and romantic narratives over tragic or ironic forms. These representational strategies expose an overriding search for unity and harmony that suppresses division and disharmony. In this project these texts express overwhelmingly monologic voices that seek to achieve authority and persuasion through the suppression and proscription of dialogue. As we shall be considering, these representational strategies exposed in the organizational culture and symbolism literature, though novel in their forms of expression, would appear to thoroughly embody the instrumental and authoritarian concerns that have been traditional in 'managementcentric' organization studies (see Benson, 1983; Smircich, 1985). Hence, the 'organization culture chaos' may be (paradoxically) understood as a coherent articulation of distinctive and privileged forms of ordering that have been oriented towards achieving organizational rationality through the persuasive bounding of the organizational irrational.

> A remarkable turnaround or critical inversion appears to have taken place [in organisation studies] in which the manipulation of the non-rational has become the latest tool of managerial control, i.e. organisations have been rendered predictable and controllable (and thus 'rational') through the management of the irrational (culture). Thus rather than 'bounded rationality' we now have 'bounded irrationality', functioning to harmonise, integrate and unify organisation. (Jeffcutt, 1989: 23)

In order to further pursue and develop these reflections on our earlier review of texts of organizational interpretation, it is here appropriate to explore representational tensions inherent in the production of analyses of organizational culture and symbolism. As we have already observed, my own contributions to this literature both exemplify and articulate the tensions of employing such representational strategies; hence they should bear further scrutiny. Accordingly, my staging of my ethnographic fieldwork, concerned with uncovering and exploring the organizational culture of an educational setting (Jeffcutt, 1989), can be understood as expressing the confessional melodrama of the epic form. This heroic transition, from seduction through corruption to redemption, was articulated through two related quests. On the one hand there was a search for the 'Holy Grail' of a unified, stable and definitive organizational culture. This was an ordeal that was initiated by my seduction by structural–functionalist theorizing; intensified by my inability to uncover a coherent, integrated and anthropomorphic cultural unit in the field; and redeemed by my recovery of theorizing (from cultural anthropology) that was able to inform the construction of an account that accommodated the diverse and paradoxical data that I had accumulated but been unable to interpret.

> In the writing up of my initial draft, I seemed to be experiencing a paradox of research, in that the more concentratedly and thoroughly I focused on my research data the more opaque and ephemeral it became. The more I sought to uncover the organisational descriptions that I had anticipated, the more diffuse and equivocal their definition appeared to become. . . . This situation caused me no end of discomfort, since I felt I was in a double sided trap. On the one hand I was unable to render the definitions I had anticipated; whilst on the other hand I was unable to adequately order or explain the complex data that I had generated. In both senses (following Turner 1988) I was threatened with being overwhelmed by data that I was unable to subdue. (Jeffcutt, 1989: 240)

On the other hand there was the search for a persuasive interpretation of my uncomfortable field experience in the research setting. This was an ordeal that was initiated through my assumption of methodological detachment within a semi-covert field role in my own workplace; exacerbated by tensions both within this role (my denial of conflict) and in relations between natives and myself (for example identification, scapegoating); and redeemed by a confessional ethnographic account that exposed my unseemly participation in the fabric of the setting as both the agency of, and an achievement of, authenticity.

> My achieved understandings of my field experience were built upon deconstructions of earlier accounts which sought to deny and distort my agency in the setting through the assumption of a supposedly neutral role (as the observer). This revelatory process brought both insight into my and others' field experience (my assumed neutrality as a means of hiding my agency in the setting), as well as the discomfort of confronting and exposing my culpability (my guilt over my complicity in the achievement of unfortunate outcomes in the setting). As Van-Maanen and Kolb (1985) observe, ethnographic researchers are fully prepared to 'betray the trust' of their informants, whilst few are prepared to deconstruct and expose their own unseemly behaviour as a participant. (Jeffcutt, 1990b: 9)

The voice in which these transitions were inscribed was that of a privileged witness. Though I clearly empathized with, sought to empower, and indeed suffered for my support of, the disadvantaged in the setting; my summative account was staged as a dramatized monologue. The voices of other indigenous participants in the setting, that I so carefully recorded and transcribed, were indeed extensively presented 'verbatim' in the text; however, the presence of these indigenous voices, though apparently dialogic, was in actuality dramatic, in which their contributions had been selected and staged as typifications of a culture to be represented (Clifford, 1989). Hence the participation of other voices in the text had here been managed by the author as supportive and confirmatory to the project of achieving a persuasive account. In this particular case the emotional intensity of the melodrama, as well as the staging of authority and credibility in the quest for persuasion, were inextricably linked to the author's need to successfully withstand the ordeal of an academic rite of passage (that is the achievement of completing a doctorate). In this situation the exultation of the hero can thus be understood not only as an artifact in the ceremonial production and consumption of academic work, but also as a product that enhances positioning in specialized divisions of labour.

> Clearly later accounts of my fieldwork experience reflect my evolving self as an author both in a personal and a research sense, in which a whole series of movings on have taken place. Also accounts are not produced in an unconsumed vacuum, at any one time a number of different accounts are possible in which the conditions of production interact with my perceptions of the constraints of the medium of expression and the proclivities of its intended audience (e.g. a doctoral thesis) . . . So when we consider that the objective of anthropological interpretation is 'to bring us into touch with the lives of strangers' (Geertz 1973), one of those strangers is inevitably yourself (i.e. as a participant in a research process whom we also have to observe). (Jeffcutt, 1989: 233)

The problematics of representation that we have been considering here, expose a number of issues that are interconnected from the perspective of a postmodern approach to knowledge. On the one hand we have the constitution, situation and interpenetration of authorship and readership (that is tensions in the production and consumption of meaning). On the other hand we have undecidability and supplementarity in the inscription of order (ie tensions in the achievement of both persuasion and seduction). It is with the further exploration of these concurrent paradoxes of textuality that the remainder of this chapter will be concerned.

Paradoxes of Textuality in the Understanding of Organizational Culture and Symbolism

As we have been observing, the 'classic norms' of interpretation constituted the social scientific author in a privileged and pivotal position in the production of knowledge. Hence, interpretative work became established as an activity that was both scientifically demanding and heroic. A lone interpreter thus 'got to the heart' of a particular culture by undergoing a process of temporary immersion in an unfamiliar social setting, with an emphasis on observational technique, aided by powerful theoretical abstractions. The crucial science of this encounter between 'natives' and a 'professional stranger' was located in the dialectic of experience and interpretation (Clifford, 1989), whereby experience was interpreted into field notes and then recast as part of a process of abstraction towards a different community. Pivotal to this process was the authorial voice of the interpreter in the translation and transformation of discourse into text for transmission to a specialized audience. By privileging the experience of the professional stranger over that of the native (participants inform whilst researchers interpret), and by theorizing parts as microcosms or analogies for wholes, distinctive representational strategies were enacted (see Silverman, 1985; Geertz, 1988). The lone interpreter had thus a commanding presence which suppressed the unruly and discordant as an account was staged that provided an integrated and unambiguous portrait of an institutional foreground against a coherent cultural background.

Building from these traditions of working and writing, the rise to authority of the organizational culture and symbolism literature can best be understood as an expression of neo-colonialism in organization studies. Not only have 'classic' representational forms been transposed here from antecedent interpretative literature (predominantly from social anthropology and sociology), but the 'classic' concerns of this literature, such as tribalism (for example Deal and Kennedy, 1982) and deviant subcultures (see Ray, 1986), have also been articulated. Indeed in an instructive paradox, as areas of the human sciences were becoming concerned with 'orientalism' and the exposure of a colonial past (Said, 1978), organizational analysis was becoming concerned with the 'orientalizing discourses' (see Turner, B., 1986) of the early corporate culture theorists (for example Ouchi and Jaeger, 1978). Hence in this literature, on the one hand, we can observe a constitution of authorship/readership that has been increasingly criticized across the 'human sciences' as nostalgic, reductionist and authoritarian (see Marcus and Fischer, 1986; Clifford and Marcus, 1986; Cooper, 1989; Clifford, 1989; Rosaldo, 1989; Linstead and Grafton-Small, 1990b). On the other hand, we can observe the importation and redescription of novel styles and forms from 'foreign' disciplines that have both embellished and revitalized a whole collection of established theorizations in organization studies (see Smircich, 1985; Jeffcutt, 1991, 1993c).

We thus arrive at a literature that largely embodies the interesting paradox of expressing a quasi-radical/subversive posture to cross-disciplinary theory-building, whilst persuasively redescribing, both overtly and covertly, authoritarian hierarchies in the analysis of organization (for example Weick, 1985; Kunda, 1986). Accordingly, the understanding of organizational culture and symbolism can thus be connected to long-established priorities and subordinations in organization studies – for example the formal/informal organization (see Gregory, 1983; Cooper and Burrell, 1988), instrumental and routinized systems of control (see Kaplan and Zeigler, 1985; Willmott, 1990), and the privileges of elites (see Weber, 1990; Reed, 1991b). Consequently, the development and establishment of the organizational culture and symbolism literature, through the continued transmission and invigoration of these traditional concerns for unity and the heroic achievement of closure, can thus be understood as a predominant process of modernization in organization studies (see Cooper and Burrell, 1988).

It is here appropriate to reconsider recurring priorities and subordinations that we have observed in the theory and practice of organizational culture and symbolism. Here, culture as an integrative force has become subordinated to structure in the theorization of organizational change (exemplified by quests for lost unity and harmony, and the suppression of ambiguity and difference). Whether interpreted as the agency by which the irrational becomes rationalized, the transient becomes transformed, or the amorphous becomes coherent, culture has thus consistently been theorized as a mediatory process that supports the bounding and redefining stabilizations of structuring. Interpretative theorizing is here explicitly expressing culture as subordinate to structure – that is as an intermediate processual tension through which structures pass in the achievement of renewed stability (evidenced by Turner, 1974; Geertz, 1983; Wuthnow, 1987; Alexander, 1988). Such theorizations in organization studies thus offer the alluring promise of enabling the disordered to become ordered, through the redemption of disorganization (see Cooper, 1990a).

At the same time these mediatory texts also privilege their mediators who, as we have been considering, prioritize their presence and experience over that of their informants or readerships. Here narrators theorize the representational form of their stagings as consequent upon prior interpretative activity (that is the translation of discourse into text). Hence interpretative theorizing through its accounts of organizational culture and symbolism has constructed a 'field' where interpretation is separated from representation. Here thinking (the researchers voice) is prioritized as near reality, with writing as subservient, being far from reality (see the separation of 'experience near/far' in Geertz, 1988).

In contrast, postmodern theorizing both overturns and conflates these separations, in a critique of the totalizing and controlling cycle of connections of interpretative theorizing (see Cooper and Burrell, 1988). Here texts are perceived to achieve an inscription of order (expressing authority, credibility, priority) through the persuasive denial of disorder (censoring, suppressing and subordinating potential alternatives). Such inscriptions, however, should be understood as aspiring hierarchies that can only express a domination that is partial, flimsy and transient. From a postmodern perspective all orderings both embody and express inescapable paradoxes of textuality. Hence on the one hand, all orderings inevitably inhabit one another (articulating 'supplementarity', see Cooper, 1989; Linstead and Grafton-Small, 1990b); whilst on the other hand, all inscriptions are inherently undecidable (articulating 'differance', see Cooper, 1989; Linstead and Grafton-Small, 1990b). As we shall observe, these inescapable paradoxes of textuality lead to the reconstitution of both the positions of author and reader (that is producer and consumer), as well as their interconnection in the evocation of meaning (that is the inscription of order).

It is thus appropriate to consider our examination of culture and symbolism in organization in terms of such paradoxes of textuality. Here, oppositions drawn to differentiate interpretative strategies (in terms of producers, their positions and products), can be understood as both establishing particular (antithetic) hierarchies in organization studies, whilst at the same time censoring their complementarity and inseparability. Accordingly the aspiring hierarchies of apparently contradictory 'modes of engagement' in the analysis of organizational culture and symbolism (for example 'corporate culture' versus 'culture in work') reveal complementary prioritizations (that is 'culture' theorized as subordinate to 'structure') as well as the suppression of their inseparability in the theorization of organization. Thus 'culture' is represented as something an organization 'has' *or* 'is' rather than 'both/and' (that is oppositions are privileged as interpenetrations are suppressed, see Gergen, 1992). Hence, as both Feldman (1986) and Meek (1988) argue, the heroic narratives of organizational culture and symbolism manage to circumnavigate the substance of long-standing debate over these issues in fields such as social anthropology, whilst extracting persuasive commodities for relocation in organization studies.

As we have already observed, struggles for authenticity between different organizational analysts have been articulated methodologically (see Geertz, 1988). However, in these 'debates' significant complementarities have been unproblematic, such as interpretation being privileged over representation, and the narrator's voice being prioritized over 'informants' and 'readers'. Indeed at the same time, the apparently contradictory authorial positions of these organizational analysts can be likewise exposed as inseparable. Here we are concerned with the much-vaunted ethical and directional separations between the so-called 'honest grapplers' of organizational symbolism research, and the 'pop-art magicians' of corporate culture consultancy (see Turner, B., 1986, Barley et al., 1988). As we have observed, the apparently oppositional interpretative texts of these contradictory sets of authors can also be exposed as revealing complementary rhetorical styles that prioritize interpretation over representation. Hence, these authors have articulated opposing stagings and persuasive strategies (seeking to establish difference), whilst denying their underlying inseparability and complementarity.

Through such stagings of authority the interpretation of organizational culture and symbolism in organization studies has become a novel, popular and valuable commodity. Hence, on the one hand we can observe interpretations which exhibit the arrogant pretensions of the professional scholar (Lodge, 1990); whilst on the other hand we can observe interpretations which exhibit the consultancy sales-pitch of the merchant trainer (Fox, 1990). However, these apparently oppositional commodifications in the interpretation of organizational culture and symbolism also expose complementary struggles for authority and privilege in bureaucratized workplaces within both academic and managerial divisions of labour. The different interpretative strategies and putative orthodoxies that have been articulated should be perceived as complementary searches for (and versions of) the 'last word' that would close the paradox of undecidability in organizational analysis. Accordingly, the mainstream discourses of organizational culture and symbolism discourses generated by researchers and consultants can be understood as fundamentally totalizing and modernizing for the understanding of organization. However, as post-modernism informs, the particular hierarchies that have been inscribed in organization studies which privilege particular readings and voices whilst suppressing and denying alternative articulations, are at the same time flimsy and transient.

Experimental Writing in the Interpretative Social Sciences

To further our analysis of such monologic neo-colonial narratives of organizational interpretation, we here need to turn from the consideration of the protection and maintenance of authorial priority in the production of meaning, to focus on its erosion and subversion in the inscription of order. In the interpretative social sciences, these issues of voice and authority have been of particular concern to social anthropology. In a series of texts concerned with the tensions between interpretation and representation (for example Marcus and Fischer, 1986; Clifford and Marcus, 1986; Rosaldo, 1989; Clifford, 1989; Spencer, 1989) both persuasive arguments for, and intriguing examples of, the overturning of authorial privileges in ethnographic writing are considered.

> Because postmodern ethnography privileges discourse over text it foregrounds dialogue as opposed to monologue, and emphasises the cooperative and collaborative nature of the ethnographic situation in contrast to the ideology of the transcendental observer. There is instead the mutual, dialogical production of a discourse, a story of sorts. We better understand the ethnographic context as one of cooperative story making that, in one of its ideal forms, would result in a polyphonic text, none of whose participants would have the final word in the form of a framing story or encompassing synthesis – a discourse on the discourse. (Tyler, 1986: 126)

Accordingly, on the one hand we have the erosion of the totalizations and privileges of authorship as enabling the progressive empowerment of the articulations of diverse and unruly 'voices' that were formerly circum-scribed; whilst on the other hand we have dialogic forms of expression as enabling the communication of ambiguity, heterogeneity and discord that had been censored, suppressed or denied by monologic forms. These over-turnings thus involve both the empowerment of indigenous voices, and the subversion of forms of expression which deny or suppress that ability. Hence, a postmodern ethnography would imply an unspecified collectivity of authors who would be confronting paradoxes of textuality (undecid-ability and multivocality) in the inscription of an order that would oppose, overturn and re-negotiate established hierarchies of representation. As our review of the field has indicated, such a representation of organizational culture and symbolism as a polyphonic, open-ended, creative dialogue between politically significant subjects has clearly yet to be achieved.

Clifford (1989), following Bakhtin (1981, 1984), describes a continuum of representational forms that stretches from monologic authorial priority, through thresholds or shades of erosion of authorial control and concomitant assertion of indigenous voices, to the dialogic heterogeneity of a polyphonic text. Here, monologic texts employ a consistent and homogeneous representational style (for example the various types of heroic narrative we earlier observed) and express a dominant authorial voice. In contrast, polyphonic texts express 'heteroglossia' (Bakhtin, 1981), heterogeneous voices and styles that interact without exclusion: 'an orchestration of diverse discourses culled from heterogeneous sources, oral and written, conveying different ideological positions which are put in play without ever being subjected to totalising judgement or interpreta-tion' (Lodge, 1990: 90). Such texts are inevitably challenging and disconcerting, representing plurality, diversity and paradoxical inter-actions that are ultimately unresolved. In Bakhtin's view, polyphonic discourses are in a state of tension with monologic discourses, expressing a 'carnivalesque' parody of the totalizations of 'canonized' genres, styles or forms.

It is indeed ironic that such subversion of established hierarchies was exactly the impetus that fuelled the critical rise to prominence of the inter-pretation of organizational culture and symbolism in organization studies. However, as we have been observing, it has also been this admirable epistemological unorthodoxy and methodological experimentation (see Turner, B., 1986, 1990; Gagliardi, 1990) that has paradoxically provided the route by which such 'radical' criticism became transformed and incor-porated into the 'classical' hierarchies of organization studies. Thus, as the interpretation of organizational culture and symbolism became an increasingly valued commodity in organization studies, experimentation and unorthodoxy became transformed into piracy and plagiarization, as authors sought novel embellishments to provide distinctive persuasive effects in struggles for authority and credibility within different settings and divisions of labour.

Despite the dominance of heroic and romantic (that is monologic) narratives of organizational interpretation, a minority of unorthodox texts of organizational analysis can be found (for example considering authorial vulnerability, and the indigenous circumscription of researcher intentions, see Linstead, 1984; Jeffcutt, 1989). To these must be added a considerable body of work of interpretation of culture and symbolism in a variety of settings (see Clifford, 1989; Rosaldo, 1989; Jeffcutt, 1991, 1992) which have sought to empower and represent indigenous voices through the erosion or subversion of authorial privileges. Yet, as we move along Clifford's (1989) continuum towards more dialogic forms, previously secure boundaries of representation (for example author/respondent and author/reader), become progressively problematized. Hence, we need to consider the potential achievement of a postmodern ethnography in relation to both the limits of representational strategies and the limits of social science.

As Linstead (in this volume) observes, the problematization of ethnographic authorship is a particularly paradoxical issue. Here, on the one hand, the majority of attempted 'escapes' from the burdens of authority appear to be effected through sophisticated forms of authorial staging (for example the dramatization of indigenous voices, see Rosen, 1988; Young, 1989): whilst, on the other hand, the philosophy underlying this project of 'escape' would itself appear to be a search for authenticity. Hence rather than escaping burdens these authors are rediscovering problems, as they re-encounter a criterion (of authenticity) which, as we have already observed, has long been significant in the adjudication of competition between the credibilities of different interpretative strategies and techniques.

As Rabinow (1986a) has argued, such a pursuit of interpretative 'truth' (that is authenticity) can, from a postmodern approach to knowledge, be considered as largely a distraction. Accordingly, in this chapter we have been concerned with the strategies through which particular 'truth effects' have been articulated, by examining the dynamics that shape thresholds and effect boundaries of representation (for example, author/respondent, author/reader). As we have been considering, these are articulations that express both licence and limitations in respect of the practice of interpretation, as well as in terms of work that is legitimate social science. Here it is appropriate to refer to the influential work of Foucault (1980, Rabinow, 1986b; Burrell, 1988) which has been concerned with the examination of discursive techniques, formations and practices as both the embodiments and articulations of power. Of particular relevance here are the disciplinary practices of disciplines (see Hopwood, 1987; Miller and O'Leary, 1987; Hoskin and Macve, 1988 in respect of accountancy). Hence, as I have argued elsewhere (see Jeffcutt, 1993c, forthcoming), the consideration of experimental writing in organizational analysis has to explore both the nature of ethnographic experimentation and the nature of the interdisciplinarity of the 'human sciences'.

The texts of organizational interpretation should thus be understood as malleable products, formed and transformed through tensions of modification and commodification. As we have been considering, these articulate, on. the one hand, representational compromises that are effected in the achievement of a persuasive commodity; and on the other hand the inhospitability of the disciplinary and logocentric parameters of social science to the expression of 'experimental' work (see Silverman, 1991).

The Understanding of Organization and the Organizing of Understanding

As the interpretation of organizational culture and symbolism has become an increasingly popular commodity in organization studies, so have its representational forms become likewise commodified. Accordingly, different orthodoxies have become canonized (articulating spuriously oppositional positions, producers and products), as experimentations have become marginalized (articulating challenges to boundaries of expression and parameters of persuasion). Hence any consideration of a significant and articulate minority of 'radical' work in organizational interpretation must be juxtaposed with the large majority of heroic monologues which have sought to maintain rather than compromise acceptable boundaries or thresholds of representation in organization studies. Creativity and challenge have thus become the significant issues that distinguish discourses here; separating the exploration of the productivity of media and styles of expression, from the employment of novel or 'radical' persuasive effects to embellish nostalgic narratives. Thus in Bakhtin's (1981, 1984) terms we have the interplay between 'canonical' discourses as authoritarian narratives that seek to offer different versions of the last word in the interpretation of organizational culture and symbolism; and 'carnivalesque' discourses that seek to subvert and parody the form of any last words as a radical unbounding of those parameters or totalizations.

With this inescapable tension between elements in paradox we return again to the nub of the problematics of textuality in the inscription of order that we have been considering. On the one hand, both perspectives in this paradox are mutually defining and sustaining (supplementarity); whilst on the other hand, these mutualities and conjunctions are in a constant state of subversion and corruption (differance). Hence the commodities which are produced from and consumed on both 'sides' of this divide, are also conjoined through media of expression and style of representation. Although, any order that is thus inscribed is both preferential and displacing, as well as contaminated and undermined. With any inscription of order being essentially undecidable, the focus of these problematics of textuality becomes not only the exposure of authority and privilege, and the articulation of censored opposition (deconstruction); but the expression of the tensions of undecidability implicit in any hierarchy and overturning. This processual tension that shapes the threshold where boundaries join is described by Cooper as 'metaphorization'. Accordingly, one is here seeking to explore and expose the process of undecidability, an existential look at 'a continuously chameleonic and indeed ultimately phantasmic world' (Cooper, 1989) that continuously seeks recursion to the closure of structuring.

To develop the theorization of this process of undecidability one can productively turn to the work of the cultural anthropologist Victor Turner (see 1974, 1986, in particular), which has been centrally concerned with tensions between structure and process. Turner's distinctive contribution to these theorizations is the concept of 'liminality', a processual state in which ritual passengers are 'betwixt and between' established structures and re-formed classifications. Clearly Turner's relatively closed cycle of loss, passage and rebirth is inappropriate here, but his account of 'liminality' as an experience of ambiguity, paradox and flux is clearly highly pertinent to Cooper's (1989) view of 'metaphorization' as one of active alternation and undecidability. Hence, I would here seek to theorize metaphorization as a process of liminality that is continuously undecidable, and therefore unable to be redeemed by any reformulations of closure.

Over the course of this chapter we have sought to understand organizational analysis as a spiralling process of production and consumption of commodities by a plurality of 'authors' and 'readers'. This is a spiral that is carried along by paradoxes of textuality ('textual transportation', Cooper, 1989), through which production and consumption become both transient and transformed (that is intertextual). Hence, inevitable in any search to decide the undecidable is the constitution of positions and products that foreclose alternatives. However, implicit in these formations is the opposition and subversion of these structurings, manifest in the reconstitution of alternative formulations (and so metaphorizingly on . . .). Thus to reinterpret Cooper (1990a) 'organization' can be understood only in relation to 'disorganization'; and this understanding (if achievable) can be effected only through exploring the inevitable and ongoing tensions expressed between the processes of organizing and of disorganizing (the metaphorization of transience and transformation).

We may thus conclude that for organizational analysis to be a legitimate project it has to be focused on the exploration of paradoxes of textuality in the inscription of order; although any attempt to articulate order in organization studies exposes the paradox of a 'heart of darkness' of textuality that continues to remain elusively unrealizable. Yet the exploration of such paradoxes of textuality in the inscription of order is, as we have already concluded, the appropriate focus for organizational analysis. The undecidability of this inevitable paradoxical spiral is well put by Samuel Beckett (in the ending of 'The Unnamable'); 'you must go on. I can't go on. I'll go on' (Beckett, 1959: 382).

In this chapter I have sought to articulate a perspective from which the understanding of organization is inseparable from the organizing of understanding. Accordingly, the choice of undertaking to 'go on' to struggle for meaning, has implicit in it the inability to go on to satisfactorily achieve the closure of meaning's attainment. In this struggle we articulate, and are articulated, metaphorizingly. Following Cooper (1989) we are written as we write; following Bakhtin (1981, 1984) we are spoken as we speak; hence we may infer that we are also organized as we organize. However, any order that is thus inscribed is at the same time subverted. Hence, we find ourselves irretrievably fixed in the paradox of Beckett's dilemma; unable to achieve the unrealizable, but unable to not 'go on' seeking. Consequently this 'quest' for understanding may be inscribed as a liminality that is both transient and transformative; appearing to offer a capacity for closure, that is at the same time irredeemably and creatively undecidable.

An Unfinal Analysis

By way of concluding, I should like to both draw in and open out the argument that I have been expressing here. As we have considered, the nature of our inextricable participation in the above paradoxes of textuality, which inscribe both order and disorder, is one of both production and consumption (Linstead and Grafton-Small, 1990b). Hence there are, on the one hand, what appear to be creative possibilities:

> Culture in work is essentially a creative process, whether the culture maker is a labourer, a machinist or a managing director . . . culture makers are inventors, artists, storytellers, mythologists, makers of possibilities. . . . In these aspects of their behaviour they do not produce outcomes but openings. (Turner, 1990: 95)

On the other hand, there is the apparent subversion and foreclosure of these possibilities:

> What was projected for [participant] transitions was also proscribed through the processes by which these passages were enacted, thus disabling rather than enabling the very outcomes that were sought to be achieved. . . . Thus the paradoxical interconnections of [participants in the 'field' setting] produced meanings which were contradictory, ambiguous and sustaining: as well as outcomes which were unsatisfactory and disabling for all. (Jeffcutt, 1989: 260)

Accordingly, our focus needs to become the tensions that constitute this threshold and boundary between articulations of order/disorder, in other words intertextuality (see Worton and Still, 1990). In this concern we are involved in what Willis (1990) describes as 'symbolic work', the ordinary and extraordinary process of mediating between the transitive paradoxes and contradictions of everyday life (see De Certeau, 1984). Here, we should be seeking to articulate the tensions of transience that express and embody the emergence and frustration of the everyday, as it becomes manifest through the settings in which we participate. In this process of inscribing order (or circumscribing disorder), we can understand ourselves as both the creators or bricolators of meaning (see Linstead and Grafton-Small, 1989; Turner, 1990; Willis, 1990), and as the sites or paths of such inscriptions (see Cooper, 1989, 1990b). Hence, it is through the tension between these paradoxical processes that everyday life is constructed and deconstructed, as we make and are made through 'culture'.

We are thus working with (and through) artifacts that are, as White (1987) observes, both textual and contextual. Such artifacts (for example organizational stories, Boje, 1991; theories of organizing, Sandelands and Drazin, 1989) can thus be understood as both catalysts and commodities that mediate between tensions (for example meaning/undecidability, production/consumption) in an active transitive process of ordering. The practice of organizational analysis thus needs to be focused on the interrogation of such formations (such as the articulation of narrative voice and style in organizational culture and symbolism) as a contribution to the productivity of such representations. Hence, it has been with an exploration of artifacts as both commodities and catalysts in the construction/deconstruction of meaning, in both the theory and practice of organization, that this chapter has been centrally concerned. Here, particular observations have been made concerning two interrelated areas of concern:

On the one hand, 'organizational culture and symbolism' has appeared to 'solve' empirical problems of organizational order and manageability by enabling the irrational to become explicable and malleable. On the other hand, organizational culture and symbolism has appeared to offer a creative multidisciplinarity through which theoretical problems of interpretation (methodology and epistemology) in organization studies could be synthesized and resolved. However, despite the generation of plausible narratives that have been seeking to give order to both theoretical and empirical disorders, these arenas would appear to be remaining (stubbornly or creatively) irrational and unharmonized. What we have instead been observing are processes of commodification within and between academic and managerial divisions of labour, whereby established privileges and prioritizations in both the theory and practice of organization have been reinterpreted and reinvigorated. Hence this chapter's consideration of this activity and work as fundamentally totalizing and modernizing.

The 'Holy Grail' of the project of culture and symbolism in organization can thus be understood as the resolution of the paradox of order/disorder in both organizing and in organizational analysis (see Quinn and Cameron, 1988; Jeffcutt, 1989). Significantly, a parallel concern for this paradox is also reflected in other issues which have concurrently been shaping the agenda of organization studies. On the one hand, we can observe a focus on 'post-bureaucratic organization' where contradictions are inherent between structure/process (Clegg, 1990) and stability/change (Peters,

1987). On the other hand, we can observe a focus on 'paradigm incommensurability' (Hassard and Pym, 1990), where contradictions are inherent between continuity/discontinuity (Reed, 1991b) and understanding/experience (White, 1987). As we have been considering throughout this chapter, the nature of the interconnection between such oppositions is crucial, both for the practice of organizing and the theorization of organization. Hence it is here important to frame these interconnected concerns in terms of the ways in which the structuring of the interrelationship between order and disorder has been pursued in organization studies. In the management of the tensions and oppositions (that is dualities) which constitute the paradox of order/disorder the following phases of structuring can thus be articulated:

1 *Prioritization*: contradictions are suppressed or denied through selective and prejudicial focusing. The explanatory power of one side of a duality grows at the expense of censoring the other. Here we have observed critiques of organization studies' overt and covert prioritizations (for example Cooper and Burrell, 1988; Willmott, 1991), as well as the exposure of the professional rationalities (for example Weber, 1990; Reed, Chapter 10 in this volume) by and through which such commodification has been pursued.

2 *Resolution*: contradictions are harmonized through the integration of oppositions. Explanatory power is developed through the generation of a perspective from which dualities are perceived as interdependent. Here we have observed the search for such resolution both in organization studies (for example Morgan, 1986; Van den Ven and Poole, 1988), and in wider social theory (Devereux, 1979; Giddens, 1984; Sahlins, 1985). Critiques have here focused on the false complementarity pursued by such epistemologies (see Hekman, 1990) as well as the covert prioritizations achieved.

3 *Overturning*: prioritizations are reordered by the privileged element of a duality becoming subverted by its inverse. The formerly censored subordinate attains priority (and censorship) over the formerly privileged. Here, as we have observed, the contradictions that perpetuate a disabling order of priorities and subordinations (for example Burrell and Hearn, 1989) also appear to provide the resources by which such privileges may be deconstructed, subverted and overturned (see Willmott, 1990, 1991; Willis, 1990; Thompson, Chapter 11 in this volume). Critiques have focused on such overturning as symbolic inversion, a process of redescription, reimposition and renewal of privilege and subordination (see Jeffcutt, 1989, 1990a; Cooper, 1989).

4 *Metaphorization*: elements of dualities are both contradictory and complementary as well as interdependent and oppositional. Such structures can be understood as truly paradoxical, where dualities are absolutely undecidable. Hence the production of order becomes consumed by disorder, whilst disorder becomes a product of the consumption of order. Organization can thus be observed as a paradox of textuality (Cooper,

1989) that is both transient and transformational (Jeffcutt, 1990a, b, 1993c). With such an inscription of order being inevitable as well as undecidable, we are drawn irretrievably into the contextualization of our subjectivity (see White, 1987; Pheby, 1988), exploring the intertextual processes through which such articulations are represented or simulated (see Jeffcutt, 1989, forthcoming; Cooper, 1992).

As has been expressed throughout this chapter, I am particularly concerned with ways of working and writing in the theory and practice of organization. My concerns here have been to expose and explore openings that express polyphony in organization studies, whilst opposing the untimely closing of monology. Indeed, throughout my long-standing activity in the analysis of organizational culture and symbolism, I have consistently participated in the articulation of diverse and critical positions in this 'field'. Over the past decade such peripheral 'carnivalesque' voices have become increasingly articulate, widespread and skilful; both as explorers of the problematics of representation in organizational analysis, and as subverters of the totalizations of 'canonized' voices in organization studies. Here I am not alone in arguing (see Cooper and Burrell, 1988; Linstead and Grafton-Small, 1990b) that a postmodern approach to knowledge has offered these voices sufficient theoretical purchase from which to mount a challenge to the modernizing momentum that had fuelled the incorporation of earlier critiques into the established priorities of organization studies (see Smircich and Calás, 1987; Letiche, 1990).

In the formulation of this creative overturning of established ways of working and writing in organization studies, I feel that it is essential to combine the analysis of the contradictions that perpetuate a disabling order of priorities and subordinations, with a praxis of leverage and empowerment.[1] Furthermore it is most important that such a praxis of overturning becomes a practice that is worked reflexively (see Atkinson, 1990) and contextually (see Hekman, 1990), exploring rather than denying our irretrievable participation in the paradoxes and contradictions of such textual emergence (see Pheby, 1988). In organization studies, in particular, this work requires the continued exposure of the commodification of texts within and between different divisions and sites of labour (both academic and managerial: see Hoskin and Macve, 1988); as well as the exploration of the parameters of persuasion and the seductive productivity of these discourses' modes of representation (see Cooper, 1992). Here, one is connecting a Derridian philosophical praxis (deconstruction/overturning/metaphorization) with a Foucauldian critical historical practice (the interdependence of bodies of knowledge and relations of power) in the understanding of both organizing and organizational analysis.

The deconstruction of ways of working and writing in both the theory and practice of organization is, as I have argued earlier, essential for the expression of an organization studies that seeks to articulate the polyphonic diversity and transience of our everyday organizational lives. To undertake such symbolic work is to expose and articulate our complete participation in the ambiguity and uncertainty of paradox and undecidability in ordering. We must be aware that our inevitable participation in such symbolic work is mediated through the practices of commodification that are contextualized within different cultural formations and settings (for example divisions and sites of labour, see Foucault, 1980; Reed, 1991b). Hence, in organizational analysis we can observe impassioned resistance to postmodern overturning from formerly prioritized positions; such as the perspectives of ethnomethodology (Giddens, 1987b) and labour process theory (Thompson, Chapter 11 in this volume). At the same time we can also observe subversive resistance whereby postmodern overturning has become subsumed and translated into pre-existing periodizations concerning both organizational transitions (for example 'industrialism/post-industrialism', see Harvey, 1989) and organization theory (for example 'differentiation/de-differentiation', see Clegg, 1990). However, both the above forms of resistance may be understood as commodifications that are focused towards the modernization of the postmodern in organization studies (see Jeffcutt, forthcoming).

Accordingly, throughout this chapter I have sought to argue that such 'canonized' hyper-modern positions in organization studies (exemplified by the heroic and romantic narratives of the organizational culture and symbolism literature) are indeed 'dominant but dead' (Smircich and Calás, 1987). Moreover, I have also sought to indicate how (through the articulations of the 'carnivalesque') these oppressive hierarchies in both the theory and practice of organization are being interrogated and actively overturned. Yet, as organizational analysis turns away from commodifying elite heroics (within both academic and managerial work) and becomes concerned with exploring and representing the extraordinary qualities of the ordinary (see De Certeau, 1984; Willis, 1990), it is most important for this work to continue to move challengingly and creatively on. As has been elaborated earlier, the symbolic inversion of 'overturning' can become (if frozen/unless continued) a reimposition of hierarchy in a process that is continually liminal. Such re-canonization (of the formerly marginal) would of course be an action of censorship and suppression on the newly carnivalesque, unless as Cooper (1989) argues, the movement of deconstruction continues into metaphorization. Accordingly, in our inevitable participation in this continuous spiral of undecidability, we experience the essential paradox of the symbolic work of structuring; and irredeemable contextual liminality through which we can only move transitively and metaphorizingly on.

As Arrington and Francis (1989) observe, such postmodern overturning makes modern life more difficult, but *not* impossible. Coming to realize that ordering comprises permeable boundaries that are at the same time fragile, brings responsibility for the inscription of structures that are inherently incapable of effectively censoring the 'contamination' of disorder. In this way the intertextual flow of paradox incisively and creatively reinvigorates the openings of possibility and opportunity from closures that are prejudicial, disciplinary and untimely.

> We may hope for a conclusion, for something like the traditional retrospective summary and judgement, a stentorian voice to restore balance and perspective to an otherwise imbalanced and volatile world. But such a return to the sanctuary of the critical voice is precisely what is denied by the trajectory of postmodern discourse. Instead we find ourselves left with something more modest, but perhaps more urgent. That is the task, not or finding ends, solutions and finalities, but of living in a world from which these privileges and certainties have been withdrawn. (Wakefield, 1990: 151)

With such a spirit this chapter has been produced; accordingly, its ending marks a position at which I both arrive at, and begin to depart from (for example Jeffcutt, forthcoming), the argument articulated here.

Notes

This chapter is based on papers presented during early 1991 to the Anthropology of Organizations Conference (University of Swansea) and the New Theory of Organizations Conference (University of Keele); my thanks both to conference organizers and participants for their interest. I am particularly grateful to Bob Cooper and Bob Grafton-Small for their comments on an earlier draft of this work.

1. Given that my later work has its antecedence in post-compulsory education, it is indeed encouraging to see the influential work of Freire (for example 1972, 1985); Willis (for example 1977, 1983); Thompson (for example 1983), and Cockburn (for example 1985, 1987) attaining significance in the practice of organizational analysis (see Burrell and Hearn, 1989; Willmott, 1990, 1991).

3

Deconstruction in the Study
of Organizations

Steve Linstead

Currently fashionable or controversial debates in 'postmodernism' are related to and grounded in historical formulations of the problems of sense-making. They have not in any sense sprung up overnight, nor are they purely a product of recent social experience (Callinicos, 1989). Their consequent importance depends upon the ways in which they self-reflexively articulate with, and are articulated by, those earlier discursive explorations (Ryan, 1982), especially where disciplinary boundaries become blurred (Geertz, 1983). This awareness is the starting point for the following discussion of the importance of 'postmodern' concepts, particularly those drawn from the work of Jacques Derrida, for organization theory and our understanding of organizing processes; and also the implications of postmodernism for ethnography as a means of studying organizations. This consideration of a possible 'postmodern' methodology for any analysis of organization produces some subtle and perhaps surprising turns in the emergence of four important analytical foci: organization as *paradox*; organization as *otherness*; organization as *seduction*; and organization as *discourse*. The conclusion offers some indication as to how the practice of investigation might proceed in developing a *deconstructive ethnography* of organizations.

Recent developments in 'postmodern' thought have established a new focus on the means by which 'truth-effects' come to be produced and consumed in symbolic structures, investigating the 'textual strategies' which stage meaning rather then the underlying principles which determine it (see Jeffcutt, Chapter 2 in this volume). As the determinacy of meaning by a flow of intentionality from origin to recipient has been called into question, so the constructive effects of the medium of transmission (language, symbol or the mass media) and the creative possibilities of the 'reader' (through 'bricolage') have been emphasized (Linstead and Grafton-Small, 1989). Knowledge becomes relative, dispersed between multiple, fragmented realities: the 'selves' who experience and produce these emerge as more of a social and shifting phenomenon than an integral cohesive one.

Ethnography is a particularly appropriate methodology for addressing what is being seen as an increasingly fragmented organizational and social world, especially in view of the centrality of language and the symbolic as modes of expression constitutive of knowledge. In organization studies, although few full ethnographies have been produced (Rosen, 1991: 22) there has been a rise in the number of studies partially employing ethnographic methods and borrowing anthropological terminology (Turner, 1977, 1983; Allaire and Firsirotu, 1984; Smircich, 1983b) which have been totalized as the 'organizational culture and symbolism' movement (Frost et al., 1985; Pondy et al., 1983; Kilmann et al., 1985; Turner, B., 1989, 1990). Although interest in ethnography has not been confined to this corner of the social sciences it is particularly worthy of attention because of the increasing acknowledgement of the importance of organization studies to the understanding of contemporary Western society (Hammersley, 1990; Stanley, 1990). Not only are formal organizations, even if undergoing some turbulence, the dominant social form, and as such commanding study; in a society of organizations they are the means by which society is itself organized, and social relations, understanding and even physical awareness are a product of organized relationships (Burrell, 1988). The understanding of organizations is simultaneously a study of the organization of understanding; and the processes of understanding have for some time been the province and problem of ethnography.

Description

All ethnographic explorations are fraught with difficulties which arise from the assumptions which are implicit in the ethnographer's way of knowledge. Despite being unavoidably committed to and grounded in a particular form of 'rationality', ethnography demands of the ethnographer that he seeks to bring his way of knowing, the world and history which he carries with him in his language and thought, into contact with that of the other. As a result, both the strangeness of the other, and paradoxically, the other's presence already within the consciousness of the observer, can be acknowledged. The excitement of ethnography is in the challenge which this poses, and which the ethnographer struggles to allow it to pose, to his own way of knowledge (Silverman, 1975: 8–9). This problem has increasingly been the explicit concern of ethnographers and anthropologists throughout the 1970s and 1980s, and centres around the difficulties of description.

Referentiality

Positivistic ethnography depends for its success on its ability to be taken as an accurate descriptive and analytic account of something other than itself – the real world of the native – yet as Stanley (1990: 624) observes, 'very few ethnographies would pass representational muster when judged by members'. On the one hand, this could be viewed as a failure of referentiality, bad technique (Silverman, 1975: 41–2). On the other hand it may be that the existence of multiple realities makes the unity of this 'other world' illusory, and the unruly nature of experience which is 'garrulous, over-determined . . . shot through with power relations and personal cross-purposes' is misrepresented in its circumscription in a cohesive account (Clifford, 1989: 25; Silverman, 1975: 59–61). Clifford argues that the failure of ethnography with regard to referentiality amounts to a crisis of *representation* in the interpretative sciences (Clifford and Marcus, 1986; Jeffcutt, Chapter 2 in this volume; see Sangren, 1988 and Birth, 1990 for an alternative view). The ability of science 'to encompass adequately the detailed reality of motivated, intentional life' (Marcus and Fischer, 1986: 165) becomes problematic, and anthropology is 'at the vortex of the debate about the problem of representing society in contemporary discourses' (Marcus and Fischer, 1986: vii).

Ethnography as Literature

One contemporary response to this problem of representation is to concentrate on the *means* by which representation is achieved, to treat language as opaque and productive of persuasive accounts and ethnography as a literary form (Silverman, 1975: 22–3, 27–30; Pearce and Chen, 1989; Dwyer, 1977, 1979; Webster, 1982, 1983; Marcus and Cushman, 1982; Clifford and Marcus, 1986; Geertz, 1988; Atkinson, 1990). This orientation has provoked the objection that

> concentrating our gaze on the ways in which knowledge claims are advanced undermines our capacity to take any of those claims seriously. Somehow, attention to such matters as imagery, metaphor, phraseology or voice is supposed to lead to a corrosive relativism in which everything is but a more or less clever expression of opinion. Ethnography becomes, it is said a mere game of words, as poems and novels are supposed to be. (Geertz, 1988: 2)

However, if ethnography achieves its persuasive force in these more literary ways then no scientific purpose will be served by suppressing it. As Atkinson (1990: 180) argues, ethnography

> cannot inhabit a world of texts where conventionality is taken for granted, or where language is treated as unproblematic. The fully mature ethnography requires a reflexive awareness of its own writing, the possibilities and limits of its own language and a principled exploration of its own modes of representation.

The problem for the post-modern ethnographer would appear to be how to write in the light of this reflexivity.

For Tyler (1986) and others this means abandoning *reference* in favour of *evocation*. Evocation is part of the poetic function of language; it evokes that which escapes reference. Where scientific language pays attention to its own rules and method, and in the pursuit of discrimination and sophistication perfects its own discourse internally by defining and qualifying its terms ever more rigorously, it becomes impenetrable. Orientated towards *theory*, it is limited to recognizing only that knowledge which can be described discursively. Referential language at the level of the everyday is motivated towards performance, and language is subordinated to the interests of getting things done, developing with the objective of getting them done perfectly. Orientated towards *practice*, it is confined to usage which produces action. However, in between these extremes of reference there is a range of association which resists tight definition, and in fact all scientific or performative statements have to be recast by their readers or recipients in terms of 'where does it come from?' and 'what does it mean to me?' with contexts, histories and associations provided in order to *make sense*. This is an 'ethnographic context' in itself, and this is why Tyler (1986: 122) states that ethnography is a 'subordinate discourse to which all other discourses are relativized and in which they find their meaning and justification'. The destruction of totalizing meta-narratives which is characteristic of postmodernism now means that 'meaning' is not universal but fragmented and locally grounded, and ethnography is the process of achieving this grounding in a context which will sustain it: in Tyler's terms, 'the discourse of the post-modern world' (1986: 123).

For Sperber (1975: 112–19) evocation is about context, the backgrounded, subconscious or implicit associations which are made at the same time as conscious, conceptual constructions. Anything can start it; nothing seems to be able to stop it. Nevertheless, we do share experiences in common with other humans, live our lives within similar conventions and are capable of making the same imaginative leaps. Accordingly broad *evocative fields* can be discerned to give us a rough idea of how particular images might be received, but this cannot be controlled, and any attempt to be deliberately evocative inevitably courts failure.

As Clifford (Clifford and Marcus, 1986: 26) argues

> to recognize the poetic dimensions of ethnography does not require that one give up facts and accurate accounting for the supposed free play of poetry. 'Poetry' is not limited to romantic or modernist subjectivism: it can be historical, precise, objective. And of course it is just as conventional and situationally determined as prose.

Birth (1990) notes this, but in common with many of the experimental ethnographers he criticizes he has no clear idea of what the precision of poetry might entail. There is no necessity for, nor should there be a call to, random signification nor a jettisoning of referential language, and Birth propounds the case for reference with some care. Unfortunately, he argues, Clifford's acceptance of stylistic precision is not carried through to the ontological and epistemological levels of placing some value on truth and some limits on relativity. A resulting byproduct of this awareness of ethnography's literary nature, coupled with the inability to set limits to interpretation, has been the analytic endeavour to achieve the emergence of *multiple voices* in the text.

Multiple Voices

The interest in multiple voices in postmodern ethnography is in part epistemological and in part ethical. The recognition of the existence of multiple negotiated realities as part of the phenomenology of the social world brings into question the coherence of traditional anthropological representations of the other (Marcus and Cushman, 1982: 32). Anthropological accounts have inevitably suppressed, selected from and synthesized these voices, and a naturalistic response to this awareness is to attempt to weave these multiple voices into the text in order to be more faithful to the cultural realities being described (Birth, 1990: 551). As Tyler (1986: 161) argues:

> A post-modern ethnography is fragmentary because it cannot be otherwise. Life in the field is itself fragmentary, not at all organized around familiar ethnological categories such as Kinship, economy and religion . . . we make do with a collection of indexical anecdotes or telling particulars with which to portend that larger unity beyond explicit textualization.

Bringing in these additional voices in the interests of realism might suggest that there is one 'real world' in the sense of Hammersley's (1990) critique which it is the task of ethnography to represent accurately, no matter how many voices it should contain. Similarly, it also privileges the constitution of that world in the speech of the participants as having greater authenticity than its appropriation by any other means, in what might be termed *multivocal phonocentrism*. There is a real risk that 'narrative realism merges innocently with realist goals and thence with positivist description of factual reality' (Webster, 1983: 198).

Such stylistic *heteroglossia* bring into question the 'authority' of the author as other voices are brought in alongside, and this alerts us to the ethical dimension which is a major objective of postmodern ethnography. Although Webster (1983: 198) argues that 'an unacknowledged status as a literary genre becomes a binding social contract for its practitioners' in works of 'dispersed authority' this may not, paradoxically, be sufficient to be 'ethical', although it may allow the ethnographer to sidestep the charge of intellectual imperialism (Pearce and Chen, 1989: 128). The risk is that a truly naturalistic ethnography would of necessity abrogate its critical capacity in reproducing the ideological presuppositions of the society under study.

> No matter how relativistically different historical contexts are conceived, it seems that the discourse through which their self-knowledge is constituted or mystified is not, as Marx would say, disembodied; consequently there is a false-consciousness as well as a consciousness to be penetrated by critical theory. (Webster, 1983: 199)

Geertz (1988: 140) argues that native voices cannot in any case speak alongside the writer in a direct and equal way, and that despite their efforts to avoid imperialism ethnographers cannot evade

> the burden of authorship . . . however heavy it may have become; there is no possibility of displacing it on to 'method', 'language' or (an especially popular manoeuvre at the moment) 'the people themselves' redescribed ('appropriated' is probably the better term) as co-authors.

Authors therefore cannot help but intervene in the process of re-presentation of the social group under scrutiny, as Clifford ultimately seems to acknowledge (Clifford, 1988: 142). This is especially so in studying organizations which are a subsection of their own society, and when their objective is to demystify that which is already substantially familiar to them (Rosen, 1991: 15). Self-reflexivity is an important part of the process of investigation, presentation and evocation of this social reality, even if that reality is multiplex and fragmented and the ideas of unity and author-ity must be brought into question. However, in regarding the problem of postmodern ethnography as being that of how to *write* ethnography in the light of such reflexivity, the problem of (and responsibility for) the interpretation of cultural forms has been displaced from the *writer of ethnography* to the *reader of ethnographies*, as reading is implicitly acknowledged as a creative process (Silverman, 1975). This need not and should not lead to a form of irreducible relativism in which any reading is as good as any other, a hermeneutic free-for-all; neither is this a conclusion which should be reached as a consequence of 'deconstruction', the critical process adopted from Derrida which is widely and inaccurately regarded as the destruction of all stability in meaning and interpretation and the cornerstone of postmodern thought.

Vulgar Deconstruction

The 'postmodern' ethnography we have discussed (see also Jeffcutt, Chapter 2 in this volume) depends upon and focuses on anthropological texts as literary creations, fictions which present themselves as fact but which have no priority to that claim over other potential orderings of the world. Unfortunately it is possible to take the idea of freeplay of signifiers as a pretext for endless interpretative games, without the necessity to pay regard to standards of logic, or ideas of truth (Norris, 1990: 152; Eco, 1990: 23–43; Bennington, 1989: 20). For example,

> giving the readings is its own end, and the value of the readings is in the act of reading. . . . All other approaches are acceptable and valid for the structuralist . . . so long as it is understood that each is merely another ordering, another myth. (Turner, 1983: 200)

As Norris (1990: 138–9) argues, this approach denies all standards of interpretative consistency, resulting in 'a kind of easy-going pluralist tolerance which leaves no room for significant disagreement on issues of principle or practice'.

Whilst Derrida has indefatigably pointed out the ways in which philosophy has rested its claims on reason, method, structure, and other concepts whose metaphorical nature it has not been able to acknowledge because of the risk to its own project in attempting to think beyond logocentrism, he has always exposed this by working *from within*. He attempts to 'solicit' this structure of concepts, to bring it down gently under its own weight, by demonstrating the paradoxes of differance and supplementarity which affect it, in the equally paradoxical necessity of *using its own tools to subvert its express functions*. As Derrida (1976: 158) argues, deconstruction 'is not easy and requires all the instruments of classical criticism. Without this recognition and this respect, critical production would risk developing in any direction at all and authorize itself to say almost anything'. There is no question of jettisoning, for example, the concept of intentionality. His exposure of the problematic factors in language demonstrates how what the text *means to say* differs from what it actually says, how intended meanings become caught up in signifying structures which are outside their control (Norris, 1990: 151). Where meaning is 'strictly undecidable in certain circumstances this cannot be taken to be synonymous with the claim that meaning is always and everywhere indeterminate' (Norris 1990: 147–8).

There is no form of *a priori* concept or principle that would restrict the freeplay of meaning, the 'play of oppositions', to those laid down by our received order of concepts and priorities through logocentrism *at the limit of language, in any final sense* (Silverman, 1975: 111; Norris, 1990: 152). Nevertheless, Derrida works with sustained care and meticulous attention to his texts at the highest analytical level, and any paradoxical positions he is able to expose are invariably hard-won through the rigorous exercise of those tools which created the very positions which he overturns. Although this is not the place for an extended discussion of Derrida (Cooper, 1989; Linstead and Grafton-Small, 1992), it is necessary to discuss the key concepts which illustrate the distance between the 'vulgar deconstruction' which characterizes much postmodern ethnography, and a deconstructive approach derived from a close reading of Derrida which might form the basis for a study of the textuality of social action in organizations.

Oppositional and Supplementary Logics

Central to Derrida's thought is the recognition that language always embodies a relationship of power between terms, one being used rather than another possible term in any text (Silverman, 1975: 20–2). That is to say, terms in language are used positively, effectively banishing those other terms from which they are differentiated. This is an oppositional *logic of identity*. Although positively valued terms require an understanding of those negatively valued terms in order to be meaningful (as 'black' *needs* 'white') they imply the absence of them. Accounts become persuasive by virtue of not presenting alternative formulations, and the act of re-presentation also becomes an act of re-pression of alternatives. Specifically, language is structured in terms of oppositions, each term depending on and being supported by the other in order to mean, and although these terms *interpenetrate* each other they exist, or are treated as though they exist, in a hierarchy, a dualism, a relationship of power with one term at any moment dominant over the other. Derrida (1976: 27–73), as Cooper (1989) explains, is concerned to reconceptualize this *oppositional either/or* as a duality or cohabitation of terms: the division between them is not a partitioning of the unalike but a joining, a mutually supportive pivotal point around which meaning turns (Cooper, 1983). The one term needs the other, a *supplementarity* of both/and. Where modernism pursues the *opposition* of terms, actively placing the one over and against the other, postmodernism resists the closure of terms, actively exploring the *supplementarity* of the one within the other. It is this subtle relationship of structure/play (or process) rather than play banishing structure which is little appreciated in postmodern anthropology (Derrida, 1976: 141–57; 1978: 289–93; 1982: 175–206). 'There is no passing "beyond structuralism" except by a constant and vigilant awareness that the structuralist enterprise is deeply complicit with the whole pre-history of philosophic reason' (Norris, 1985: 222–3).

Differance

What Derrida calls the 'metaphysics of presence' is a response to the problem of reflexivity, in that no utterance, writing or text can guarantee its own truth and must necessarily resort to a meta-level of reference in order to derive its authority (Lawson, 1985). Any sign thus *defers* to another level of meaning, and simultaneously *defers* its presence: writing denotes the absence of speech, the word denotes the absence of the object it is supposed to represent. The word necessarily differs from the thing in that it can be separated from it, and is in this sense *more* than the object; simultaneously it is *less* than the object as it does not re-present the object in its fullness (Lecercle, 1985). It has a life of its own which is not controlled by any referential links: the world we know is the world as represented, 'reality' being undecidable (Derrida, 1973). Remembering that terms also depend for their meaning on the terms from which they *differ* and yet contain within themselves their own negation in order to become meaningful, we have a curious internal *difference* of terms from themselves. The combination of differing and deferring, a continual, never-fixed movement, a play of spacing within the 'text', Derrida (1973, 1978) calls '*differance*'. It is this paradoxical, fluid, contradictory process that is crucial to a postmodern understanding of organization.

Supplementarity

Derrida argues that later ideas always take precedence over what was initially there, but are nevertheless shaped by the '*trace*' of those earlier often implicit and unacknowledged ideas and responses. This adding on is one effect of *supplementarity* which is taken up by Gergen (1992: 220) in his concept of 'social supplementarity' which he sees as reflecting the need to complete the terms used by others to determine what they mean. The 'marginal' amplification, although de-centred, is actually necessary to 'fix' the term itself, although the term is never finally fixed and one can disappear into a vertigo of social supplementarity (cf. Garfinkel, 1987 and his incongruity procedures). However, Derrida's supplement is rather more than the codes which actual human subjects apply to the deciphering of terms – it carries the sense of the opposite, the negation of the term itself being necessary for the term to mean at all, as well as reflecting the never-satisfied need for something to be 'added' to determine its meaning.

Supplementarity is therefore a subversive quality in which a *term* is *necessarily inhabited by its opposite*, and hence possesses the potential for its own corruption. 'Social' supplementarity as an activity is a recognition of and response to the inadequacy of language which paradoxically drives it to excess, endlessly to pursue closure. It is a *human* response to the self-destructive quality of supplementarity *within the term itself*, which goes beyond it in an attempt to resolve the problem of the undecidability of terms, to 'gloss' or 'bracket' the problem. Derrida (1976), however, emphasizes the need to recognize the problematic nature of positive terms by placing them 'under erasure' – crossing through them whilst allowing them to remain legible – which undermines their fixed appearance whilst acknowledging their necessity as a heuristic, however inadequate. This forms part of the process which Derrida calls 'deconstruction', which is founded on an understanding of 'supplementarity' and 'differance'.

Deconstruction

Based upon this understanding of supplementary logic deconstruction is the means by which Derrida operates on texts – and the world itself can be viewed as 'text' (Cooper, 1989: 481; Eco, 1990: 23). Deconstruction is a means of revealing the contradictions inherent within texts, a means of exposing their logocentrism, their reliance on the metaphysics of presence, and of revealing their inescapable qualities of differance and supplementarity despite repressive textual strategies. Although deconstruction seeks to avoid the mystifications of other texts, it is nevertheless trapped within language and is bound to share some of the blindspots, and fall into some of the traps which it exposes in other writing. There is therefore no solid independent ground on which the deconstructionist can stand, and the

method can and *must* be turned back on itself. In attempting to open up
the closures of the texts he studies, *entering into them and using their own
terms against them*, Derrida attempts to avoid merely setting up a meta-
level of critical terms and thus becoming incorporated into the logocentrism he critiques. Cooper (1989: 483) refers to the two movements of
deconstruction as *overturning* and *metaphorization*. In the first movement
Derrida focuses on the binary oppositions of terms which we have already
noted, existing in a hierarchy in which one term is suppressed. Of course,
simply overturning the hierarchy at any moment, centring the marginal
and marginalizing the central, remains an oppositional strategy, and itself
creates another hierarchy which in turn requires overturning. Much so-
called deconstructive criticism gets no further than this. The second movement of metaphorization is necessary to keep the process in motion, to
resist its degradation and ossification into structure. This entails the
recognition that the positively valued term at any moment is defined only
by contrast to the negatively valued term and that they interpenetrate and
inhabit each other. In Derrida's writing this emerges as a ceaseless moving
between terms, giving his work an elusive quality which is nevertheless an
essential feature of his project (Derrida, 1982).

The De-centring of the Subject

Derrida's deconstruction of the metaphysics of presence has important
consequences for the understanding of the nature of human agency, identity, and subjectivity. Geertz observes that the Western (and hence
logocentric) conception of a person is of

> a bounded, unique more or less integrated motivational and cognitive universe,
> a dynamic centre of awareness, emotion, judgment and action, organized into
> a distinctive whole and set contrastively against other such wholes and against
> a social and natural background. (1983: 59)

Silverman notes in contrast:

> writing and reading are always acts of production – of societies, of selves. And
> that production is both mine and not mine alone. Mine because in my acts of
> production I re-member my-self. Not mine because 'I' exist in and through a
> dialogue with a tradition that always already precedes me, and with an emerg-
> ing social order that will be the readings of my text. (1975: 42)

Derrida argues with some similarity that presence is always already
mediated by the absent trace, which is to say that self-consciousness is not
direct, pure, authentic, originary and unmediated experience but is
indirect, contaminated, on the rebound, secondary, delayed, reflected and
already formed and mediated. The subject is not natural but fabricated
(Venn, 1984: 150): subjectivity is an artifact. Social and historical traces
enter into the structuring of consciousness; indeed in Lacan subjectivity
is the process of finding a place in the language of the other (Harland,

1987: 38–9). That is to say individual subjects are constituted through a symbolic system which differentiates and fixes them in place whilst remaining outside their control. Even awareness – the structuring process which guides and determines their formation – is always other, always de-centring them from the seat of author-ity at which logocentrism places the self-aware, self-present, self-conscious subject of Western psychology. The constitution of the subject in this way is seen by Sampson (1989) to be the result of an ideological practice which conceals its own contingency as it 'represses the fluidity and indeterminacy of process in the name of a fixed point of origin' rather than allowing to emerge a picture 'of a subject who is open-ended and indeterminate except as fixed in place by the culturally constituted symbolic order'.

The integrated subject of ego-psychology, depending as it does on its being 'centrable', is no longer tenable. Derrida sees its 'sovereign solitude' as being displaced, existing rather as a 'system of relations between strata' (Derrida, 1978: 226–7). It is a site which emerges as an overcrossing of traces, society, the world, the psyche, other texts, other times. It is a weave, a texture, fragmented but intertwined rather than hierarchical and integrated, a process and a paradox having neither beginning nor end.

Organization, Text and Subjectivity

The consequences of this for the study of organizations are profound. Organizations as a symbolic product are 'written' and can be regarded as 'texts', but our view of 'text' can have no integrated originary 'author'. Rather, any consciousness of 'author-ity' emerges from the process of producing the text – the author is as much a product of the text as the text is product of an author (Barthes, 1981). But the text cannot exist as mere words on a page, symbols in the air or actions in the world until it is read or made to mean – therefore it depends upon its re-creation by a 'reader' or recipient. Because of supplementarity and differance, we can no longer regard the process of reading as deciphering the meaning inscribed into the text by the author – the author having already been 'written' through the trace. The text is formed by the overcrossing of other traces, other meanings, *other texts* and is read in terms of them. It is disentangled rather than deciphered (Barthes, 1977: 159). The text has an *intertextuality*, a multiplicity of meaning which is inherent rather than a result of a variety of interpretations.

Organizations, as texts, are therefore partially constitutive of the subjectivity of those who are involved in their production. Similarly, they seek to constitute the subjectivity of this readership, their style, strategy and context 'interpellating' them, inviting participation in a certain way. Nevertheless, 'readers' bring their awareness of other texts, other cultural forms, other evocations and explosions of meaning to their reading of any text, and enter into the text, changing its nature and re-producing it as they consume it. As differance illuminates, consumption is an inseparable part of production; as supplementarity confirms, the author is completed and de-centred by the reader. Both authors and readers, creators and consumers, are inseparably bound together in, and are constituted by, the continual process of the emergence of meaning. So it is with organizations as members, be they managers, professionals, superiors, subordinates or amenable to any other taxonomy, are immersed in this unselfconscious negotiation and emergence of their own identities within and without the corporation.

Organization as Paradox

Current approaches to organizational analysis are dominated by the oppositional approach which sets integrated, whole self-conscious and centred individuals against each other, hierarchically arranging and aggregating them in groups, subgroups, subcultures and cultures, and many of the problems of organizational analysis are a logical outcome of this analytical practice. This is recognizable as the embodiment of logocentrism, the philosophy of presence that assumes 'natural' categories (for example individual, organization, group, structure, function) which become prioritized and normalized.

This habit is deeply ingrained in the social sciences, in theorizing, research practice, and pedagogy, and in the study of organizations becomes emblematic in one form in the overwhelming concentration on the concept of 'shared meaning' as definitive of cultural forms; as does the alternative but complementary formulation of subcultural fragmentation. Supplementarity indicates that 'shared meaning' is impossible, always incomplete; differance that it exists in continual fluidity with its own negation, paradox and ambiguity being its essential qualities rather than occasional surprises or problems at the margin. *'Shared meaning' is nothing more than the deferral of differance.* Viewing 'organizational culture' in this way we should *expect* it to be paradoxical, being unsurprised by Young's (1989) observation that strong cultures may mark strong internal division – this embodies the supplementary principle of return that is entirely to be expected. However, we must look elsewhere than to the aggregation of self-conscious rational minds pursuing their interests at a group level to explain or respond to its emergence.

Organization then is continuously emergent, constituted and constituting, produced and consumed by subjects who, like organizations, are themselves fields of the trace, sites of intertextuality. The emphasis in investigation then must be away from oppositional, interpretative strategies towards supplementary, representational ones, towards those processes which *shape* subjectivity rather than the process by which individual subjects act upon the world.

Organization as Otherness

The significance of the Other as a principle which structures meaning whilst appearing to be subordinate becomes important for postmodern organizational analysis. A necessary focus then is on the ways in which the *principle of return* can operate, the negative simultaneously working against the positive. Canetti (1962) defines power as the expression of order via command, command having two dimensions: *momentum* and *sting*. The momentum is the force upon the person to act, but the sting remains behind, invisible, indestructible and silent, perhaps for years, after every command is obeyed (Cooper, 1983). What it is waiting for is the chance to be rid of the original command, to avenge itself, to free the recipient of a 'deference order' which distorted the relationship, to make the relationship 'whole' again in differance. The sting inhabits the trace: the trace in this sense is deferred sting, and this has particular significance for the concept of organizational culture. Within such a command-based structure the most powerful formative influence on 'culture' may well be the invisible and unarticulated tissue of *deferred stings* embodied in the trajectory of traces of past commands delivered throughout the organization.

The tendency to seek to make 'whole' embodied in the principle of return is a fundamental drive to regain a *supposedly* lost and anterior unity – the point of origin, the logos – from which all division and differentiation stems (Cooper, 1983). The very existence of *another* is information which tells us that we are not *complete*, and the fundamental, intractable compulsion in social life is to reconcile this difference, to complete what is missing to being, to fill our own lack. This drive, this *desire*, emerges in one form as the desire for recognition, the desire to be valued and completed in that sense. Where formal organization emphasizes partitioning, division and difference, the drive of *desire* towards the imagined Other, where there are no inequalities or discrepancies, a 'desired yet impossible absence' continually subverts rational arrangements (Cooper, 1983). Organizational membership then is a mere epiphenomenon to social being.

Organization as Seduction

Jackson and Carter (1986) have followed Deleuze and Guattari (1984) in distinguishing between Desire and Interest, the one represented by the corporate image, intentionally developed by the organization, the other by the counter image or images produced as a response to the former. The role of management, as they see it, is to manage the tensions between the fictionalized corporate image and its inevitable negation in counter-images, to perpetuate Desire (the lack of the many for the benefit of the few) at the expense of Interest (the benefit of the many).

The corporate image is a means to capitalize on the fundamental drive of ontological *lack*, the desire for the other which drives social structure, by manufacturing a synthetic lack which is engineered by consumerism, and which offers access to the desired world of the other (implicitly, at an ontological level) through access to the desired world of a particular social milieu. The desire of the *supplement*, the more fundamental drive, may then serve to implicitly or explicitly overturn the manufactured image, producing the counter-image, perhaps informed by the trace of class interest. The corporate image, or corporate culture, is a seductive device, designed to operationalize manufactured lack into a desire willingly to be controlled.

For Schultz (1989) the corporate culture offers 'identity, importance and the great orgiastic amalgamation with the collective' which we recognize as the desire for the Other. However, the culture is a *simulated* response to a *simulated* lack which occupies the same symbolic space as the ontological lack, and thus appears to have the potential to fill it. Corporate culture then follows the aesthetic *form* of meaningful experience without its *substance*. As Alvesson (1990a) puts it: 'pseudo-events, pseudo-action and pseudo structures, i.e. phenomena which have the effect of producing effects on people's impressions and definition of reality are important features of modern management and organization'.

We might consider Silverman's discussion of Castaneda (Silverman, 1975: 62–75) to relate corporate culture to the concept of 'non-ordinary reality' and 'special consensus', albeit in a somewhat debased form. The Yaqui Indian *brujo* (or shaman) Don Juan's 'little smoke' provides the means needed to transport a man 'beyond the boundaries of himself' into a world where, although not cut off from everyday life, and where the component elements were stable and consistent relative to each other, they were nevertheless 'singular'.

> [E]very detail of the component elements was a single individual item; it seemed as if each detail was isolated from others, or as if details appeared one at a time. The singularity of the component elements seemed further to create a unique necessity, which may have been common to everybody: the imperative need, the urge, to amalgamate all isolated details into a total scene, the total composite.

'Non-ordinary reality' is sustained by 'special consensus' which has to be prepared and guided. Although there is not space here to develop the linkages, I am reminded in reading this of the 'hyperreality' of the corporate world, the flickering images on the Wall Street computer terminals which sucked their dealers into the hollow vortex of the Crash of '87 (Rosen, 1990); the unreal moral states into which corporate managers are drawn and initiated (Jackall, 1988); and the activities of internal and external consultants in the manipulations of symbols and semi-religious events (Hopfl, 1991). This works to simulate in organizational members the trance induced by the 'little smoke' creating the common but *non-ordinary necessity* for a composite 'culture' to arise.

Corporate culture is 'a medium of changing the simulacra of an original identity in the organization which does not exist' – and which in itself is a simulacrum of the Other – 'and thus erase the member's feeling of the history of the organization. The history of the organization thus becomes the copied "basic" values of the moment, and yesterday's copy is a far distant past' (Schultz, 1989: 14; see also Baudrillard, 1988b, and de Certeau, 1984: 177–89). However, this cannot escape the effects of the inevitable reciprocating forces of sting, gift and desire, through the trace operating to overturn the asymmetry which the corporate culture perpetuates and through its drive towards its own fictionalized ontological ideal reasserting differance. Ordinary reality does inevitably re-emerge.

Organization as Discourse

Following Derrida's demonstration of power, repression and censorship being inevitable in linguistic construction Foucault (1979, 1980; Burrell, 1988; Parker, 1989), expands on the relationship between knowledge and power, power existing as a condition rather than a property, knowledge being constituted as an outcome of the systematic articulations of language grounded in social practice. That is to say, technologies or the 'micro physics' of power govern and reproduce specific discursive practices which have the effect of constituting knowledge. Power in this formulation is implicit in organizational discourse, structuring the rules and procedures which determine different forms of knowledge (Foucault, 1970, 1974); the definition of distinct fields (illness, madness, criminality, competence); the relationships within repertoires of concepts; the establishment of 'truth'; the delimitation of what can and what cannot be said; the emergence and presentation of 'subject-positions' (a sort of 'role' in discourse) which distributes and hierarchizes the field of unequal relations.

In this sense, power is the right to speak 'in the name of another (person, authority, etc.)'. Discourses emerge as regulated systems of statements (which can include symbolic phenomena drawn from other 'languages') which have both ideational content and implication for social practice, and cannot be reduced to either. Discourse produces 'rules' which systematically 'delimit what can be said, whilst providing the spaces – the concepts, metaphors, models, analogies – for making new statements within any specific discourses' (Henriques et al., 1984: 106) and for articulating with other discourses. Gergen implicitly acknowledges this when asking 'Why do we find it congenial to speak of organizations as structures but not clouds, systems but not songs, weak or strong but not tender or passionate?' (1992: 207). It is not therefore difficult to see how organizational or corporate cultures could be seen as discourses, especially in view of the significance of establishing internal and external boundaries. Discourse cannot be closed, although it may be relatively so, because it has to articulate with other discourses. Thus, just as science and literature compete over their relative battlegrounds, the one nevertheless inhabits the other in supplementarity, with each discourse being 'a practice of production which is at once material, discursive and complex, always inscribed in relation to other practices of production of discourse' (Henriques et al., 1984: 106). Scientists read novels and write poetry as well as doing science, and these alternative vocabularies are always available to them, and are necessary to define 'not-science'. The problem of understanding organizations could be formulated as that of understanding which discourses constitute and come to constitute them as complexes, what effects they have, for what reasons and what resistances they incur.

Foucault (1979) demonstrates that the logocentrism of 'writing' when translated into formal organization revolves around discipline. Discipline, he argues, revolves around controlling the minute details of the lives of those subjected to it whatever the organization. The technology of this is the Gaze, the imagined gaze of the Other as a controlling device, as we sit not perhaps in a total institution, but in a world in which 'the institutional organization of our lives is total' (Burrell, 1988: 232). As Letiche (1990) points out, however, the response to the Gaze is the 'Look' (as in 'appearance') and it may be possible for the appearance of compliance to satisfy the condition of surveillance whilst subverting, and paradoxically, controlling it by providing false information. It is central to the concept of discourse that it is reproduced, can be resisted and is subject to change and 'negotiation': the emphasis of study therefore should fall on the conditions which make reproduction more or less likely, and the detailed responses made in actual organizational situations by social actors.

There is, however, always the tendency of the contingent to ossify, as one particular view or version of events temporarily predominates over others, and contestation becomes weaker or less frequent. This hegemonic tendency, as one ideological formulation gains ascendancy, raises or supports the elevation of one subgroup over other subgroups, bringing economic, political, intellectual and moral unity within its compass. However powerful at any moment this solidification may be, it must be reproduced and sustained, can be resisted and deconstructed, and is never *permanently* normalized. As Hebdige observes

> Commodities can be symbolically 'repossessed' in everyday life, and endowed with implicitly oppositional meanings, by the very groups who originally produced them . . . the struggle between different discourses, different definitions and meanings within ideology is therefore always, at the same time a struggle within signification: a struggle for possession of the sign which extends to even the most mundane areas of everyday life. (1979: 16–17)

Many 'corporate culture' initiatives attempt to determine or lay claim to the sign without realizing that any sort of struggle is entailed or inevitable, even though it may well be asymmetrical. What researchers have so far inadequately considered in the context of organizational culture are the contours of the field of power relations against which symbolic determinations are played out, at particular historical moments in particular economic contexts, and which shape the coding possibilities and evocational fields which enable, constrain and prefer particular meanings without limiting them.

The Margins of Organizing: Deconstructing Everyday Practice

In this context postmodern anthropology is potentially responsive, as it sets itself specifically against *holism*, and the attempt to produce totalizing narratives. In this sense it has some similarities with metaphorization. Yet the examples of *'cultural critique'* which Marcus and Fischer (1986: 137–64) term *'defamiliarization by epistemological critique'* and *'defamiliarization by cross-cultural critique'* give several well-known examples of 'overturning' which do employ more or less holistic approaches, or at least employ theory at more than a local level (Geertz, 1983; Pearce and Chen, 1989). Rosen (1985, 1988, 1990, 1991) argues forcefully that a holistic approach enables ethnography to demystify as well as defamiliarize the taken for granted. Linstead (1985a) uses Levi-Strauss's methodology for the analysis of myths to analyse everyday discourse on a factory floor, arguing that this both demystifies managerial formulations of 'corporate culture' and delineates contours of resistance. He also (1985b) uses anthropological conceptualizations of the body in the analysis of industrial sabotage in the same setting, effectively to problematize the definition of the act itself. If fragmentation as a concept is to be at all useful in analysis, then it must be constantly brought to bear on conditions and structures of integration, at textual, conceptual and analytical levels whilst these integrating structures are simultaneously brought to bear on conditions of fragmentation (Burrell, 1989). In this way we might begin to understand the passionate embrace of supplementarity in which structuralism and deconstruction are energetic bedfellows. If we are correct in assuming that thought is 'nothing more and nothing less than a historically locatable set of practices' (Rabinow, 1986a: 239) then the devices which connect thought and organized society must feel the focus of this attention.

Accordingly, traditional ethnography has developed a capacity for critique at an epistemological or social-institutional level by a comparison of the thought-processes or social structures of other societies with its own. Where ethnography has developed 'at home' into subsections of society, occupations, locations or organizations, it has relied on a process of demystification through theorization, applying theory already developed or developing theory 'grounded' in its ethnographic context. In either case its critical leverage has depended on its ability to be taken for an accurate account of the social milieu in focus – to be taken as 'fact'. It is in their approaches to the representation of 'facts' that traditional, postmodern and deconstructive ethnographies differ crucially.

Postmodern ethnography interrogates traditional practice, asking of every representation 'is this fact?' and refusing to come to any final conclusions (Birth, 1990: 555). It throws into question its own authority as an account, and whether it introduces the device of co-authorship or multiple voices or not, it nevertheless points to the possibility of an infinitude of interpretations and accounts. However, this has posed a problem for those who believe in the critical and ethical purposes and emancipatory potential of ethnography. With no claim to factual superiority, how can it contest the accuracy of other accounts? How can it avoid the charge of nihilism if it recognizes no absolute authority and all facts, values and assumptions are undecidable? How can it enable choice between accounts if all are substitutable and none have priority? How can it deal with non-epistemological issues (Morgan, 1983b: 403; Jackson and Willmott, 1987: 364) – ideology, politics, ethics, morality – if its 'relativization of the new' leaves it no means to challenge the 'hegemony of the old' (Webster, 1983: 202)? In short, how can it contribute to praxis? (Jackson and Willmott, 1987).

These questions go further than those accusations of relativistic paralysis which assume that some form of absolute knowledge is a prerequisite for action. Empirical 'objective' knowledge cannot be absolute: situated in history it is 'circumscribed by a seriality it cannot transcend . . . possible only through material processes of production whose empiricity contradicts its ideal absoluteness' (Ryan, 1982: 213). Ethnography can neither be defended nor attacked through this paradox. However, acknowledging the falsity of meta-narratives of truth does not inevitably lead to the postmodern pragmatism of Rorty or Lyotard, in which truth and power become more or less equated (Norris, 1985: 18). The work of Lyotard (1984) has particular relevance for organizational ethnography in that he sees the old patterns of social centralization and control breaking down under postmodernity, as the influence of information technology fosters the growth and diffusion of information networks. As these networks become more densely interactive the need for absolute legitimating truths will dwindle, and truth will be based on a consensus of whatever is held to hold true for a given society at a given stage in its cultural evolution. Linguistic practice (conformity to a language-game) and performative power (its furtherance of the present aims of knowledge) become the only truth criteria (Norris, 1985: 16).

Lyotardian ethnography would provide detailed studies of fragmented information networks, clarifying linguistic practices and adding to the store of accessible data that would contribute to performativity and the development of the aims of knowledge. The fact that philosophy has debunked the objective truth is for Lyotard grounds for the optimistic assumption that with the spread of information and the 'free circulation of ideas' (Norris, 1985: 16), knowledge and instrumental reason will collapse into each other and their attendant social and political structures will inevitably follow. Baudrillard (1988b), less happy with this 'naturalized relation between history, reason, and present day consensus values' (Norris, 1985: 9) is profoundly disillusioned and pessimistic about the possibilities of transcending the simulated reality of the hyper-real disseminated by the new media. *Baudrillardian ethnography* could do no more or less than record experience as the flickering of images on a television monitor, as his more recent writings do – whatever is 'caught' by such means is fleeting, ephemeral, and misleading, appearance rather than essence.

Neither Baudrillard not Lyotard offers a satisfactory response to the problem of ethnographic critique. Lyotard's (1984) focus on knowledge, despite his disillusionment with the world as it is, leads to a virtual suppression of what Jackson and Willmott (1987) term 'non-epistemological' issues as truth and power become more or less indistinguishable. For Baudrillard the problem, or impossibility, of distinguishing truth from appearance seems to lead to a wallowing in the image and the abandonment of the pursuit of anything more substantial.

This criticism of insufficient attention to the moral/ideological dimension can also be levelled at what is a much less extreme and, at first sight, far more attractive approach to the problems of social knowledge and its investigation. Morgan (1983b) has extended Rorty's (1979, 1982) concept of *'reflective conversation'* into the methodology of the social sciences. Based on interaction between researchers and research paradigms, traditions and activities, its object is 'mutual edification and self-awareness with regard to the conditions and consequences of research strategies' (Jackson and Willmott, 1987: 365). Its advantages are proposed as the appreciation of a variety of voices in the conversation of research; the adoption of a tentative rather than absolute status for any truth claims; a detachment from normal presuppositions; and an increased awareness improving choice of research strategies or their modification. Jackson and Willmott (1987: 366–70) offer an extended critique of the flaws in this potentially attractive approach, which I will summarize. First, 'reflective conversation' takes language as unproblematic, ironically ignoring the non-epistemological (ideological and other) influences which it evokes and symbolizes. As Derrida has demonstrated, language inevitably suppresses and privileges: as Jackson and Willmott argue, it is not sufficient to acknowledge that this takes place but to examine *what* becomes privileged. The possibility that the sort of dialogue that 'reflective conversation' proposes can take place is in considerable doubt because of the influences embodied in the language-games of different scientific paradigms which may well be incommensurable (Jackson and Carter, 1991). Positivism, for example, limits its self-reflection to the authorial inspection for bias which Geertz (1983: 145; also Webster, 1983: 190) notes.

Second, the process and possibility of 'reflective conversation' depends on a value-neutral logos which powers, or is powered by, a sort of altruistic goodwill amongst social scientists. This linguistic free market – 'there are no constraints on enquiry save conversational ones . . . only those retail constraints provided by the remarks of our fellow inquirers' (Rorty, 1982: 165) – fails to connect with both the consequences and the sources of scientific motivation outside science, and their relation to practical interest and action in that arena, rather than the internal means–ends epistemological concerns of scientific communities. This form of 'conversation' may be both a substitute for action, and distorted by the more powerful and loudest voices, as Morgan acknowledges. However, as Jackson and Willmott argue, it is the *near certainty* that this will be the case that should be the centre and starting point of consideration, rather than a marginal note.

Ethnography under 'reflective conversation' or *Rortyan ethnography* would look very like 'postmodern' ethnography, sharing as it does similar formative influences. *Deconstructive ethnography*, however, takes as its starting point not the postmodern frame 'is this fact?' (Birth, 1990), but the deconstructive interrogation 'how could this come to be considered as fact?' and 'what are the consequences of treating this as fact?' Its grounding in philosophy is important, for as de Man (1984: 124, cited in Norris, 1985: 15) argues: 'philosophies that succumb to ideology lose their epistemological sense, where philosophies that try to bypass or repress ideology lose all critical thrust and risk being repossessed by what they foreclose'. This latter condition is ironically one of the consequences of pragmatism and a risk which is run by 'reflective conversation'. Deconstructive ethnography gives attention to the historicity of epistemology (Rabinow, 1986a: 241) as well as its textuality, and drives to demystify both traditional theoretical concepts, including those which it applies itself, and the workings of common-sense or naturalized perception (Norris, 1985: 8–9). Insofar as it embraces holism it is as

> the articulation of a diverse differentiated plurality: a unity or a whole or identity of a 'totality' is never anything but that anyway. Once it is thought to be anything else, an absolute identity or totality for instance, authority must be wielded to make the material world correspond to the ideal form and make the technological construct of totality or identity seem natural. (Ryan, 1982: 215)

Deconstructive ethnography then also works on the forms taken by this authority through its representations, linguistic, symbolic, 'textual' in its widest sense to demystify them through revealing their own internal contradictions rather than the application of an external theoretical or moral standard.

Conclusions: Organization and Deconstructive Ethnography

The tension between organization and disorganization (Cooper, 1990a), the drive to organize originating in the inherent 'undecidability' of terms in language and hence the nature of 'truth' (Cooper, 1989; Linstead and Grafton-Small, 1992) is discernible in all human structures. Derrida approaches this through 'deconstruction', a procedure which works closely with the 'texts' presented to use their own terms and contradictions within them first to overturn, then to 'metaphorize' or keep them in motion, not allowing them to rest in a final meaning. Deconstructive ethnography approaches social and organizational life as a 'text', entering into its terms and using them to disrupt our conventionalized consciousness of their significance. In deconstructive ethnography the use of theory is a device to resuscitate the subordinate terms, to elevate them, to amplify the silenced voices in order to problematize the dominant understanding and rather than create a new hierarchy, to re-construct a duality of awareness within conventional consciousness. However, this device is not merely the pursuit of theoretical novelty for its own sake, and must arise from a close and relevant reading of the 'text' *in its own terms* (Norris, 1990). It is in the rigour of the analysis which proceeds out from the text that the value of this analysis lies, rather than in its imaginative departure from the stimulus of the text into unlimited semiosis and unbounded interpretative pluralism or the semantic tyranny to which it subjects the text in order to 'fix' it.

In the context of social action in organizations, this deconstructive rigour will demystify in terms of the pursuit and identification of the *sources* and *consequences* of specific formulations and truth-effects, within the specific organizational, social, historical and economic contexts in which they occur. It will also examine the particular paths which evocation takes in such contexts, exploring evocative fields alongside the consideration of the discursive fields within which conceptual and referential language forms knowledge–power relations (Foucault, 1970, 1974, 1979, 1980). This is not to resurrect the idea of traditional individuality but is entirely consistent with the constitution of self within community. Just as the organization is a discursive field, the individual is a field of traces, 'a locus in which an incoherent (and often contradictory) plurality of . . . relational determinations interact' (de Certeau, 1984: xi). Just as 'reading' is a formative process, the *consumption* of organizational artifacts, be they products, relations or images, is a significant and neglected part of the process of the re-creation of subjectivity. De Certeau argues that modern 'production' systems (including the producers of *images* – television, urban development, commerce, etc.) increasingly 'no longer leave consumers any *place* in which they can indicate what they *make* or *do* with the products of these systems'. However, despite this marginality which De Certeau argues is 'massive and pervasive' the cultural activity of the non-producers forces the culture to mean and re-mean again and again in the assertion of supplementarity in 'organizational bricolage' (Linstead and Grafton-Small, 1989). These emergent practices may well seem mundane, but as Young argues they are the very substance of organizations. The exploitation of the margin, in Derrida's sense, is to turn the meaning of the term, to overturn the direction of the discourse, to de-construct culture, to dis-organize.

This will require of the ethnographer a self-reflexive capacity in order to recognize the processes of self-construction within accounts, and complement this with a self-deconstructive capacity; it will also require, in the process of 'getting close to the earth' (Webster, 1983: 202) evocatively a poetic capability for self-negation and openness in the face of the other. Poetic rigour and conceptual rigour will ultimately combine in the production of the account, which will employ explicit literary and figurative devices poised in the space between 'fact' and 'fiction' where 'truth' is manufactured. Articulating the tension between unity and dispersal, structure and play, will avoid closure but nevertheless identify some real limits to interpretation as this paradoxical precision teases out the critique which is *always already* implicitly present within all organized social/textual formulations: as we write we are written upon (Silverman, 1975: 111).

4

Eco and the Bunnymen

Gibson Burrell

Let me crave the reader's indulgence and begin by explaining how the present piece has come to be written: with exceptional reluctance. Had it proved possible I would have much preferred my compilation of pieces of video-tape entitled 'Eco and the Bunnymen' to have stood in stead of this article. The weeks spent in preparation and learning the technologies of video-editing were some of the most interesting and exciting I have experienced for several years. The final product was hurried, clichéd, distant from my original envisioning of it and lacking, unfortunately, in originality. Nevertheless, the complete experience from conceptualization to presentation will remain dear to me even if the finished version of the tape does not.

The fact that it has proved necessary to *write* this piece then is personally disturbing. No blame, I hasten to add, is attached to the current editors who have been most understanding. Other forces are the culprits. Writing, as a meaningful activity, is profoundly painful as an undertaking. It represents a struggle against uncertainty and the tyranny of the white; it stands for a personal inability, known to a small but increasingly vocal group of collegial technophiles to come to terms with computerized word-processing. (I grandly call my machine 'Ulysses' but that's really a sort of anagram.) But if one can't get the mind to process words acceptably how can a machine possibly help?

More disturbing still is the reaction of some close and some distant colleagues to my attempt at 'videocy' (Denzin, 1991: 8). This term represents a description of the movement towards the visual, video image and away from orality and the print media. There is displacement of the old media, logics and formats by new technologies which turn everything into theatrical spectacle – the diverse fact connected by the bizarre (Baudrillard, 1981: 115). The audience, indeed, can become part of the production as in for example, the slot in Noel Edmond's TV programme entitled 'NTV'. Here the deliciously uncertain viewer is viewed by other viewers as secret cameras enter the observer's home and appear to view from inside the TV itself. As Connor (1989: 153) states, 'we are not sure . . . whether we were watching them or watching them watching themselves'. Videocy then produces an ecstasy of communication (Baudrillard, 1988a) and an over-abundance of meaning.

My video-tape is an effort in this type of format. It as an attempt to reject the authority of the author. There was a refusal to answer questions during or immediately after the presentation of the tape at Keele. Since my understanding of its meanings were as constrained and relative as every other viewers' there was an obvious ploy on my part to leave interpretation open. In personal terms, my management of this process did not work, however. For whilst the tape was offered in a postmodern spirit, its compiler was unable to escape classic modernist and academic conventions. The very absence of questions (which, of course, had been formally requested) in the immediate post-presentational interactions encouraged me to think the tape had been a 'failure'.

These feelings were compounded dramatically some months later by a Salaries and Promotions Committee in my own Department. Not unkindly, it was made clear to me that the video-tape produced for the conference and appearing on my C.V. was not deemed to be a paper, still less a publication, and that perhaps the effort I had devoted to it in some way was not a sensible utilization of Professorial time. The implication that experimentation outside the media of print remained unrewarding both for the Department and for me personally was difficult to ignore.

My immediate reaction was to attempt to 'publish' the compilation under the auspices of the Keele conference and its associated publications. The knowledge that it would sell even less copies than the very brief video-tape of 'Great Newcastle United Teams of the 1980s' worried me little. However, it soon became apparent that the copyright laws would not permit a compilation of the kind represented by 'Eco and the Bunnymen'. Back to the written word.

Thus, writing this piece engenders very mixed emotions including feelings of rejection, memories of confrontation with legal systems, perceptions of pleasure turned into pain based on issues of career and careerism. So why the present chapter? First, let me protest it is not some attempt to re-ingratiate myself with professorial colleagues. No, I have done that in other ways. Rather it is an (perhaps vain) attempt to create a climate of opinion in the area of management studies where 'performativity' (Lyotard, 1984) can begin to be questioned and where alternative forms of presentation, of raising of arguments and of critique, become possible. For if it is not possible for someone with a relatively privileged institutional position to attempt the unusual, how much more difficult will it prove for the untenured lecturer with her more radical and youthful stance to such issues? To use Lyotard's terms, the present chapter and its reluctant replacement of the video-tape is meant to be part of a postmodern, figural, paralogical system of representation which stands at odds with more university-based, rational discursive systems of representation (Lash, 1988). So it is to this task that I must now address myself.

For some, the university-based disciplines represent the epitome of scientific achievement and require wakeful defence in the face of the 'anti-aesthetic, anti-institutional, anti-intellectual impulse' (Denzin, 1991: 10) which runs through and around postmodern productions. High modernism, found in those 'ivory towers' where long-term inhabitants carrying out the key tasks of research and discovery shy away from the tourists' gaze and their vacational mess, stands opposed by postmodernist notions. Postmodernism is dangerous for it questions discipline, totalizing attempts, rationality and truth. It seeks to criticize innovation, novelty and dynamism (Berman, 1982), which is what modernism has stood for since the Enlightenment. It is akin to that activity so antithetical to the Edwardian university; trade (Clegg, 1990: 15). But, of course, modernism and its institutional expression in the university has also created untold misery.

First, its reliance upon 'discipline' which both defines an area of intellectual activity and what goes on within it and specifies what is acceptable, normal behaviour on the part of the member of the discipline, creates a controlled intellectual space (Kuhn, 1970; Foucault, 1979). This 'cordon sanitare' keeps out the enemy and restrains the pulsating forces within. The Modernist tower blocks envisaged by Le Corbusier were designed to free the inhabitants from the poverty of the 'ghettos' but also and equally important to be 'the grave of the riot'. What they succeeded in doing was to replace one form of imprisonment with another (Harvey, 1989: 36).

A number of writers in the sociology of science have also noted the ways in which scientific fields develop power structures, through which careers are managed and those who bow not to discipline are marginalized. Ravetz's work here is important (Ravetz, 1971). He speaks of the ways in which 'shoddy science' can develop as influential figures within disciplines gain control over publication outlets, privileged access to research funding, sponsorship of young researchers and achieve refereeing centrality. These figures, who are known to exist in most fields of human intellectual endeavour but are sometimes more visible in particular disciplines, can so control the progress of an idea, conceptualization or individual that it makes a nonsense to talk of peer assessment. The infamous Velikovsky controversy in the 1970s highlighted the lengths to which a group of disciplinary leaders would go in order to suppress the work of a non-standard entrant into their debates. Commenting on the characteristics of Venus, Velikovsky was totally at odds with conventional astrophysical beliefs. When the first few attempts at landing on that planet suggested the 'normal science' view of its origins and composition were unable to predict the results obtained, and Velikovsky's predictions, based as they were on historical and mythological research, were much more accurate, a controversy developed in which his work was totally denigrated. The alternative views which Velikovsky articulated were deemed to be so threatening to the dominant disciplinarians that he was subject to appalling professional attacks. This sort of debacle is a concomitant of modernism within university settings.

Second, and connected to the previous section, is the growth in bureaucracy within those organizations known as universities. The relatively isocratic nature of decision-making within the community of scholars has given way to the power of key research managers within the contemporary academy who organize hierarchically. Once one fuses modernism, bureaucracy and the university one finds knowledge becomes hierarchically organized and falls into the hands of those who claim to profess this body of science. Within the United Kingdom, the Jarratt Report made these lines of responsibility and discipline very clear, putting to an end any thoughts of a defence of an intellectual communitas by effectively reducing the power of the professional academic for the benefit of university administrators and 'senior' professors.

Third, there is the arena of cultural capital and the vast amount of time that is spent in acquiring it. Featherstone (1991) is particularly incisive on this. The intellectual is a producer but also a consumer of symbols in particular and cultural capital in general. As goods become more widely available, one's position or rank in the cultural order cannot be read off from mere possession of commodities. One needs to demonstrate discriminating judgement in order to draw and redraw social exclusivity. There are high barriers to entry of social groupings and very effective mechanisms for exclusion. Key amongst these is the extraordinary investment in time required in order to maintain knowledge about positional goods and services and facilities and how to use them 'correctly'. Up-to-date knowledge of what, how and where to consume comes to have great value. And the universities are certainly no exception to this emphasis on consumption knowledge. Those who are economically unable to support an interest in the growth of the market for positional goods face exclusion from class-status groups. In some senses the British university system has always marketed itself to consumers of positional goods, but this tendency has developed in an accelerating way throughout the 1980s. On the other hand, Featherstone argues that an openness and dynamism in what is conceptualizable as a positional good has developed in precisely the same period. This has led, he opines, to a lowering in the barriers of what is termed 'culture' which threatens those university disciplines reliant upon defending High Culture.

Fourth, Featherstone is very keen to build upon Stallybrass and White's (1986) discussion of carnivals, festivals and fairs. In Featherstone's discussion the carnival and the fair are not fully distinguished. Both are seen as the locus of fattening food, intoxicating drink and sexual promiscuity. But the fair was also a *local market* as well as a site of pleasure where 'spectacular imagery, bizarre juxtapositions, confusions of boundaries and an immersion in a melée of strange sounds, motions, images, people, animals and things' (Featherstone, 1991: 23) used to meet the observer and participant.

As the civilizing process (Elias, 1982) developed, however, the market functions of fairs began to overtake the grotesque and pleasurable elements locked within them. The commodification of everything, the control, measurement and analysis of human interaction through the 'value' it held and the metaphor of the market in governing life transformed the premodern fair into today's modernized equivalent – the academic *conference*. Let us take as our example the American Academy of Management's annual meeting in August of each year. The British Academy of Management is yet but a pale reflection of what I am about to describe, but unfortunately there are those who wish it were much closer in form and content than it is presently.

For three or four days each summer, full-time academics at all institutional levels, from doctoral candidates to the professoriat of Ivy League universities meet at the Academy of Management in their thousands to see and be seen. For the novitiate, Featherstone's description of the fair (above) conceptually describes first impressions, but it is important to remember and hang on to the distinction here between observer and participant. For the British 'observer' there is always likely to be some personal investment either as a paper-giver or as someone who is attempting to raise his/her level of intellectual capital. But this marginal role of brief investor is very different from being in the labour market itself. One is not a full participant and so the full fascination of this market for intellectual meat strikes the peripheralized observer very forcibly. Everything is commodified, everything is status-driven.

Doctoral candidates, looking for university positions, are glaringly obvious in the hotel lobbies. The males dress in blazers and grey trousers, the women in blue suits. Prestigious professors dress in Bermuda shorts and sandals. One's position in the hierarchy therefore is marked by dress, so the 'smarter' the attire the lower is one's standing. Full professors of note call breakfast meetings with talent they have spotted or which has been pointed out to them. A number of years ago, someone who is now a very well-known professor of organization theory, turned up by invitation to a breakfast meeting expecting to be involved in a dialogue with a shaven-headed, powerful, male academic from an institution of some standing in North America. As it turned out, a dozen other academics (all male) were also there, and my colleague's appointed position was way down the table, well below the condiments. Even at that developed stage in his career he was not yet 'worth his salt'. Yet to be invited was something. The message was clear. Work hard, publish much and year by year you will creep closer to the salt. Seven or eight years later, subject to appraisal, you will sit next to the great man. In a decade, said the fairground's message to my colleague, you could be that great man. Meanwhile, be grateful.

From balconies above, the observer notes that the reception halls are spatial representations of power. Key figures in management form the centre of magnetic fields of attraction, surrounded by less powerful but still significant figures, with the marginal and peripheralized tenure-seekers looking for access into the charmed circle of the powerful. For the doctoral students such access is not possible. On their first evening they hand over a copy of their C.V. (Vita) to a centralized bureau with a list of universities they would wish to join. That night, all night, representatives of these universities sift through the copious applications, rejecting, judging and considering, until by dawn a list of interviewees has been constructed. Throughout the days of the meeting, interviews will be held in each university's suite of rooms until eventually enough new blood has been attracted. For the student, the second morning of the annual meeting means a flood of desirable invitations, or perhaps, a few enquiries from the less prestigious universities or nothing at all. Your market value becomes immediately obvious on opening your mail, in a way which almost instantaneously, finally and irrevocably places your self-image in a more inter-subjective context. This is not what we have all faced; rejection from a particular institution. This is a rejection by and an ejection from the market in its continental whole.

The Academy of Management represents, then, to someone who is outside the culture, strange sounds, images and people. It is the fairground, however, not in a premodern sense but in its modernist form. Like many academic conferences it drips power, bureaucratic hierarchy and patriarchy. It reflects the institutions from which its membership is drawn. In common with its species it is the modern fair in which we and our relationships are all commodified. It is a three-day market in which we are all likely to be bought and sold – unless we are very, very careful.

Fifth, modernism highlights linearity; linearity in space, linearity in time and, most importantly, linearity in thought. For example, Le Corbusier was keen to pronounce the straight line much superior to the curve (Harvey, 1989: 36) and in the view of time established in the West, the metaphor of 'time's arrow' became popular. Within thought, however, the metaphor of the line has predominated the Enlightenment's vision of itself. Linearity, therefore, invades all aspects of the university's self-conception. Essays, theses, examination answers and reports must have a beginning, a middle and an end. They must tell a story, with some development of narrative discernible within them. Argumentation is deemed to be incremental, building up to a conclusion which all must accept if sufficiently clear in its expression. But this form of accounting, of a retrospective construction of 'the scientific method', belies the construction of multiple mosaics and bountiful bricolages which are much closer to many forms of human understanding. As McLuhan noted, this one dimensionality of thought creates a conservatism and closure which specifically excludes other forms of understanding.

Thus, whilst postmodernism may threaten the achievements of modernism and its attempts to shed light on the dark corners of the macrocosm and the microcosm, the former also offers hope and new openings. But this hope arises from a reconceptualization of knowledge and, equally importantly, of the university. For how can any understanding of the 'universal' be sought if postmodernism is correct in its orientation? What role can an institution which often claims to seek

Table 4.1

Modernism	Postmodernism
Differentiation	De-differentiation
Language	Desire
The authority of the author	The author as powerless
Auratic art	Popular art
Discursive signification	Figural signification
What does a text mean?	What does a text do?
Literary format	Visual format
Literacy	Videocy
The reality principle	The pleasure principle
Aesthetics of interpretation	Aesthetics of sensation
Theatre of intelligence	Theatre of cruelty
Educated ear	Savage eye
Discipline	Spectacle
Consensus and homogeneity	Dissent and paralogy

universal truths play within this new cultural milieu? Let us crudely summarize, in Table 4.1 some of the relevant elements.

It must be noted, of course, that the very act of differentiating between the two 'cultural orders' as I have done here is a typical Modernist activity and is part and parcel of the left-hand column, reflecting in quite close ways the assumptions laid out there. New ways of presenting arguments must be developed in order to escape from our literary presuppositions and presentiments – but more of that, earlier and later.

The University under Modernism

Classification, separation and categorization, as Foucault has shown, are essential elements in the development of discipline, and this is accompanied, of course, by the formulation of academic disciplines. Differentiation of fact from value, the sacred from the secular, the ethical from the theoretical, is central to the movement generated within modernism. Out of these dichotomies comes the appearance of value neutrality, of distanciation from the issues at hand, of a rejection of old theology and an embracing of the modern sociology. In this movement, language (words and sentences) comes to be subject to detailed analysis. It is unpicked, phoneme by phoneme, and subject to ever closer scrutiny for its true meaning which resides within the author's intentions. To know the author is to seek authority in a more perfect understanding of a text's real meaning. If the author was to say she did not mean to say what she has been interpreted as saying, then it would fundamentally undermine the validity of the interpretation in question. There is an aura around works of art such as the novel, the painting, the poem, the key textbook, which encourage a hagiography and icon worship either in the form of prized institutional collections or the honorary doctorate for the author.

Discursive signification is highly valued in the modernist university. Here, words are prioritized over images, and the meanings of these words and how they are packaged is given tremendous emphasis. The spectator of these words and discourses is kept at a distance from the object of culture in question and is meant to articulate an impression of the object through rational discourse and debate. Literacy and the literary format reign supreme in committee work, issues of promotion and evaluation of contribution. In Freudian terms the viewer must be kept on course by the reality principle, subjecting his or her views to rational tests on a regular basis. Similarly, questions of interpretation must always be discussed through the medium of language and the aura and authority allocated to the author. In terms of university teaching and seminar work, kudos is attached to the 'theatre of intelligence' where an appeal is made to a clearly segregated audience's intellectual faculties and the erudition and eloquence of the speaker. The appeal, when there is one, is made to the 'educated ear' of the lecture hall's audience. In sum, the modern university relies upon disciplines for discipline, the hierarchical labelling of individuals by academic performance and upon the historical presumption that academics are motivated by the search for consensus and homogeneity.

The University in Postmodern Times

'Beneath the pavement, the beach.' So said the graffiti on the walls of Paris in 1968. Beneath language, according to several postmodern theorists, lies *desire*. In the beginning there is not the word, there is the id and its impulses. There is the visual impact of the seen upon the seer which is to be felt not upon the thinking eye but upon the savage eye. It is visceral, in the gut, not at the level of the cerebellum. In a crude sense it is not so much organismic: it is more orgasmic. It is to do with the sensual and not the intellectual. It is to concern ourselves in the universities with the 'erotic' and not the cerebral.

But in what senses, if any, does the interest in 'desire' found in Lyotard, Deleuze and Foucault, impinge upon the British university and its concern for disciplinary development? When William Blake talks of 'dark, satanic mills' he does not only mean the textile industry. In Plate 15 of Jerusalem it is fairly explicit that universities, with their then contemporary acceptance of Newtonian physics in all disciplines, were dark and satanic also. They and their membership were cogs within a machine, teaching mechanistic predictability and unfailing order, in a way which we would now say was both bureaucratic and modernist. Since Blake prefigured postmodernism with its questioning of unity in history, its playfulness and wit and its rejection of rationality, it is unlikely that he would have seen the universities of the *1990s* as either being postmodern or capable of treating desire seriously. This is probably true of many of us!

Let us be clear here. The pursuit of knowledge of a universal kind which gives the university its name is essentially a modernist exercise. Rationality, regularity, science and technology, calculability and prediction are almost always predicated upon a modernist project. Therefore, attempts to conjure up postmodern forms of organization or pursue postmodern analyses with a view to publication may well be contradictions in terms. This is not to say we should embrace modernism ever more tightly simply because postmodernism is pragmatically oxymoronic (Power, 1990). We should, in my view, seek to understand postmodern thought and accept its influence on our being, but not necessarily believe it can much affect our doing. The irony in Chaos theory within mathematics is that it seeks to find order in chaos; it seeks to reduce postmodern concepts to modernist calculation. If we follow this path of control and use, then we lose the radicality and inventiveness of the concept. We one-dimensionalize it so that practice abuses theory (Parker, 1992a).

In the case of desire, however, I am advocating a fusion of theory and practice in order to affect our doing. At the risk of sounding naive and out of touch let me suggest that modern universities in a generic sense have within them the capacity for reflecting desire.

With regard to one important but narrow part of desire, namely sexual relations, the attempted suppression of sexuality has been less successful in universities than in many other organizational forms. Single-sex colleges were the historical norm but homosexuality was never repressed effectively. Heterosexuality was discouraged through architectural and other disciplinary means but the modern campus university in Britain, designed in the 1960s, does not have the full paraphernalia of desexualization. Penalties exist, of course, and the role of the cleaner as moral policer is ever as it was, but one does not immediately assume that universities are relatively devoid of homosexual and heterosexual activity (Cockburn, 1991; Burrell, 1992a). Nevertheless as Table 4.2 shows, there is much disjuncture between what is and what might be.

Perhaps the very old distinction between the formal and the informal organization is relevant here? Might it not be that the student body lives a postmodern life whilst staff inhabit a modern world? Might it not be that instead of saying with some perspicacity that 'youth is wasted on the young' we go on to complain that postmodernism is wasted on the young? Perhaps they live a life as close to that described in the right-hand column as is currently possible?

Suddenly I am frightened. It is two days since I completed the last sentence and I have re-read the complete text. How does one write about a university based on the pleasure principle when the evidence before our eyes is so at odds with such a conceptualization? How does one write as

Table 4.2

The modern university?	A university in postmodern times?
The reality principle	The pleasure principle
Language	Desire
Control and suppression of the erotic	Enhancement and development of the erotic
The erotic narrowly defined	The erotic broadly defined
Drug abuse	Drug use
'Egological vision'	The seer
Mass leisure	Spontaneous involvement of the 'masses'
Bureaucratic organizational forms	Every form of social organization
Crowd control and public order	The carnival
Desexualization (that is the attempted suppression of penetrative homosexual and heterosexual activity)	De-eroticization (the attempt to reintroduce sensuous polymorphic emotions into human life)
Doing	Being
Performativity through disciplined action	Ecstasy through joyous serenity

a middle-aged male about such issues without being deemed to be priapic? How is one to be sure one is not priapic anyway? I feel like Dr Vorless in *The Day of the Triffids* (Wyndham, 1954: 122).

Is the notion of free speech so deeply entrenched in my institution that the advocacy of drugs use, the erotic, desire, the carnivalesque and the involvement of the masses found here, will be viewed without prejudice? Or will I be subjected to discipline? Doesn't all this sound like a hollow romanticism for the late 1960s when at the time the universities seemed to some to be central institutions of reforming zeal? In answer to these questions I am reminded yet again of Kafka's short story (some say, novel) entitled 'Give it up'.

Yet Gergen (1992) has helpfully attempted to construct an argument which points 'toward postmodern theories of the organization'. He distinguishes between romantic, modernist and postmodern approaches to the organization. The first two have proved to be cultural 'leitmotifs' or 'hegemonic bodies of discourse' (Gergen, 1992: 208) from which organization theory has drawn its sustenance. Already, however, the romantic has been replaced by the modernist discourse, and in turn the contemporary Zeitgeist witnesses the slow dismantling of the rhetoric of modernism.

The romantics had a vision of the person in which 'the deep interior' was what was truly significant. To see this hidden place required great sensitivity and sophistication, but if this was available, the interior became revealed as a place of energy, passion and madness. 'Know oneself' became the motto of the romantics and their orientation is made visible, says Gergen, in the work of the Tavistock Institute, Japanese management theory, neo-human relations approaches and those following Jungian archetypes (Gergen, 1992: 210). Is not much of the search for 'New Age' thinking with its concern for freer expression a reflection of this type of approach?

This vocabulary, however, according to Gergen, is in remission. It is less easily found today, having been displaced by the modernist world view. This has 'left an indelible mark on theories of organization from early in the century to the present' (Gergen, 1992: 211). For modernists there were essentials to be uncovered using reason and observation, to be expressed, clearly and unambiguously, in language. Language here is the servant of the essential; it can be rectified by an ever closer contact with the real.

But postmodernism, of course, questions this posited relationship between the real and language. The real becomes replaced by the representational so that we can no longer be sure that the 'real' exists outside of some group's tendentious, ideologically motivated project. According to Gergen, representation is a communal artifact so that psychological, individualized explanations are thrown into question. These are often essentialist types of reasoning and within a postmodern view of the world are highly dubious.

Rather than the situation being one of me expressing relationships through language, relationships are now seen as expressing themselves through me (Gergen, 1992: 214). If this is so, the role of the theorist is deeply troubled by an irony. All is representational and there can be no 'real' world against which to argue or on which to base critical commentary.

Gergen provocatively sketches some solutions adopted to the problems raised by this ironic self-reflection. Derrida, for example, deconstructs his own writings in elliptical fashion. Kristeva seeks to develop a non-androcentric form of expression. Citing Sloterdijk, Gergen says 'others propose that the scholar should play the fool or the dandy, or more provocatively, go piss in public'.

How far then has organization theory moved towards pissing in public? Gergen answers that there has been progress, but his arguments here fail to convince. He maintains that postmodernism has practical significance and intelligibility. Further, it should be able to draw upon modernist and romanticist notions. It should also be able to offer up new options for action within the organization (Parker, 1992a). But is this really the situationist or anarchist view of the warm glow which comes from urination over the feet of the bourgeoisie as they climb the steps of the Paris Opera? No, this is more that of the consultant who wishes to plunder postmodernism for the radicalization of conventional organization design. Very similar in fact, to my previous section on the postmodern university!

The problem remains this, therefore. Should postmodernism be seen as practically useless since it offers nothing but a plurality of competing representational vocabularies in a world where facticity has disappeared, or should it be neutered, tamed, harnessed further to imbue consultancy-speak with another argot upon which to draw? Gergen believes harnessing is possible. My earlier sections argued that our own organizations could be improved by the embracing of postmodern notions. But is that all that postmodern ideas represent – a template for better university structures based on a call for 'heteroglossia' (Bakhtin, 1981: Gergen, 1992)? I'd rather piss in public than believe that.

Indeed, there have been times since the Keele conference when I wish the video-tape of 'Eco and the Bunnymen' had been blank and an audience had been forced to watch a black screen flicker away 30 minutes of their time. I sometimes wish the frothy liquid in my water pistol aimed at Mike Reed's head had not been designed 'for hands that do dishes'. I wish . . . I wish. . . . At least, a Spoonerist title for another video has just suggested itself (always supposing one's nerve could be relied upon to carry it off in the face of collegial hostility or indifference). How about 'glands that do wishes'?

5

Modernism, Postmodernism and Motivation, Or Why Expectancy Theory Failed to Come Up to Expectation

Pippa Carter and Norman Jackson

In this chapter we identify Expectancy Theory as a prototypically postmodern theory of motivation to work, which distinguishes it from any other available such theory of its time.

Expectancy Theory rejects the principle of transcendent rationality characteristic of modernism, and introduces the voice of subjective understanding into the issue of motivation to work, thus making it impossible, in theory, to sustain treating workers as mere passive objects of motivational strategies. However, Expectancy Theory has failed to realize its promise because its arena of operationalization, management, is quintessentially modernist. We argue that, typically, theories of motivation to work have exhibited the characteristics of modernism, being rooted in formal logic and universal reason. Failure to explain motivation fully has been addressed by increasing sophistication. This process of development led inevitably towards inclusion of subjective experience as a significant element, yet it was this very move which placed Expectancy Theory outside the bounds of transcendent rationality. A postmodern reading of Expectancy Theory both explains its fate and indicates what could have happened had its precepts been taken seriously.

Because of the diversity surrounding concepts of modernism and postmodernism and their relationship to each other, we begin by offering an interpretation of these concepts, which focuses on the issue of rationality. The impact of a conceptualization of postmodernism which characterizes it in terms of its informing ideas (ontological and epistemological in particular) (see Carter and Jackson, 1991), is, partly, that it emphasizes the absence of an identifiable break between modernism and postmodernism. They have been, and are, coexistent, concurrent – at most it could be said that one may have been more dominant. Thus it has been possible to see, retrospectively, some writers long gone as representing postmodern approaches, such as Weber (see, for example, Turner, C., 1990), or Simmel (Weinstein and Weinstein, 1990), notwithstanding the lack of such a concept in their time. The development of postmodernism has been spasmodic and has varied enormously in different fields of knowledge and discourses. This very intermittence can be highly informative, if it is possible to identify work which signifies divergence from modernism towards postmodernism.

Central to understanding postmodernism is awareness of key events which mark the passing of the modern and the emergence of the post-modern. This is important for a number of reasons. Postmodernism emerges as a reaction or an antidote to the perceived failures of modernism – in other words, when the modern can no longer explain social phenomena we turn to the postmodern explanation. If we can identify the key shift, we should also be able to identify the crisis which brought about the shift, although neither crisis nor shift may have been recognized at the time. If we can re-construct, de-construct, re-interpret this event, we may be able to identify obstacles to social progress. The particular significance of this is that, given that modernism is perceived to have *failed* – that is, it has not produced the promised solutions to social problems – there is an immeasurably greater possibility that such solutions might be found if we can understand why modernism failed, and/or in what sense it failed. Identifying the crisis and the shift are the first, crucial steps in this process. Having done that, we may then also be able to see where postmodernism leads, in terms of providing an efficacious basis for praxis. This is our intention in identifying, in the general field of organization studies and the particular arena of theories of motivation to work, Expectancy Theory as marking the shift from modernism to post-modernism.

Modernism and Postmodernism

Postmodernism is generally conceptualized in contradistinction to modernism, which, it is held, it is now succeeding: we are entering the postmodern epoch (*pace* Bradbury (1990), who implies that it is already over). However, what is not so clear is whether postmodernism stands in opposition to modernism, or is the latest stage of development of modernism (Lyotard 1984; Turner, B.S., 1990). Whilst the distinction is not necessarily crucial here, it is useful to try to understand the relationship between modernism and postmodernism.

Given the frequent and liberal usage of the terms modernism and postmodernism, it may appear that the concepts lack any coherence or significance. Indeed, this conceptual diversity is itself an aspect which is frequently subjected to searching analysis (see, for example, Harvey, 1989; Boyne and Rattansi, 1990; Featherstone, 1991). The heterogeneity of each which is thus analysed tends to be addressed at the level of the sign, with a focus on materiality and attendant imputed meaning. Thus, for example, in the visual arts, it is perfectly feasible to see both realism and surrealism as manifestations of modernism (as also implied by Harvey, 1989), but, at the level of the art objects produced, their differences seem far more demanding of attention than the unity of their underlying logic. Harvey (1989: 30) notes that '[m]odernism . . . took on multiple perspectivism and relativism as its epistemology for revealing what it still took to be the true nature of a unified, though complex, underlying reality'. In other words, despite the diversity in manifestations of the modern, there is an informing logic, a meta-level, which is common to all this diversity. It is on this commonality that we wish to focus, rather than be distracted by the inevitable plurality that occurs when the human mind attempts to translate a meta-concept into a social phenomenon, be it a painting, a building, a novel, a social policy, an organization, etc.

Modernity is popularly regarded as a product of the Enlightenment and quintessentially represents the use of scientific logic (objective rationality) to explain causal relationships – in Habermas's (1981: 5) terms, 'modernity lives on the experience of rebelling against all that is normative'. The preceding (premodern) epoch was dominated by theological explanations of causality. The superseding modernism was seen to have better explanatory power, central to which was the claim of superiority for scientific, non-ideological, rigour over theocratic dogmatism. Truth was to be discovered in the causal relationships of a transcendent and pre-existing natural world. Truth could no longer be prescribed by the powerful – by the Church or the aristocracy, for example – but was embodied in some neutral concept of Nature, equally available to all, without fear or favour. This had clear immediate applications in the context of the natural world – for example, scientists no longer had to concur with a geocentric universe because of the power of the Church, but could acknowledge the overwhelming evidence for localized heliocentrism, which has given rise to the cosmology of the last 400 years. However, the impact was equally powerful with regard to the social world, giving rise to a social science modelled on the natural sciences. Social science could discover social laws, in the same way that natural science could unlock the laws of the natural world, and through human intervention solve problems and enhance human existence. Harvey (1989: 27) comments: 'The Enlightenment project . . . took it as axiomatic that there was only one possible answer to any question. From this it followed that the world could be controlled and rationally ordered if we could only picture and represent it rightly.' It is, of course, just such principles which inform Scientific Management. Another manifestation is the concern with motivation to work and attempts to discern regular relationships between, for example, reward and performance.

The implication of all this was that modernism had the potential to solve social problems. All that was necessary was the application of rational thought to an empirically accessible reality. But modernism has obviously failed to realize this project. War, ignorance, hunger and pestilence are still rife in the world; and, at the organizational level, for example, amongst many other problems, modernism has failed to solve the problem of motivation to work. Far from pushing out the boundaries of what is accessible to rational thought, spreading enlightenment to the unenlightened, enlightenment has come to be characterized as culturally specific rather than universal. Even where rationality has conquered it is now suffering a loss of credibility, and not only does it seem to have reached its limits but also the gains once made are undergoing reversal: preventable diseases once eradicated are now recurring; illiteracy rates once diminishing are now again increasing; the general concern to make work satisfying has given way to an acceptance of its degrading and dehumanizing qualities; and there are myriad other promises that modernism offered that have not, even temporarily, been fulfilled.

No matter what our position in the social world we cannot fail to recognize that these things are happening. So what can be done to put them right? In its most basic form the choice is between only two alternatives. Either modernism is fundamentally sound but has been inadequately and/or incorrectly applied, in which case we must preserve the spirit of modernism and redouble our efforts to apply it more successfully (see, for example, Habermas, 1981; Harvey, 1989; Kellner, 1989; Jameson, 1991). Or modernism is fundamentally flawed and we must reject its informing logic (for example, postmodernism). The problem with accepting the former position is the assumption that modernism is allowed to address the problems that it seeks to solve unfettered. But, even though the meta-theory of modernism works from the basis that it is ideologically neutral – that is, rooted in nature – in practice this clearly is not and never has been the case. The explanations for this range from the benign view that, because people are involved in implementing the meta-theory, an ideological bias is inevitable though unintentional, through the argument that, because of the way research is socially controlled, some ideological interests are inevitably better served than others, to the strong version that, because societies are dominated by ideological systems, solutions to problems are, first and foremost, subject to tests of ideological acceptability: if rational thought demonstrates that y is the solution to x, but y is ideologically unsound, y will not be implemented. So, for example, in the arena of theories of motivation to work, despite their proliferation, even a cursory examination will reveal that they are subject to a limited number of acceptabilities, which do not include, for example, the possibility that motivation to work is important *per se*, rather than just as an epiphenomenon of profitability (an ideologically specific category), or that it may be against the interest of any individual worker to work harder. Some solutions are simply inadmissible, notwithstanding that they might, if given the chance to be tested, offer the solution to the problem under consideration.

The extended analysis of what has gone wrong with modernism has revealed, *inter alia*, the ideological superstructure in which this avowedly neutral rationality has had to operate (for example, Marcuse, 1964; Foucault, 1974; Lyotard, 1984). Postmodernism's response is to claim the need to abandon transcendent rationality as a precept, not least on the grounds that it is an unattainable condition. Failing the opportunity ever fully to test modernism's power to solve social problems, the other alternative is to reject modernism's meta-theory, its totalizing rationality, and this is what postmodernism does (Burrell, 1989). In the questioning of the probity of modernism, it is the precept of absolute rationality which has been seen as fatal to its potential to fulfil its promise, in particular to solve social problems through 'the rational organization of everyday social life' (Habermas, 1981: 9), whether in relation to health or education, happiness or productivity, and so on. Again, motivation to work can be seen as a relevant field which exemplifies this process of rejection, having suffered a substantial decline of belief in its efficacy and effectively being replaced by a concomitant increase of faith in the power of leadership – not, however, rational/legal leadership, but charismatic leadership (Carter and Jackson, 1989). In other words, the loss of faith in the rational has led to an increase in faith in the mysterious and the magical. Thus, the three epochs can be characterized as shown in Table 5.1.

Table 5.1

Premodern	Modern	Postmodern
Dogmatic rationality based on theo-logic	Objective rationality based on scientific logic	Subjective rationality based on mytho-logic

It must be stressed that the term mytho-logic should not be seen as pejorative, but simply indicative of a logic based on myth. The etymology of 'myth' relates it to muthos (mouth) and thus to the subject and to subjectivity (Olson, 1970). (For an expansion of this use of myth to characterize human understanding, see Jackson and Carter, 1984.)

Thus, what is particularly significant about postmodernism is the replacement of belief in the power of *the* rational explanation by belief in the *subjectivity* of rational explanation. Whilst, in its abandonment of rationality, this might seem to represent a regression to the premodern, postmodernism distinguishes itself in its rejection of *all* totalizing metatheory – it rejects both the modern and the pre-modern, as shown in Table 5.2. It can be suggested, indeed, that in these terms modernism and premodernism have more in common with each other than postmodernism does with either of them (see also Turner, C., 1990).

Postmodernity, even more than modernity, has been characterized by multiplicity of interpretation, and indeed this diversity is itself actively celebrated by many of its proponents. It has become a commonplace for

Table 5.2

	Premodern	Modern	Postmodern
Meta-theory	Yes	Yes	No
Rationality	Transcendent/Dogmatic	Transcendent/Objective	Subjective/Rhetorical

writers to preface their remarks on postmodernism with the caveat that it is effectively impossible to define (for example, Harvey, 1989; Boyne and Rattansi, 1990; Lash, 1990; Featherstone, 1991). This not unreasonable qualification clearly serves to disarm other writers on the topic who, while equally eager to disclaim authority, are nevertheless happy to challenge definitions with which they do not agree. This is, no doubt, very postmodern. But while there is indeed enormous variety in postmodernism – even to the point of contradiction – (a condition also found, as noted, in modernism), and while we would agree with Jameson's (1991: xxii) argument that such diversity in usage needs to be retained to 'prevent the mischief of premature clarification', we would also argue that for postmodernism to be a meaningful concept distinguishable from other concepts, there must be, at some level, a commonality which permeates all this diversity. (See also Boyne and Rattansi, 1990; and, on the inevitability of meta-narratives, Kellner, 1988a; Jameson, 1991; and, although such an approach may seem to contravene the precept of abandonment of meta-theory, it is appropriate also to note the implications of Bauman's (1988a) distinction between postmodern sociology and a sociology of postmodernism.) To employ Robbe-Grillet's (1977) distinction between information and meaning – 100 per cent information contains no meaning and 100 per cent meaning contains no information – if the term postmodernism is to be of utility it must have information *and* meaning. If it does no more than supply a label to be stuck on to a multitude of apparently disparate and incomprehensible phenomena, then 'postmodern' contains enormous information and no meaning and is unintelligible. If, on the other hand, it is a term which can be applied independently of any substantive characteristic, then it contains only meaning and no information, and is redundant (see also Featherstone, 1991: 1). For it to be useful it must first be understood as a meta-level concept. It is our contention that, just as the underlying logic of the diversity of modernism can be seen as faith in the power of transcendent rationality, it is the abandonment of this faith which provides a commonality for the diversity of postmodernism, which distinguishes it as a useful concept.

People who write about postmodernism reflect the diversity apparent in its manifestations. There is a marked tendency to treat it as a cultural phenomenon – thus, for example, Lash (1990: 4), from a sociological perspective, has declared it to be 'strictly cultural . . . a sort of cultural "paradigm"'. Jameson, wishing to avoid treating postmodernism as a strictly cultural category, develops a more social–theoretical approach linking cultural logic and a new socioeconomic stage of capitalism (see also Kellner, 1988a) – perhaps echoed by the architect Richard Rogers's (1990) characterization of postmodernism as 'an obsession with money and fashion' with poor problem-solving capacity. Rather than dealing with postmodernism at the level of effect, other writers have placed the emphasis on epistemology (for example, Lyotard, 1984), or on postmodernism as an epiphenomenon of poststructuralism (for example, Cooper, 1987), though Jameson (1991) puts this the other way round. Perhaps most usefully, and subsuming elements of all these approaches, Harvey (1989) sees it as a historical condition. The diversity is underscored by Foster's (1985) contention that postmodernism can be seen as having two broad 'modes', the 'postmodernism of resistance' and the 'postmodernism of reaction'. In other words, Foster argues that postmodernism is capable of being either expansive and liberating or repressive. However, all such commentators on postmodernism, intentionally or otherwise, examine the effects and/or causes of the abandonment of transcendent rationality.

Harvey's (1989) chronological approach highlights the point that some change has taken place, over time, from the modern to the postmodern, though whether this can or should be identified as a moment has been much disputed. On the one hand, Jencks, perhaps tongue in cheek, dates the end of modernism to a particular minute – 3.32 p.m. 15 July 1972, 'when the Pruitt–Igoe housing development in St Louis (a prize-winning version of Le Corbusier's "machine for modern living") was dynamited as an uninhabitable environment for the low-income people it housed' (Harvey, 1989: 39) – while, on the other, Lyotard's (1984) constant nascent state approach would seem to make periodization both impossible and irrelevant. But if some change has taken place it *has* taken place in time, and there is general if tacit acceptance of this point among writers on postmodernism. Even if it is not possible to be as specific as Jencks, some general delineation is possible. Thus Harvey (1989: 38) opts for the period 1968–72 as marking the 'moment' at which postmodernism became recognizable, if still incoherent. But if it was coming into bloom then the seeds were germinating much earlier, and it is this which leads us to identify Expectancy Theory as embryonically postmodern in the field of motivation to work.

Theories of Motivation to Work

Motivation to work (MTW) is one of the key areas of interest in organizational behaviour, and theories of MTW can be found in most management teaching. Yet nothing new has been produced in MTW theory for the last 25 years (see, for example, Robbins's (1991) catalogue of contemporary theories of MTW). In fact, we would argue that MTW theory effectively came to a halt with Expectancy Theory. We will further suggest that Expectancy Theory represented a break with modernist MTW theory, to the extent that modernist management (see later) found it impossible to use. We will use the exposition of Expectancy Theory by Vroom (1964) since this constitutes the major attempt to theorize Expectancy Theory in the management context (but see also Porter and Lawler, 1968). However, some of the imputations we are making are not those of Vroom. It must also be added that, in the following, we are not particularly concerned with the validity of any theory of MTW, only with the logics and contradictions, and that we include theories which have been used as theories of MTW even though that may not have been their original purpose, such as Taylor (1947), Maslow (1943, 1954) and McGregor (1960).

Labour productivity has always been a concern of those with control over labour, and attempts to affect it have usually centred on threat/reward systems. As regards threat, the exercise of raw power, as in slavery, is an extreme example, but the application of financial sanctions, such as fine systems (see, for example, Doray, 1988), can also be cited. Strategies of reward can be seen to include the power to give work to those who needed it (for example, hiring fairs) and the use of bonus payments (see Marglin (1980) on the practice of tying handkerchiefs to spinning frames). However, prior to the work of Taylor (1947), the justification for labour intensification tended to exhibit the characteristics of the premodern, insofar as its legitimacy was rooted in the caprices of power, and the emphasis was usually on attendance rather than actual performance. Taylor's work marked a radical shift to modernist approaches, using a scientific framework to focus on the concern with productivity rather than attendance, and to analyse *processes* of labour which enabled him to demonstrate through empirical data how productivity could be enhanced.

Taylor was an engineer and used an engineer's approach to his study. He saw labour very much as just another 'mechanical' component in the manufacturing process. Workers were basically machine animals who could be encouraged to perform with a more refined economic threat/reward system whose distinction lay in the precise specification of activity which would prompt threat or reward. During World War I when productivity problems occurred in the munitions factories the work by people associated with Myers, and what was to become the National Institute of Industrial Psychology, added scientific sophistication to Taylor's approach and demonstrated, counter-intuitively, that productivity could be increased through reductions in hours worked and attention to experienced boredom and monotony (Rose, 1988). Thus developed the idea of the worker as a social animal, associated most famously with the Hawthorne Studies. With the advent of Myers into the arena of concern with productivity the science of psychology took over from engineering, and stayed in command for the next 50 years. Psychology's intrinsic concern with the individual naturally led to that focus in the work context and, perhaps inevitably, evolved into the next stage, Needs Theories. These added the psychological dimension to the model of the worker, epitomized in Schein's (1980) 'Complex Man'. And with neo-Maslovian approaches – essentially behaviourist attempts to operationalize Maslow's insights in the management context (for example, McGregor, 1960; Herzberg, 1966) – MTW finally becomes a topic in its own right.

What can be seen in this progression is a classic scientific line of development, such as described by Kuhn (1970): the role of science is to solve problems, and scientific theories undergo a process of constant refinement in order to enhance their problem-solving capacity. At no stage is the commitment to science itself as a means of solving problems in doubt, and it is this which makes it possible to characterize motivation theory to this point as classically modernist. The line of development is basically evolutionary, certainly in the neo-Maslovian case, which can be taken as representing the most refined explanation. In this model motivation was to be achieved through self-actualization via increased job satisfaction. But the model can be seen as incorporating the approaches of its predecessors. The physiological and safety needs of Maslow's hierarchy (compare Maslow, 1943, 1954) represent the concern with material needs of Rational Economic Man. These needs having been satisfied, for motivation to be sustained required the presence of social motivators such as might be supplied by the social organization of work: the affiliation and esteem levels of the hierarchy – this was the essence of Human Relations Theory. Once social needs were satisfied they too ceased to motivate, and this left the worker ripe for self-actualization, which represents an infinitely renewable motivator. In terms of conventional interpretations of Maslow's theory, self-actualization only comes into operation as a motivator once the other levels of need have been satisfied.

Expectancy Theory, however, negated the possibility of assuming that any of the lower-level needs were satisfied, no matter what actions had been taken to this end. If the individual did not feel that lower-level needs were being met, then, effectively, they were not met – higher-level needs would remain an irrelevance. (Yet it must be noted that the *development* of Expectancy Theory is entirely consistent with the scientific line of development already suggested.)

The application of rational thought through the medium of science to issues of productivity has always reflected the interests of managers as agents of ownership. It is, after all, managers who perceive productivity as a problem, rather than that productivity is a generic scientific problem in the way that, for example, gravity might be. Thus, even at the level of problem definition, scientific approaches to MTW have suffered the fate typical of modernism's attempts to solve problems – constraints of ideological acceptability. What characterizes all these early approaches is that what constitutes a motivator is determined by managers, armed with appropriate constructs furnished by academia. Thus, in operationalizing neo-Maslovian theory it was to be managers, or their representatives, who: (a) determined what constituted a satisfying job and (b) determined when these conditions had been achieved. At no point did the understanding of the worker as to what constituted a satisfying and/or enriched job enter into the assessment. It was for managers to prescribe. That is, managers were to prescribe what workers should experience as enriched. The entire history of the development of MTW strategies up to that stage can be seen as rooted in managers introducing increasingly sophisticated techniques to encourage workers to be more productive. The means by which managers assessed whether their MTW strategies had been successful or not was in terms of increased productivity. In other words, the outward (indeed, the only) sign of motivation has been taken to be, in a most basic interpretation, performance – even though there has been increasing awareness, evolving over a long period of time, of the tenuous nature of the relationship between satisfaction and performance, to the extent that the direction of causality, if there is one, is contested (Cooper, 1974; Vroom, 1964). In effect, what MTW strategies really amounted to were increasingly sophisticated *incentives*. Nonetheless, the underlying problem of low motivation (as perceived by managers) remained untouched. New approaches had no more than a cosmetic effect.

Expectancy Theory, however, broke with this tradition by emphasizing the key factor of individual understanding/perception. Motivation was a function of the individual's desire for a particular outcome, and the perception of how likely a particular course of action was to achieve that outcome. Thus, for example, the relationship between the experience of any particular job and satisfaction becomes a function of whether satisfaction is perceived as a desirable outcome from work and how likely the experience of doing that work is to create satisfaction. The implication of this for MTW theory is that blanket approaches prescribed by management would only succeed *if* all workers shared, to a significant extent, a desire for job satisfaction *and* all perceived it as being achieved through the same course of action *and* this course of action happened to be the same as the one prescribed by managers. It must be conceded that this is an unlikely constellation of events. Thus, as Vroom (1964: 286) says: 'We will merely note one of the most general implications of the model – . . . job satisfaction and job performance should be regarded as joint functions of *individual differences* in motives and *cognized* or actual properties of work roles' (emphasis added). Treating workers as a homogeneous group would thus be inappropriate, as would assuming that managers knew what constituted a satisfying job for anyone else. Furthermore, two people confronted with an identically enriched job might perceive it differently in terms of the satisfactions to be gained from it; and if a job deemed by managers to be enriched was not perceived as enriched by the worker, then job satisfaction would not be experienced and the worker would not be motivated. The neo-Maslovian behaviourists would see satisfaction as reinforcement leading to repeat behaviour, with no room for free will on the part of the worker. For the behaviourist there must be a law-like relationship between job enrichment and satisfaction – if subjective understandings and experience are allowed to intervene then the relationship and the consequent motivation collapse. But even from a behaviourist point of view, if satisfaction were not experienced then behaviour would not be reinforced. Nevertheless, behaviourist approaches did, and do, concentrate on collectivist models. After Expectancy Theory, however, omnibus approaches to MTW could no longer be adopted, whatever their provenance: each worker had, potentially, to be treated as an individual. This was an impossibility for management.

Another problem, post Expectancy Theory, was the issue of desirability of outcomes. A behaviourist approach, rooted in the normative ethical orientation to work as a good in itself, assumed that workers would work for satisfaction (bearing in mind that the carrot of more money for extra effort was now out of fashion). Expectancy Theory admitted the possibility that workers might not view work as a good in itself, that they might not want to work more productively (Vroom, 1964: 36): the desire for (job) satisfaction might be low and the perceived likelihood of achieving satisfaction through work might also be low. For motivation to occur, both desire and expectation must be high. Yet perception of these two elements is profoundly individual. Thus satisfaction was no longer to be seen as an objective property of the job, but was a subjective appreciation of the individual: 'The important feature of the model . . . is its view of behaviour as *subjectively rational* and as directed towards the attainment of desired outcomes and away from aversive outcomes' (Vroom, 1964: 276, emphasis added).

Expectancy Theory as Postmodernism

Whilst Expectancy Theory certainly has scientific (modernist) pretensions epistemologically and methodologically (Vroom, 1964: 5, for example), it clearly represents a theory of the individual (Vroom, 1964: vii), rather than a theory of management; that is, it is a theory of labour not as a homogeneous reactive group but as fragmented and proactive, instantly denying the possibility of collectivist approaches to managing MTW. Thus whilst in the context of individual psychology the theory could be seen as firmly within the classic tradition of modernism, in the context of management theory it exhibits the signs of rejection of modernist assumptions which we would now understand as emergent postmodernism.

A rationalist explanation of management would see it as a resource possessed of certain techniques for the efficient achievement of particular goals. Part of this process is the employment of labour to perform certain tasks and the objective of management should be to extract as much productivity as possible from labour during the hours which are bought. Unfortunately for management, labour does not instinctively share this desire to be as productive as possible. But management has available to it certain techniques to encourage compliance on the part of labour. For Expectancy Theory to have utility in this respect it must facilitate this compliant contribution of labour.

In its simplest form Expectancy Theory argues that motivation is a function of the desire for a particular outcome and the expectation that a particular course of action will provide that outcome. Thus, from a manager's point of view, the desired outcome is that workers have desires, material or psychological, which they believe can be fulfilled by the accomplishment of the work which management wants them to do. Given that workers can perceive that relationship, they would then be motivated to do the work. Yet if we briefly deconstruct the terms desire and expectation it immediately becomes clear that Expectancy Theory may be fundamentally inappropriate to managers' concerns. To fit in with the modernist model of management, workers would have to desire outcomes that managers could provide, and to believe that they were achievable by doing whatever management required them to do. But this is certainly not what Expectancy Theory says – it does not say that desire is the desire for what management is willing to provide, but that it is potentially polymorphous. There is nothing in Expectancy Theory which warrants the assumption that there is a necessary connection between the satisfaction of desire and work. It is quite reasonable to suppose that people might desire outcomes to the achievement of which work is a positive obstacle; for example, sexual desire. Thus, in the very defining terms of Expectancy Theory's hypothesis there is nothing to suggest that the supposedly transcendentally rational prescriptions of management should be shared, individually or collectively, by workers. This in itself is an abrogation of the modernist principle of universal reason. All Expectancy Theory does is posit the existence of desires and expectations, and a relationship between them. It does not prescribe what they should be – that is, it is not a normative theory – and thus can as easily explain chaos as order, anarchy as hierarchy, absence as presence, play as work.

Not only does Expectancy Theory violate the precepts of modernism, but it also contains within it elements which can be seen as prototypically postmodern. In conjoining the two, we take as key Vroom's statement, quoted above, that behaviour is subjectively rational and directed towards attainment of desired outcomes. The popular normative assumption in the literature of management of a congruency of goals between various organizational actors, whether from a unitary or a pluralist perspective, is, by this claim, exposed as at best a pious hope and more likely an unwarranted ideological bias. Vroom points out that motivation will occur in terms of *desired* goals, not *prescribed* goals. That the goals of any actor might be organizationally dysfunctional *and therefore irrational* can no longer be sustained as a premise, since rationality is now by definition subjective – the issue of irrationality is irrelevant. Whereas it has been common to conceive of work organizations as part of the great social machine in which each component fulfils a necessary social role which contributes to the overall systemic good – as epitomized by Parsonian structural functionalism – with Vroom's statement organizations come much more to resemble arenas for the pursuit of individual self-interest, *as subjectively defined*, as noted by Robbins (1991). Not least of the implications which follow from this is the conceptualization of organizations as coercive rather than consensual.

But, however profound the shift from objective rationality to subjective rationality which Expectancy Theory represents, we would not want on this basis alone to claim it as prototypically postmodern. Whereas explanations for behaviour had traditionally been rooted in science, with Expectancy Theory it became incumbent for explanations of behaviour to be sought in individual perception. Similarly, whereas the search for law-like generalizations of causality had characterized the history of MTW theory, with Expectancy Theory causality became firmly located in subjective experience. The concern with structural relationships, such as management/worker, or motivation/hygiene factors, was replaced by a sharp primary focus on the individual *qua* individual. Expectancy Theory's acknowledgement of the process whereby desires are made logical and legitimate by reference to individual rhetorics exemplifies the change of emphasis to ordinary discourse from scientific discourse.

Modernist theories of MTW centred round the search for transcendent knowledge, for understandings and indeed strategies which were consistent in space and time. In terms of Expectancy Theory, however, the concern for consistency and replicability becomes irrelevant – with the emphasis on individual perception and experience what motivates today need not motivate tomorrow: the desire may change and so may the perceived valency (Vroom, 1964: 34). Equally, modernist MTW had an overriding concern with form. Thus, for example, in the case of job design, modernist theories concentrated on producing strategic packages for managers which could be implemented whatever the organizational context, because the stimulus to motivation was always the same. With Expectancy Theory, not only is the stimulus potentially different in every case, but whether motivation occurs at all is dependent on the worker's experience of the content of any strategy to motivate him/her, even to the extent that workers could be highly motivated in the total absence of the conditions held to be necessary for motivation to take place, or thoroughly demotivated in the presence of all such conditions.

A Foucauldian approach to the analysis of modernism sees management as a discourse, subject to all the immanent processes of inclusion and exclusion that characterize any discourse (Foucault, 1970, 1971). Modernist MTW theories are aptly so described, in part because they clearly exclude certain 'voices', in particular the voice of the object of motivational strategies, whose role is simply to be passively manipulated. One of the impacts of postmodernism has been, at least potentially, to redress this imbalance, to empower those who were disempowered by modernist discourse. Authority becomes a contested issue. The question of who is empowered to speak is a crucial element of Expectancy Theory, with its insistence on the prime significance of workers' subjective understandings and preferences, which need show no allegiance to the aims of management. Although as originally drawn, it was assumed that, operationally, managers would be able to impose their will to control preferred outcomes, this does not (as noted) follow from the theory and, as subsequent experience has shown, this has proved impossible to achieve (see later).

What we see in Expectancy Theory is the end of the meta-narrative, of the attempt to produce totalizing explanations of organizational existence, which end is so much the epitome of postmodernism. Expectancy Theory signifies the emergence of the pre-eminence of relativity over rationality, of the subjective over the objective and, most importantly, of subjective order over objective order.

Modernism has been seen as representing the embodiment of neo-Darwinian bourgeois order (compare, for example, Baudrillard, 1988b). The early theories of MTW we have cited reflect this pattern. They are deterministic and naturalistic; they reinforce the apparent immutability of hierarchy, and define the *raison d'etre* of the worker as to work; they are reductionist in failing to incorporate non-work influences on MTW, allowing workers to be conceptualized as workers rather than as people; they are paternalistic in denying the relevance of workers' own perceptions of work. But these characteristics gradually became transformed into constraints as it became increasingly acknowledged that they failed to supply a realistic appreciation of MTW. Thus it also became imperative to approach MTW from a radically different perspective which answered these shortcomings, though it might have shortcomings of its own. Not only does the rejection of these certainties implied in Expectancy Theory signify it as emergent postmodernism, but it also signifies (if taken seriously) the end of the traditional bourgeois conception of management. The same process of rejection of certainty has been taking place in many discourses at various historical moments, and always signifies that a discourse has reached the very limits of what modernism can offer it and, in order to sustain itself, must turn to some new approach. This is the point at which postmodernism is born.

Management as Modernism

As previously noted, modernism can be seen as rooted in the Enlightenment, in the triumph of the scientific over the theological explanation of the cosmos. Knowledge could no longer be claimed by reference to dogma but had to be demonstrated according to certain empirical rules based on formal logic and universal reason. Whereas science may initially have had a role devoted to explaining the macro-functioning of the cosmos, it became associated with the ability to solve social problems: 'the idea of being "modern" by looking back to the ancients changed with the belief, inspired by modern science, in the infinite progress of knowledge and in the infinite advance towards social and moral betterment' (Habermas, 1981: 4). This appreciation of science spread to all areas of human action, including the Arts.

Management is an essentially modernist activity rooted, *prima facie*, in the application of formal logic to the solution of problems (Clegg, 1990). The particular problems that management deals with are commonly held to be the efficient conversion of resources, which can be epitomized in the concept of productivity. This concern is not just modernist but has a long history. Thus in the premodern period productivity was encouraged by theological exhortation, the need to propitiate the gods, to acquire intercession. With modernism it was recognized that the cause of productivity would be better served by the application of science than of theology. In the arena of MTW in particular theodic management was superseded by scientific management – compare, for example, Ure (1965, first published 1835) with Taylor (1947). Later developments such as the Human Relations School and the neo-Human Relations School can be seen as further refinements of this logical approach (notwithstanding contradictions). The Human Relations School added the science of society to Taylor's mechanics, and post-Maslovian theory added psychology, so that with, for example, the work of Herzberg (1966) we get a well-rounded view of the individual: a physical being able to perform, a sociological being influenced by social interactions, a psychological being requiring emotional satisfaction.

Yet there is little to suggest intrinsic variety in the individual, who was subject to standard assessment and practice. Taylor's workmen could, in theory, all perform at the same rate and, if they could not (though a paradox) were got rid of. With an emergent social science and industrial psychology modelled on natural science, this scientism penetrated deeply into management theory, as it did with the other humanities. Thus while the Human Relations School and Maslow might have dealt with more abstract concepts than earlier theories of management, they were none the less scientistic – as, indeed, is the case with Vroom's work. And in work study we have the concept of Standard Performance. In general, management theory is still very much underwritten by the assumption that standard management practice will produce standard performance and standard results – the classic scientific model.

The attempts to operationalize and test Expectancy Theory clearly demonstrate this point. It has been noted that the major significance of Expectancy Theory is that it helps understanding of MTW but does not specifically solve motivational problems (Luthans, 1985): it will explain the motivation of an individual but will not tell managers how to motivate groups of employees. Attempts to assess the theory on a comparative basis have not been successful (Arnold et al., 1991; Robbins, 1991), because Expectancy Theory deals with differences within a single individual and not with similarities between individuals. But since management is not capable of dealing with MTW on the basis of single individuals, the focus of operationalization and testing has tried to shift this emphasis towards usage with groups (Hackman and Porter, 1968). One impact of this is the much-noted proliferation of variables and emphasis on definition and measurement which has rendered the theory extremely, even unusably, complex (Lawler and Suttle, 1973; Schwab et al., 1979; Gibson et al., 1991). Another impact has been the transfer of emphasis from psychological satisfactions to material rewards (Robbins, 1991) which, as Bartol and Martin (1991) note, runs into problems with perceptions of equity. Several commentators have stressed that a severe difficulty relates to organizational/managerial constraints on what can be considered as a desired outcome (for example, Gibson et al., 1991) but this is seen as a weakness of the theory rather than of the operational context (for example, Robbins, 1991). There is a wide acceptance that Expectancy Theory is a good model of motivation and an equally wide sense of bewilderment that it is so difficult to utilize. Given the type of reason cited for this, it must be noted that the problems are *not* problems of the theory, but arise from attempts to force it into the modernist managerial straitjacket.

While modernist management had modernist MTW theories to use there was a certain congruence in terms of theory and practice. When a MTW theory emerged which violated the precepts of modernist management there were obvious problems of utilization – *in no case* is it conceivable that a modernist practice could realize a postmodern theory without doing violence to it ontologically and epistemologically, since the latter is defined by its rejection of the former's meta-theory. There is a temptation to view this as a Kuhnian revolution, but this would be an over-simplification both of the concept of paradigm incommensurability and of postmodern ontology (Jackson and Carter, 1991). However, it can be said that, superficially, there is a fundamental incommensurability between modernism and postmodernism. In the field of MTW this explains the virtual impossibility of operationalizing Expectancy Theory in the management context. The impact of this was that that line of development of MTW, notwithstanding its far superior explanatory power, effectively died out. MTW theory has, since Maslow, only seriously attempted to continue development through its modernist forms, continuing to utilize, if sometimes implicitly, the insights of the needs hierarchy – for example, QWL.

Whilst we do not want to be side-tracked into issues of temporality, it is noteworthy that, simultaneously with the development of Expectancy Theory, there was development of modernist extensions of Maslow's work, epitomized perhaps by the work of Herzberg, and sustained by belief in the relationship between job design, job enrichment and motivation. This represents, arguably, the most refined state of modernist theory in the field. But that such blanket approaches failed to produce blanket responses is now well known. Yet this particular relationship still has lasting appeal for managers. There are two reasons for this: there has not been, nor is it possible that there could have been, any further development of modernist theories of MTW, yet management as a practice is committed to modernism and perhaps inimical to postmodernism. But were such theories to be developed they would inevitably have to include the centrality of subjective perception, and would then fall prey to precisely the same fate as befell Expectancy Theory.

Conclusion

We have suggested that Expectancy Theory, as associated with Vroom, was prototypically postmodern, and have used this to highlight a crisis in understanding MTW, albeit one which has lain dormant for the last 25 years. However, whilst we are identifying Expectancy Theory as prototypically postmodern, it is important to stress that we are not suggesting that Vroom himself was consciously an early postmodernist. As we have noted previously, it is unresolved whether postmodernism is a late form of modernism or anti-modernism, and it would be invidious to talk about Vroom as a postmodernist. In fact, Vroom's approach is classically modernist in the traditional sense, with a commitment to science, belief in the relationship between job satisfaction and motivation and a fairly conventional view of the roles of management and worker. It could be argued that Vroom failed fully to recognize the key element of his own argument, that of subjective rationality. With the inclusion of this feature Vroom inadvertently introduced a theory which went beyond the bounds of what modernist management could accept. In fact, Expectancy Theory is deeply problematic as a theory, because it is a postmodern conceptualization nested in a modernist epistemology. Had there been a correspondence between conceptualization and epistemology, Vroom would have been laying the basis for a radically different conceptualization of management itself, one where the myth of consensus would have been exposed as just another Foucauldian discourse. In the event he introduced something into the discourse which was not admissible, and his theory suffered the processes of exclusion and marginalization which characterizes reaction in such cases. A new ingredient had been introduced into MTW theory, but its significance has been wilfully ignored. Not surprisingly, MTW theory has since spent the last 25 years on a merry-go-round, going nowhere. We would argue that it can never go anywhere until the issue of subjectivity is integrated into the concept of management (see Jackson, 1986).

Expectancy Theory has received a great deal of attention, but with a marked resistance to the possibility that subjectivity cannot be confined to the context of productivity. A postmodern reading of Expectancy Theory is informed by the requirement to oppose the appropriation of subjectivity and emphasizes that understandings of MTW cannot be bounded by what is acceptable to management, by what organizations are prepared to offer to workers. This paper identified Expectancy Theory as a 'moment' at which the limits of modernism were exceeded, and new voices were admitted to the discourse. The processes of exclusion have so far managed to deny those voices. Had they been heard they would have fundamentally challenged the prevailing wisdom about the role and significance of organizations, management and work in our lives.

There is evidence that the shortcomings of modernist theorizing are actively being reflected in changing management practices with moves towards more individualistic approaches, some of which can readily be characterized as postmodern, for example, the interest in charismatic leadership. But because of the aborted programme of MTW theory as a result of the impact of Expectancy Theory these developments remain mostly under-theorized in terms of contributions from the field of organizational behaviour. Paradoxically, Vroom pointed the way forward, but it led to a brick wall – the way forward now requires that this brick wall be demolished. Perhaps this is the role for the consciously postmodernist.

6

What can Organization and Management Theory Learn from Art?

Dag Björkegren

Postmodern thinking, with its interest for cultural and social rather than technological and economic change, has recently started to influence the field of organizational studies (Burrell, 1988; Cooper and Burrell, 1988; Berg, 1989; Cooper, 1989). Perhaps in connection to this a renewed interest in rhetorics in the social sciences can be noticed (McCloskey, 1985; Geertz, 1988; Van Maanen, 1988). In organization theory Czarniawska-Joerges (1988) describes management consultants as merchants of meaning and beautiful words, and Czarniawska-Joerges et al. (1990) compare management consultants with the ancient Greek sophists and their rhetorical skills. There also exist attempts to regard organizations as texts, and analyse them as such. Cooper (1989), for example, applies the French philosopher Derrida's deconstructive methodology to the field of organizations and talks about the writing of organizations and the organization of writing. Kreiner sees working in organizations as 'the torrent of words in a text without structure, without punctuation, without sentences' (Kreiner, 1989: 12). Kreiner also makes the observation that the vast attention paid to autobiographies of well-known industrialists, such as Iacocca (1984), indicates that what society is willing to accept as truthful presentations of organizations does not have to be connected to any scientific method. This might depend on the fact that science has no special right to the 'truth' any more, and everybody has a free hand on the market of organizational theory. The demarcation line between what passes as art and as science is becoming blurred.

In this chapter the relationship between art and science, and what organizational theory possibly can learn from art, is discussed with the help of postmodern thinking. Postmodernism is generally not regarded as a coherent and unified theory. It is usually perceived as a patchwork of ideas that exist in various artistic and academic fields (Berg, 1989). One common denominator within postmodernism is the rejection of rational discourses that assume the existence of all-embracing explanations of social and cultural functioning. Another common assumption is that there are no deeper truths in the world to be discovered. Within linguistically oriented postmodernism efforts are made through various forms of textual analysis to show that what is perceived as 'true' is a social construction rather than the discovery of an aboriginal world (Norris, 1987). In the following this postmodern assumption is used as an epistemological guide to understanding the production of art and scientific knowledge. The chapter constitutes an attempt to describe how what is perceived as science and art is a product of the practices of science and art, thereby illuminating differences and similarities between these practices and their products.

The chapter starts off with a description of different views on what is considered to be art and scientific knowledge. This description makes no pretensions to be exhaustive. I merely want to give a picture of what is considered to be characteristic for a work of art and for scientific knowledge. After this the production of art and scientific knowledge are compared and significant similarities are found. The final products also have similarities but exhibit significant differences since art's aim is to create aesthetic experiences while science aims at creating 'true' knowledge about the world. A final argument is made that what might be learned from art about organizations and management probably lies more in the artistic form than in the artistic content.

Beauty

The word aesthetics means to pay attention to something. Aesthetics as a science is the study of the arts, their differences and similarities, under what conditions art is created, and from what criteria art manifestations are judged as good or bad (Brunius, 1986). An aesthetic object is usually associated with an artificial object whose main purpose is contemplation. If a bottle-rack is assigned the function of an aesthetic object its function is changed from bottle-keeping to an object for contemplation. Aesthetic contemplation implies a concentrated observation of a certain object and its characteristics, where the observation of the object is more important at the time than possible consequences for action (Berefelt, 1977). According to Brunius (1986) and Becker (1982) anything can be art, but what actually becomes and is experienced as art is restricted by prevailing art conventions.

Systematic thinking about art started around 400 BC with Plato and Aristotle (Ödeen, 1988). The oldest known view of art is based on inspiration and ecstasy. Such emotional states were supposed to be a consequence of contact with the gods. Such contact could be established through the intake of various drugs. The artist was a medium of the gods.

In ancient Greece there existed a certain group of professionals (the rhapsods) who specialized in inspired art through the recital of the Homeric poems. Plato's dialogue *Ion* describes a conversation with the rhapsod Ion. Through Socrates, Plato criticizes Ion for being only a medium for the gods without any skills or knowledge of his own.

In the dialogue *The Republic* Plato puts forth his mimesis-ideal for art (Plato, 1976). In this work Plato elaborates on the poets' mission in his ideal state. Mimesis means to imitate nature and puts art's relation to reality in focus. As an example, Plato used the representation of a sofa. The idea of a sofa is the sofa's ideal form, which is common for and exists in all sofas. Next to the ideal sofa form is the carpenter's sofa in the material world, which imitates the ideal form. Furthest removed from the sofa's idea is the artist's painting of a sofa. It is but a distorted picture of an imitation of the sofa's idea. Such distorted pictures of imitations were forbidden by Plato in his republic, where the poets gently but firmly were led to the door. The art that could be allowed was such art that praised desirable ideals and fostered moral character, that is art with a political value.

Aristotle, who was Plato's disciple, took a more benevolent attitude to art and tried to study the arts on their own merits. He argued that imitation of nature did not have to imply distorted pictures of things' ideal forms. Instead works of art could be a first step towards knowledge about nature. Aristotle also took an interest in rhetorics (the art of eloquence). Rhetorics is interested in audience reactions to an artistic performance and how to influence an audience in a desirable direction. This pragmatic and technical conception of art became fairly dominating during the Middle Ages. According to Horatius the poet's mission was to entertain his audience. Horatius gave recommendations on suitable subjects, composition and style for art performances.

The pragmatic and the mimetic views of art remained dominant until the end of the 18th century when expressive art theories came into being with romanticism. The artist was viewed as the divinely gifted poet who mediated the truths about nature in an ecstatic state. The philosopher Kant amplified this esoteric and transcendental tendency through his speculations about the things in itself, and the artist as the mediator of the essence of things. Art for art's sake became the slogan of the romantic age.

The mimesis-ideal was toned down since the romantic artist expressed himself in a symbolic language. Hence, the oldest known art view had arisen anew, but with one important difference: until romanticism the work of art had been the centre of attention. It had been customary that paintings and poems had been ordered in the same way as houses. A poem or a painting should have certain motives, be painted and written in a certain style and be of a certain size, all decided by the buyer. Who wrote or painted was of less importance as long as the person in question was in possession of the necessary technical skills (Wolff, 1987). During the romantic age the artist became the centre of attention as the chosen and divinely gifted person. The notion of the artist as the lonely genius, set above the rules of the rest of society, originates from this time. Creativity was a matter of emotion and intuition and not based on artistic skills and knowledge.

During the 19th century various notions about art started to succeed each other with an accelerated pace. Realism and naturalism came as a reaction against romanticism. Symbolism and expressionism were romanticism's reaction against realism. Futurism signalled the machine's march into the world. Plato's utility ideal, in combination with the mimesis ideal, rose again during the 1930s in Stalin's Russia in the form of social realism. The rhetoric ideal gained a forceful renaissance in the entertainment and advertising industries that evolved through mass media, where it was of prime importance to gain an audience's attention (Gitlin, 1985; Leiss et al., 1986).

After World War II a slightly new view of art came into being. Within this view the work of art was regarded as a world of its own, obeying its own rules, independent of the artist's intentions (Beardsley, 1981). The interesting thing to study became the formal composition of works of art. Structuralism and poststructuralism are examples of this formal conception of art. It can be said to have its origins in Aristotle's analysis of drama's formal construction.

Within high culture the formal and the Marxist view of art have been the dominating views since World War II. Within popular culture the rhetorical view has been the dominating view, combined with the romantic conception of art in the form of star-worship.

Truth

Research or production of knowledge generally refers to the creation of increased knowledge about the world and the way it works. Our picture of how the world looks is called ontology. Our belief about how knowledge about the world is acquired is called epistemology. Since the way we acquire knowledge about the world is influenced by the way we think the world looks, an epistemology implies an ontology.

How do we then know when something is scientific knowledge and not some other form of knowledge? Through the years many attempts have been made to determine this. The positivists of the 19th century argued that scientific knowledge was characterized by the use of a scientific methodology. Such a method of inquiry was objective and quantitative. The early 20th century's logical empiricists added that only directly observable phenomena could be investigated scientifically.

The philosopher Karl Popper (1986) argued in the 1930s that even more important than an objective and quantitative method of inquiry was that the research results were falsifiable. If not, it was metaphysics instead of science. Kuhn (1970), in a polemic against Popper, suggested that what was perceived as scientific knowledge was determined by the prevailing scientific paradigms. What counted as production of scientific knowledge took place within the framework of the paradigms' theory and methodology conventions.

The three described views of what scientific knowledge might be all have the common denominator that they are based on a realist ontology. In contrast to an idealist ontology realism presumes that the world has an existence of its own, independent of our thoughts and feelings about it. Idealism assumes that what exists depends on ourselves.

The positivists, whose aim is to verify theories, base their epistemology on a perceptual realism. Perceptual realism, which was originated by the English philosopher David Hume, involves the assumption that reliable knowledge about the world can be acquired directly through our senses. Accumulated data should therefore be influenced as little as possible by theoretical assumptions. The assumption of the existence of a real world implies a striving to establish the truth of theories and hypotheses through an attempt to confirm the concordance of the disposition of theories with reality.

Popper's falsifiability principle is based on a critical realism. He considers perceptual realism a utopia. We need assumptions about the way the world works in order to be able to produce meaningful interpretations of what we experience. If we succeeded in freeing ourselves from all our assumptions about the world, it would appear incomprehensible. For the world to be comprehensible we must ourselves create a meaning in what we see. There is no given meaning in the world which can be absorbed through our sense impressions. On the other hand, our assumptions about the way the world works can be more or less reasonable and functional. The question of whether or not there is a true reality seen from this point of view (constructivism) becomes less important. We can never attain any true reality that there may be if we constantly see the world through our assumptions about it.

There have been attempts within the tradition of positivist research to solve this problem through a universal, scientific language, independent of the individual. No-one has, however, succeeded in constructing such a language. Judging by, among others, Kuhn (1970), this is probably a utopia. The solution Popper suggests is the falsifiability principle. Given that we can never know whether or not a true reality exists, neither can we know when and if we attain any truth that there may be. We can therefore probably never attain true and absolute knowledge. Our knowledge will always be more or less imperfect. According to Popper, it is therefore better to attempt to falsify rather than to verify theories.

Kuhn, in his polemic against Popper, is of the opinion that production of scientific knowledge happens the way in should according to the positivists. Kuhn makes a difference between normal science, where the researcher solves problems within the existing paradigm, and revolutionary science, where a shift of paradigm occurs. In real life scientists do not try to falsify but to verify their theories. When it becomes impossible to explain away anomalies a paradigm-shift occurs where the old theories are replaced with new ones that can explain the anomalies.

But no matter if it is a positivist, a Popperian, or a Kuhnian who is speaking, there exists an outer reality that can 'talk back' and verify or falsify the theories. The proponents for the renewed interest in rhetorics in the social sciences take another, more intertextual view of what becomes scientific knowledge (McCloskey, 1985; Geertz, 1988; Van Maanen, 1988). Traditional philosophy of science focuses its interest on the theoretical content and the relation between theories and their empirical reference-objects. Rhetorics takes its prime interest in the theoretical form and theories' relation to other theories. What becomes scientific knowledge is mainly seen as an issue of rhetorical form. The important thing with scientific texts is that they appear credible to the reader, not that they are 'true' no matter what the reader might think. Important rhetorical means of assistance to accomplish credibility are the usage of methods that are regarded as scientific, and references to other scientific texts. Through such stylistic means a text becomes grounded in the scientific discourse. The crucial thing for a person who wants to be perceived as a scientist is that he should not deviate from existing norms for how scientific knowledge is produced.

Cummings and Frost's (1985) description of the research community of organizational scientists in the US gives some support to this notion. Their book indicates that scientific form might be more important than scientific content. Cummings and Frost's book consists of a collection of articles about how to write scientific articles in the organizational sciences. Indirectly the book describes the research community of organizational science in the US. In this world the best way to generate organizational knowledge is through the publication of scientific articles in scientific journals. Competition is supposed to promote the development of knowledge. The high rejection-rate (90 per cent or more in the high-status journals) is a good sign that the wheat is separated from the chaff. The incentives to write scientific articles are very high since publication in scientific journals is necessary for academic advancement. To write books has very low or no academic value since book manuscripts are accepted for publication on commercial instead of scientific grounds. For an article to have any chance of getting published it must be of a specific form and length, and not divert from the prevailing theories and methods in the field of research. It is of less importance that the article contains anything new or ground-breaking. Senior researchers are allowed to deviate from the research norms to a larger degree than junior researchers. Network-building via participation in academic conferences is recommended as a way to increase the chances for publication.

The Production of Truth and Beauty

From a rhetorical perspective the production of scientific knowledge has significant similarities to the production of art. Cummings and Frost's book can be compared with Ericson's (1988) study of the Stockholm art world. Ericson, who is an anthropologist, describes what becomes art in the Stockholm art world as a social construction process. Ericson starts her study of the Stockholm art world with an investigation of aspiring painters' education. To become an established serious painter in Sweden a degree from the Academy of Arts in Stockholm is more or less mandatory. An important part of the artist's education consists of, apart from gaining knowledge about prevailing art conventions, a socialization process where the art student learns the work-ethic and acquires the right gallery contacts. An exhibition at one of the six elite galleries in Stockholm is necessary for getting the leading art critics to write about the aspiring artist's paintings, hopefully acknowledging them as serious art. When the aspiring painter has gained acceptance as a legitimate artist the artistry becomes a 9–5 business. The work-ethic is very hard, far away from the romantic and bohemian work ideal the artists cherished during their student days. Ericson also investigated Swedish art critics' work. What is regarded as serious art in Sweden has a Lutheran character. Serious paintings are pure and simple, often portraying scenes from nature. It should be evident that a lot of work lies behind the painting.

So, if artists exhibit their paintings in art galleries for the approval of the art critics and fellow-artists, organizational scientists exhibit their research findings in scientific journals for the approval of fellow-scientists. And just as fashion trends emerge in art there are fashion trends in science. Abrahamson (1988, 1989), for example, shows how the popularity of quality circles in the beginning of the 1980s to a large extent was a fashion trend. The quality circles' goal was to raise productivity, although the companies were not all that certain that the implementation of quality circles really would increase productivity. On the other hand the companies were afraid that they would be regarded as unmodern if they did not have quality circles, which all the other companies seemed to have. If you strayed away too much from the behaviour of other firms there was a risk that you might be regarded as out of tune with the times.

Evaluation of art's quality is usually made on high culture's terms according to Gans (1974), who focuses his interest on differences between popular culture and high culture. Gans argues that the difference is that serious art is art on the artist's terms and popular art is art on the audience's terms. In high culture the creation process and the artistic form is of prime importance. The artistic content is expressed in sophisticated and subtle ways, where introspection and development of character are more important than the action plot. In popular culture the emphasis is on the content and action plot and the artistic form is simpler. Since it is mainly the high culture's art products that gets the mass media's attention, popular culture's art products are also evaluated with high culture's values. Popular culture is therefore often accused of winning people's attention in crude and unsophisticated ways. That popular culture often receives negative reactions from the art critics depends on aesthetic disappointment, according to Gans.

Stablein's (1989) analysis of how the scientific debate within organizational theory in the US is conducted has similarities with Gans's analysis of how the cultural debate functions. According to Stablein the scientific debate in the US mainly deals with methodological issues. Underlying ontologies and epistemologies are usually not discussed. Since positivism is the dominating epistemology in the US this causes almost all management research to be judged from this world-view. Even if epistemologies other than positivism allow subjective methods of inquiry and the use of qualitative data, the research results are considered unscientific since such methods are not scientific methods from a positivistic point of view. Increasing doubts have been raised in the US as to whether American organization and management theory creates any factual information about the managerial world (Webster and Starbuck, 1988; Bedeian, 1989; Byrne, 1990). Bedeian, a former president of the American Academy of Management, expresses worries over the fact that most of the research produced by the Academy's members is driven by methodology instead of theory, and therefore has a tendency to establish already well-known facts. Webster and Starbuck argue that industrial psychology, which has been extremely a-theoretical due to a strong emphasis on a positivist research methodology, has accomplished a growth of knowledge equal to zero since the 1950s when this field of research was established. Byrne questions the American management research's relevance for practitioners. One might therefore wonder whose reality has been talking back – the managers' or the scientists'?

Judging from Byrne's critical investigation of how American management research is conducted, it seems to have been mainly the scientists who have been talking back at each other:

> The papers are largely written to please an inner circle of academic experts who must approve an article before it can be published. Morris Holbrook of Columbia University has called the lengthy review process 'a socially approved form of intellectual sadomasochism'. Delays of up to two or three years are common because reviewers often demand pages of revisions. (Byrne, 1990: 51)

The dean of New York University's graduate school of business takes a very grim view on the relevance of the research when Byrne interviews him:

> 'It's often crap', he says of academic writing in learned journals. 'They say nothing in these articles, and they say it in a pretentious way. If I wasn't the dean of this school, I'd be writing a book on the bankruptcy of American management education. (Byrne, 1990: 50)

Scholarly research at American business schools started in the 1950s as a way to improve the business schools' academic legitimacy on the college campus, since they were at that time mainly seen as vocational schools. This strive for academic legitimacy seems to have led to the creation of what can be labelled a scientific hyper-reality.

The term hyper-reality originates from linguistically oriented postmodernism. A basic assumption within postmodern linguistics is that the relationship between a concept and its reference object, that is the extra-linguistic world, is arbitrary and socially determined (Norris, 1987). Because of this an artificial hyper-reality (Eco, 1987; Baudrillard, 1988b) is supposed to have arisen, consisting of pictures, signs, words and concepts that float around in various media such as television, radio, movies, books, newspapers and commercials. Eco, for example, gives a description of how the phrase 'New Orleans' floats around in the ultimate hyper-reality that Disneyland constitutes according to Eco:

> When, in the space of twenty-four hours, you go (as I did deliberately) from the fake New Orleans of Disneyland to the real one, and from the wild river of Adventureland to a trip on the Mississippi, where the captain of the paddle-wheel steamer says it is possible to see alligators on the banks of the river, and then you don't see any, you risk feeling homesick for Disneyland, where the wild animals don't have to be coaxed. Disneyland tells us that technology can give us more reality than nature can. (Eco, 1987: 44)

In a similar way a scientific hyper-reality seems to have been created within American management research, where scientific words and concepts such as 'management' and 'organization' float around in academic journals and at conferences. One might then wonder if science and art are just different forms of fiction, where aesthetic and scientific experiences are created via different rhetorical devices, and the relationship to the extra-linguistic reality is of no importance? The case of Harvard Business School seems to shed some light on this question. Harvard Business School is not considered a part of the American management research hyper-reality:

> most academics look askance at writing for the *Harvard Business Review*. 'It's not quite whoring, but if it's given any value, it's seen as educational instead of scholarly'. (Byrne, 1990: 52)

At the same time the research results at Harvard Business School stand out as the most relevant research for practitioners:

> The survey found that Harvard business school is a bastion of research, producing far more insight and relevant information for executives than many other schools that have long-held reputations for traditional scholarship. (Byrne, 1990: 51)

This might depend not only on the fact that the research performed at Harvard Business School is presented in a pedagogical manner, but also on the underlying research method. Organization and management research at Harvard Business School is still influenced by Roethlisberger's (1977) clinical method to a significant degree.

The clinical method originated in the 1930s within the Human Relations School of thought. The foremost representative of this method was F.J. Roethlisberger, who founded the Human Relations School and the clinical research method with Mayo in the 1930s. Roethlisberger subsequently developed the method gradually in conjunction with his teaching at the

Harvard Business School. The clinical method is characterized by the fact that the research phenomenon is studied in its natural environment. Adaptation to the situation under investigation takes place in terms of the researcher finding out what is important for the people he is confronting, and not just directing his attention to the data his theories say he should be collecting. The clinical method attempts to enable the researcher to proceed from the research subject's theories about the studied reality in his analyses. According to Benson and Hughes (1983), among others, this is an advantage since people's behaviour in a social context is normally controlled by their own theories and not by accepted scientific theories.

Via this clinical research method the research conducted at Harvard Business School hence seems to have become grounded in the world of business and management. This might explain the practitioners' high opinion of research coming from Harvard Business School, and low opinion of the rest of the American management research which, if one is to believe Byrne, seems to have lost contact with managerial practice to a considerable extent.

From this a fairly pragmatic conclusion can be drawn. Given the postmodern assumption that there does not exist any aboriginal reality to test different world-views' validity against, it becomes more reasonable to test different world-views' usefulness. Instead of asking if a certain view of the world is true it might be better to ask what it would mean to believe in the world-view in question, what consequences it would have, and if these consequences are desirable or not (Bruner, 1990). In this particular case it would mean that if one aspires to an academic career in America it makes sense to believe in a positivistic world-view, irrespective of whether this world-view is 'true' or not. If the goal, on the other hand, is a consulting career it is probably better to put one's faith in Harvard Business School's clinical research paradigm.

Discussion

Is it then possible to learn anything about organizations and management from art? Waldo (1968), Guillet de Monthoux (1988) and Czarniawska-Joerges (1989) are some who are of that opinion. They demonstrate how novels that take place in administrative settings can tell us quite a lot about how organizations affect people. Novelists can more easily than scientists take into account people's private experiences of organizational life. Scientific descriptions of organizational life are usually expressed in a quantitative form and are narrower according to Waldo. Waldo stresses that administrative novels can give a more balanced view of organizational behaviour since the organizational activities are seen in a wider context than what is usually the case in scientific studies of organizations.

One important difference between art and science is that art is fiction, and not based on facts. However, art does not have to be false because of this. Scientific theories are also reconstructions of the world, although based on 'facts' (Alvarez and Cantos, 1989). Sandelands and Srivatsan (1989) even put forth the idea that the artist might create more 'true' knowledge about the world than the scientist. This might be so because art is based on direct sense-impression to a larger extent than science. The scientist sees the world through abstract concepts while the artist sees it directly. According to Sandelands and Srivatsan the artist therefore sees the world as it 'is'.

The suggestion that art would portray reality better than science seems to stretch the qualities of artistic representation a bit too far. The goal of art is, after all, to create aesthetic experiences and not 'true' knowledge about the world. It is the relationship between the work of art and the observer that is the important thing, not art's relation to reality. If, for example, a novel deals with the eternal questions, the thinking is profound and the critique of existing living conditions and society is important and well-founded but the novel in question is poorly written it might not be perceived as much of a work of art since it will not evoke much of an aesthetic experience with the reader. If, on the other hand, a novel deals with banal questions, the thinking is artificial and shallow and the critique of existing living conditions and society trivial but the novel is skilfully written it might be perceived as more of a work of art, since it will evoke more of an aesthetic experience with the reader.

Such a view of art, which assumes that what is perceived as art ultimately depends on the potential art object's ability to evoke aesthetic experiences, and that this ability lies more in the artistic form than in the artistic content, is by no means undisputed. It has been an ongoing debate since the beginning of aesthetics about where the stress is to be laid, on artistic form or content, on art's emotional or intellectual impact. It started with Plato when he formulated his aesthetic theory based on reason, in a reaction to the earlier view that was based on emotion.

Eagleton (1990) shows how aesthetic philosophy has shifted between these two poles through history. Kant, the originator of modern aesthetics, spent a lot of time thinking about how man through a detached (that is aesthetic) attention to the world and the sensory impressions it evoked, could refine the direct sensual and primitive sensations, thereby becoming more civilized. David Hume, on the other hand, argued that if man became slave under his emotions this would create civilized manners since the good would manifest itself as the beautiful, and the bad as the ugly.

These two approaches, to either let reason or the emotions govern the aesthetic side of life, have continued to dominate aesthetic philosophy. Philosophers such as Schiller, Hegel, Schopenhauer and Kierkegaard continued in Kant's cognitive tradition with various proposals about how the emotions could became reason's servants. Nietzsche returned to the body and its sensations as the foundation for social life. The 20th century's cultural modernism meant a return to reason. Art's mission was declared to be to criticize bourgeois society and rationalize aesthetics through a systematic exploration of the different artistic materials' possibilities.

The 1980s postmodern aesthetics meant yet another return to the emotions as the organizing force (Lash, 1990). Postmodern aesthetics has its origins in the surrealistic movement of the 1930s. Surrealism was based on Freud's psychoanalytic theory, and wanted to portray the bodily desires in non-discursive ways. This could be achieved by letting reason be invaded by the subconscious. One technique for accomplishing such an invasion was automatic writing. Automatic writing was based on the psychoanalytic free-association technique where the patient is encouraged to say whatever comes into his mind. Automatic writing meant that the poet wrote whatever came into his mind without editing it. This perception of art is revived by postmodern aesthetics. The subconscious instead of the conscious is to be the organizing principle. Postmodern art therefore becomes non-discursive and figurative. Art's mission is to transmit emotional energy through the portrayal of bodily desires. The film medium is considered especially suited for such art, given its visual and non-discursive qualities.

The postmodern view of art is almost identical to Sontag's (1966) art view from the 1960s. Sontag argues that the tendency to make art into something else than art originates from Plato's thoughts about art's relation to reality, and in fact questions the value of art. That something is mere art is not enough. It must be something else. From this descends the separation of artistic form and content, with the content as the most important. This turns the interest from the aesthetic experiences a work of art evokes on a sense-level to a detached analysis of the content on an intellectual level. Artistic intellectualism is also a way to protect the observer from the emotional impact a work of art might have on him. Many artists have tried to avoid such intellectualizations of art through various form-experiments at the expense of the content. Sontag argues that one way to let art remain art would be to create a work of art whose surface is so dense and pure, and whose effect is so fast and direct, that any analysis becomes impossible. The creation of such works of art is possible in the movies, where Ingmar Bergman's films are mentioned as an example of this. The visual intensity and beauty of Bergman's films is so strong and direct that it neutralizes the films' often pseudo-intellectual dialogues about the perils of human existence.

From such a perspective Sontag advocates an increased attention to artistic form instead of content. Bordwell and Thompson (1986) demonstrate how it is possible to analyse movies without bothering about their content. By studying narrative technique, *mise-en-scène*, cinematography, sound, shooting and editing it is possible to form an opinion about a film's artistic form and how it creates cineastic experiences. Within the world of literature Welleck and Warren (1967) reach the same conclusion. It is the literary form and its ability to evoke literary experiences that is of importance, not the content's relation to reality.

Perhaps it is therefore a work of art's artistic form rather than content that can contribute to increased knowledge about organizational behaviour. Sandelands and Buckner (1989), for example, show how not only the content of work but also its form influences job satisfaction. Berg (1979) uses the concept of narrative structures to study a case of organizational change, and Schultz (1989) demonstrates how semiotics can be used when studying organizational culture, two commonly used techniques in film analysis.

Drazin and Sandelands' (1989) speculations on the possibilities of writing down organizational behaviour in a simple formula and checking the formula's validity via computer simulations to see if the forecast behaviour pattern emerges, bear strong similarities to synthesizer-programming, which is built on the formal properties of music. Also the thematic analysis which Zaleznik and Kets de Vries (1984) advocate for studies of leadership originates from the world of music. The word *theme* is originally a technical term used in music to describe a recurrent melody in a piece of music, with the help of which the work in question can be identified. In the context of leadership the text is to be interpreted not from a musical but a social point of view, and it is expressed in words and actions rather than tones, so that the theme is seen to be recurrent topics of discussion and/or actions on the part of the actors being studied. Alvarez and Cantos show, in an analysis of the Harvard Business School's case method, regarding the cases as a particular type of narrative fiction, how the use of narrative techniques can enhance the literary quality of business cases, thus making them more enjoyable to read.

So even if the production of truth and beauty has similarities, one should probably not over-emphasize the similarities of the final products, and demand of art that it should be something other than art. This is not to say that a work of art cannot have an influence on the extra-textual world, but that its influence resides more on the art object's aesthetic qualities than on its correspondence to the extra-textual reality. Neither is it to say that art is not capable of sometimes making significant observations about the extra-textual world's functioning. And we can definitely learn a lot from art about the use of rhetoric. Because if works of art sometimes happen to provide factual information it is perhaps less common that scientific texts evoke any aesthetic experiences.

7

The Play of Metaphors

Mats Alvesson

During the 1980s metaphors have received considerable interest as a focus for understanding organizational analysis and for inspiring new theoretical ideas. It has been argued that we conceptualize organization through seeing it as something, that is using a metaphor, and that the metaphor used is of decisive importance for understanding the research object as well as for thinking and theorizing in general. The works of Morgan (1980, 1986) have been central in this regard.

Morgan talks about metaphors used to conceptualize the whole organization, or at least all those elements of an organization that are focused upon by a particular school or theory. (Metaphors can also be used to illuminate more delimited phenomena – for example, when one talks about 'higher' and 'lower' positions in a hierarchy or of 'sending' and 'receiving' as elements in communication.) His basic idea is that: 'schools of thought in social science, those communities of theorists subscribing to relatively coherent perspectives, are based upon the acceptance and use of different kinds of metaphor as a foundation for inquiry' (Morgan, 1980: 607).

According to Morgan, the following metaphors have guided or are appropriate for organizational analysis: machine, organism, population-ecology, cybernetic system, loosely coupled system, political system, theatre, culture, text, language-game, enacted sense-making, accomplishment, psychic prison, instrument of domination, schismatic, and catastrophe. In some of these cases there are hardly any examples of studies in organization theory informed by the metaphor in question. Other suggestions for metaphors summarizing existing work and development lines in organization theory have been proposed by, for example, Berg (1982) and Mangham and Overington (1987).

The major point of this chapter is not, however, to suggest new metaphors for organizational analysis. Instead the purpose is to look a bit more carefully into a few existing (that is established) metaphors and see how these are used. I will argue that the metaphor is, sometimes or even normally, best understood through another framework or idea informing and guiding the use of the metaphor. This is in opposition to, for example, Morgan, who believes that through the use of a metaphor a clear picture or image emerges, which provides the starting point for a coherent analysis. I argue that metaphors normally give a broad and imprecise picture of the phenomenon, unless they are structured in a particular way. This structuring only to a limited degree takes place through the combination of the object of study and the metaphor (metaphorical concept), the principal subject and the modifier, as Ricoeur (1978) calls them. Metaphors for organization such as culture, organism, machine and political system provide, in themselves, only very general guidelines for theoretical and empirical work, and are open to very different images. The nature of this structuring of metaphors (metaphorical concepts) will be investigated and ideas for understanding the topic of metaphors in general and in organization theory in particular will be suggested. I will here utilize the concept of *second-level metaphor*, in contrast to the more explicit metaphors which Morgan and other authors refer to as guiding their analysis, and indicate how 'hidden' metaphors put imprints on the explicit or espoused metaphors (metaphorical concepts).

The interest in metaphors can be linked to the broader issues related to postmodernism and poststructuralism. Authors advocating these orientations often stress the figural nature of language and the role of images as central in our way of relating to our worlds (for example Berg, 1989; Daudi, 1990; Lash, 1988). They reject the traditional view of (scientific) language as literal and representative, as well as the possibility of formal, accountable frameworks guiding research and, over time, being controlled through hypothesis-testing procedures. The, at the same time, problematic and inspirational role of second-level metaphors producing conceptualizations of research objects will in this chapter be related to various views on postmodernism and poststructuralism. My point is that these second-level metaphors raise doubts regarding the coherence of frameworks guiding analysis, but also offer new inspirations for creative thinking.

After a brief review of the concept of metaphor I will further address how the structuring of metaphors can be understood through the application of the second-order metaphor construct. Then some texts proceeding from a metaphor relatively common in organizational analysis, organization as game, will be investigated. It will be shown that the texts use explicit metaphors with different meanings and produce different analyses. The second-order metaphor idea will be used to illuminate the different images informing the way 'game' is treated. Finally, the chapter suggests some ideas for how second-order metaphors can be used in organization theory, both for generative and critical purposes.

On the Metaphor Concept

Some time ago metaphors were mainly thought to be useful and necessary for poetry and rhetoric, but less appropriate for rigorous thinking and expression. In contrast, the precision of science demanded literal expressions and well-defined usage of words. Even today, many people adhere to this stricter view (for example Pinder and Bourgeois, 1982), but opinions on the role of metaphors and metaphorical thinking and expressions have changed, so that they now appear as vital for understanding social research (and language use in general) and as a necessary element in creativity and the development of new approaches to research objects.

A metaphor is created when a term is carried over from one system or level of meaning to another, thereby illuminating some central aspects of the latter (and shadowing other aspects). A metaphor allows an object to be perceived and understood from the viewpoint of another object. It thus creates a break from literal meaning: 'a word receives a metaphorical meaning in specific contexts within which they are opposed to other words taken literally; this shift in meaning results mainly from a clash between literal meanings, which excludes literal use of the word in question' (Ricoeur, 1978: 138). A good metaphor means the right mix of similarity and difference between the transferred word and the focal one. Too much or too little similarity means that the point might not be understood and no successful metaphor will have been created.

Metaphors are used in different senses. In a narrow and traditionally held sense, metaphor is viewed as an illustrative device. Here both words with 'improve' language through making it richer or more pleasant and formal models can be seen as metaphors (Brown, 1976). In a very broad sense it can be argued that all knowledge is metaphorical, so that it emerges from or is 'constructed' from some point of view. So are our experiences, for 'our ordinary conceptual system, in terms of which we both think and act, is fundamentally metaphorical in nature' (Lakoff and Johnson, 1980: 3). This has consequences for our understanding of everyday life as well as science. Empirical 'reality' or 'data' do not appear by themselves, or talk directly to the researcher. It is metaphors of various aspects of the research object which partly determine 'data'. Related to this view is the idea of the root metaphor, that is a fundamental image of the world on which one is focusing. It is primarily this sense that the metaphor concept is of interest in the present context.

The major advantage of metaphors is often said to be their generative power, their ability to open up creativity and new insights (Czarniawska-Joerges, 1988; Morgan, 1980; Schön, 1979). (This argument refers not exclusively to root metaphors, but to metaphors with some cognitive depth in general.) Reflection on metaphors also draws attention to the partiality of the understanding gained by a particular approach which builds its inquiry on a particular root metaphor. Limitations are then better understood and a more tolerant view for other approaches is, hopefully, encouraged. Such tolerance should not, however, lead to an uncritical view of metaphors or metaphor usage (Tinker, 1986). Tolerance concerns the fact that there are different metaphors, that different opinions and statements can be understood only if the metaphor behind these is appreciated, and that critique of research based upon one metaphor proceeding from another might not be fair if the differences between metaphors are not taken into account.

A focus on metaphors is also useful for the exercise of critique. A critical, and constructive, purpose of interpretation of metaphors is to examine the more basic assumptions of a particular conceptualization of a phenomenon and bring these more clearly to the 'surface'. The search for and reflection upon the metaphors which guide research texts might facilitate a 'better' understanding of research. Beyond rhetoric, formal definitions and so on, the gestalt of the research object might appear different from what the words used indicate. We must therefore make interpretations and critical analyses instead of just examining definitions, and focusing on the metaphorical level is important for such scrutiny. Here it is often necessary to go beyond the explicit or surface metaphors used, and look for the underlying image. Sometimes jargon and vocabulary indicate a particular metaphor, but this can be misleading. In culture studies, for example, many authors use anthropological concepts, but in such a way that their principal metaphor of the organization seems to be closer to a machine than a 'real' culture. Culture is sometimes treated as a building block in organizational design (Smircich, 1985).

This critique is directed to issues of consistency, problematic assumptions, and so on, but does not relate to criteria associated with scientific progress in a more strict sense, such as ability to predict and explain phenomena. A common critique against researchers advocating metaphors as central in research focuses on more traditional epistemological concerns (Tsoukas, 1991a, b), but falls beyond the focus of this chapter.

The point in addressing metaphors for the sake of critique and reflection does not appear to have much to do with the generative abilities of metaphor, at least not in the first step. It is not the new, explicit metaphors as much as the 'old', implicit ones which are the suggested targets of interest. However, focusing on the implicit, not clearly recognized aspects of metaphors in research may result in them appearing in a new light. Critique can thus facilitate creativity. By signifying the implicit and by discouraging 'bad' ideas, new ideas might be encouraged.

Second-Order Metaphors

Authors advocating metaphors as a construct for understanding and developing research tend to portray a metaphor as a relatively sharp and coherent picture or image of the principal object (the object to be understood). But, as earlier remarked, the interaction between principal subject and modifier (the inferred concept which produces/activates the metaphor) often opens up a broad range of different images. This is particularly the case when the degree of overlap between object and modifier is too great. This is often the case in organization theory. In fact the most commonly used metaphors for organization overlap the principal subject to a considerable degree: for example political system, organism and culture.

If we take perhaps the most popular metaphor of the last decade, organization as a culture, there is enormous variation within the images, perspectives and analyses conducted based upon this metaphor (for example Alvesson and Berg, 1992; Smircich, 1983a). This can be understood in terms of the broad and fuzzy concept of culture being rather similar to the also rather broad and fuzzy concept of organization. The culture metaphor potentially opens up not just one new understanding of organizations, but a broad range of quite different possible understandings. (Here I am not referring to differences on the puzzle-solving level related to detailed quarrels as to how to define concepts, but to much more profound differences, which are best illustrated by the fact that the culture metaphor is utilized by researchers belonging to different paradigms, cf. Alvesson and Berg, 1992.)

Something similar can be said about the organism metaphor. According to Morgan (1980), a number of schools within organization theory ranging from human relations and sociotechnics to contingency theory and strategic choice are based on this metaphor. So if we here talk about a single metaphor, it also must be very broad and imprecise, having very little generative power. Alternatively, we are more able to say that all these orientations actually proceed from different metaphors, and that organism in itself functions more as a label or umbrella concept for these.

It could be argued that the 'espoused' metaphor provides only a very broad and general view of schools and orientations in social science and organization theory, and that one word, if viewed as a metaphor, can often actually be better understood as summarizing a number of different metaphors. One way of dealing with this is to say that culture, organism and other explicit and recognized metaphors in themselves are metaphorically structured when they are put into concrete 'action', that is they produce a distinct image, function in a generative way and guide particular coherent perspectives. If authors such as Brown (1976) and Morgan (1983a) are correct in saying that all seeing is metaphorical, then this must also be valid for metaphors in themselves (that is for the modifying part in a metaphor). We can then talk about different metaphors for culture, organism, etc. We can refer to these concepts, which function as metaphors for organization, as first-level metaphors, while the metaphors structuring the understanding of the metaphors (the modifiers), can be seen as second-level metaphors. (The number of the order is a consequence of what the primary object to understand is, in our case, the organization.)

Instead of two elements producing an interaction effect (the metaphor), we now have three elements producing a particular image, through the interaction of two metaphors (three elements producing two interactions; the first- and the second-level metaphors). If, for example, the organization is seen as a culture and the culture is seen as a holy cow, then organization/culture is the first-level metaphor, while culture/holy cow is the second level. In order to understand the culture view on organization, the holy cow metaphor must be invoked. In another study (Alvesson, 1993), I interpreted a number of culture studies and suggested that these were informed by very different second-level metaphors, ranging from exchange-regulator and compass to a set of blinders and non-order. While the culture metaphor is explicit and rather superficial, the second-level metaphors are implicit and often 'deep'.

This argument can be illustrated by the following figures. In Figure 7.1 we have the first-level metaphor. The large overlapping area signifies that the two components are rather similar. The modifier gives only a rather crude hint of how the principal subject (an organization) is seen (what it is seen as). In Figure 7.2 the second-order metaphor is included. It is the area that overlaps all three components which really produces the metaphor that guides the researcher's view on his/her object of study. Here we have the 'true' metaphor (that is a more elaborated view of the metaphor); the demarcated picture and conceptualization that can function generatively. Of course, the interplay of metaphors does not start or stop here. It is also possible to include additional levels of metaphors into the picture, but for the purpose of this chapter I am content with addressing second-level metaphors.

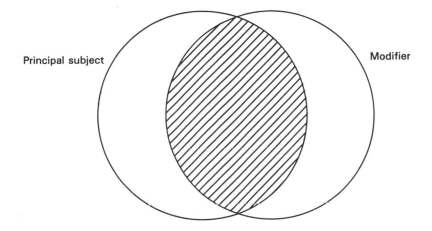

Figure 7.1   *First-level metaphor (hatched area = metaphor)*

I will now illustrate my point and show the importance of considering second-level metaphors. In order to promote a refined understanding of second-level metaphors I have chosen not to look at a case where the first-level metaphor is obviously broad and opens up very different metaphors, but to discuss and interpret a metaphor that might appear to provide coherent perspectives. I will also try to show that it makes sense to investigate it from a second-level metaphor perspective. I have chosen a relatively common metaphor in organizational analysis: the game metaphor. Two illustrations of it will be provided.

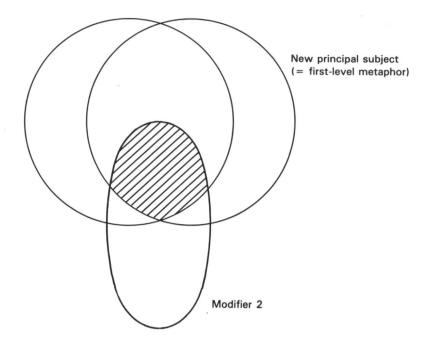

Figure 7.2   *Second-level metaphor*

The Game Metaphor

The idea of viewing the organization as a game has most distinctly been
proposed by Michel Crozier (1985; Crozier and Friedberg, 1980). More
elaborately, Crozier and Friedberg (1980: 57) suggest that the organization
'is conceptualized as a collection of interdependent games'. Actors in
organizations are then viewed as players of such games. The meaning and
implications of this image are far from evident at the first sight and the
authors distance their opinion from some of the associations which
perhaps most immediately come to mind when one thinks about games.
They assure the reader that 'to say that the players play games in no way
implies that there is any initial equality whatsoever among them, or that
there is any consensus as to the rules of the game' (1980: 57). The game
is a mechanism for integrating actors in organizational settings and for
avoiding conflicting (damaging) objectives between the involved actors
and the organization as a whole:

> Men have developed the game as an instrument to regulate their cooperation.
> It is the essential instrument of organized action. The game reconciles freedom
> and constraint. The player remains free but must, if he wants to win, adopt a
> rational strategy which conforms to the nature of the game, whose rules he
> must accept. (1980: 56)

Crozier and Friedberg emphasize the impact of the rules of the games, which rational actors – and actors are rational according to the authors – are wise in following or, rather, not breaking. Occasionally, actors can choose strategies that bring about a modification of the game itself. But it is also important to note that rules are not in themselves controlling behaviour. Rather they produce constraints and are inputs in the game which is played, they are also viewed in a longer perspective, the product of relations of force and of prior bargaining. The games offer organizational participants ways of promoting their own interests without disturbing or counteracting the overall functioning of the organization:

> A good game is the real organizational trick. Suppose the field is structured and the problem redefined so that people can still pursue their own interests, while their winning and losing will not alter the collective goodwill, in fact, improve it. (1980: 6)

This approach to organization theory and the basis for proposing the game metaphor is founded in certain ideas and assumptions about the nature of people. According to Crozier and Friedberg, man is basically *egoistic* – driven by self-interest. This has become more salient over the centuries as a consequence of the vanishing of the religious, moral and patriotic taboos of the past. Man is also *rational* – interested in using his capacity and the margin of liberty, for example, by playing upon uncertainties – and, which is seen as closely related to rationality, *free*: 'man is first and foremost a head, or, in other words . . . he can exercise his freedom' (1980: 19).

Associated with these attributes of man, Crozier and Friedberg believe, is this 'basic fact: power and its hidden counterparts, manipulation and blackmail, are unavoidable components of any collective endeavor' (1980: 12). Power is viewed as 'a relation of force from which one party can obtain more than the other, yet in which neither party is totally defenceless' (1980: 32). To have power with regard to others, it is proposed that an actor must partially satisfy their expectations of him (or her), and consequently, such expectations become a constraint for him (her). Power then is a central feature of organizational life and it can in no way be reduced to a formal authority structure. But the organization nevertheless regulates the development of relations of power, for example, through formal hierarchy and other organizational structures. This determines where relations of power develop which affect organizational members' capacities to play the game. Crozier and Friedberg do not view normative integration as an important aspect of organizational life, and certainly not as the major vehicle for the achievement of organized action. Instead they reject the idea that 'the actor responds passively to normative injunctions' (1980: 49).

When Crozier and Friedberg talk about games they do so in a particular way. As remarked above, many of the most salient aspects of games – or at least possibly the central ingredients in an understanding of them – are not a part of their picture. Players are not (necessarily) equal but might have very different formal positions, the rules are not very strict or clear and can be changed by players, and the game is not played for its own sake but concerns particular stakes and is thus tightly coupled to instrumental motives. A relaxed, playful attitude is lacking. When people play, they seem to be very serious; they are not, in the 'normal' sense of the word, 'playing'. Through Crozier and Friedberg's text runs a particular understanding of the nature of people and of social relations:

> the organization is in the end nothing more than a universe of conflict, and its functioning is seen as the outcome of confrontation between contingent, multiple, and divergent rationalities employed by relatively free actors using the sources of power available to them. (1980: 46)

They talk about the organization as 'a theatre of confrontation and conflict'. But the game concept indicates that these features are latent rather than overt. In normal organizations these forces converge into game-playing which, on the whole, serves the interest of all involved.

Behind the use of the game metaphor, Crozier and Friedberg can be interpreted as operating with another metaphor which is not espoused, although it is hardly hidden. This metaphor can be said to structure their use of the game metaphor in a particular way. They use the game concept so that certain aspects of the game are highlighted while many of the aspects salient in normal language use are not present. Crozier and Friedberg might be said to proceed from a 'second-level' metaphor of *'domesticatable jungle'*.

This metaphor draws attention to a view of social life as basically jungle-like – with divergent interest and actors individually seeking to maximize their interest in accordance with their strength, which is not very much constrained by normative regulations – but which it is also possible to regulate and control. The last elements are, however, uncertain and precarious. The tension and contradiction between these two elements – everybody's war against everybody and the prospect of domestication – are central and inform Crozier and Friedberg's use of the game concept so that this expresses a 'meta-understanding' produced by the overlap between the game and the domesticatable jungle concepts.

The relevance of this point can be illustrated by considering other possible metaphors for the game, which would give it another meaning, for example, 'high culture'. A 'culturally ordered' game metaphor would be very different from the one proposed by Crozier and Friedberg. Here a refined system of rules, matters of prestige, acknowledgement and status, and a more specific understanding of what would be at stake if the game was played by thoroughly socialized players (who would deny that there is a game going on) would be salient. (The writings of Bourdieu can be understood through the combination of these metaphors.) The idea of viewing an organization as a game does not determine the metaphor used in concrete analysis, but in itself only provides a rough guideline for analysis. How the game metaphor influences analysis if put into operation will be clearly illustrated by a couple of examples using the game metaphor.

In Crozier (1985) the concept of game is used in order to explain some phenomena in two different organizational contexts: French public administration and hospital units. In the former case the Crozier and Friedberg position reviewed above seems to be present. In relations between mayors and other top officials in French regions, political games appear to be important. It is, for example, suggested that

> Regulation is not achieved by command, evaluation and control, but indirectly by the results of games where each partner fights for his own interests without regard for his peers and superiors and must cater to the wishes of a stronger partner over whom his superiors and the whole milieu have an influence. (Crozier, 1985: 114)

In the other case, the one of hospital units, the meaning of the game metaphor appears to be very different, even though this is not explicitly stated by Crozier. He also here argues against a traditional view stressing organizational structures and notes that four hospital units showed considerable differences in their ways of working and social relations, despite the same structural conditions. Two of the units were characterized by clear-cut role distinctions, hierarchical relations, a strong priority given by physicians on their technical functions, a very poor communication system and complete passivity of the patients. The other two showed a relative blurring of the professional roles, more developed relationships, participation by patients and a relatively open and active communication system. Crozier says that in the first case 'the various partners play a formalistic game of isolation and non-communication', while in the second 'they play a game of open communication' (1985: 110). If we consider the second case with its more open, multipolar system and its progressive involvement of nurses and patients, it is clear that Crozier's understanding of the 'game' involved here is quite different in character from that suggested by Crozier and Friedberg's general remarks referred to above.

Still, Crozier applies the game concept and in this sees the explanation of the various work arrangements and social relations in the various units. The key variable is 'the collective capacity of the people concerned to handle the tensions these games create' (Crozier, 1985: 112). At other places in the text capacity is viewed as a means for power, but in the case of these humanistic, open systems it is a bit difficult to understand the relevance of this aspect and of the political and power-laden nature of the games which Crozier, at least in the case of French administration, and Crozier and Friedberg (1980) stress so firmly.

I have some difficulties in seeing the merits of the game metaphor in the context of the humanistic units and in the explanations of differences between the four hospital units, but leaving this doubt aside, I think that it is important to emphasize that game is used in a quite different way here. In terms of a second-level metaphor the one of 'domesticatable jungle' is not salient. Instead game is equated with something like 'health-care philosophy'. Consequently the nature of the game is not only different, but the basic way of understanding what a game is – the metaphors used for the game – differ when the two progressive hospital units and the French administration are described and analysed.

To the extent that my remarks are 'correct' or fruitful, it is worth noting that the metaphorical usage of a particular metaphor can change – without explicitly being explained or perhaps even noticed by the author – within one and the same text. Different second-order metaphors might govern the use of the 'same' (first-level) metaphor (which only on the surface remains the same). This can be called '*metaphorical drifting*'. While complex words in general are difficult to ascribe fixed meanings because they vary according to context and situations where they are employed (cf. Wittgenstein's 'language game' idea), words with a 'strong' metaphorical meaning exhibit a special likelihood of drifting because of the nature of a metaphor (that is non-analytic, involves fantasy, etc.). To think in terms of the possibility of different second-level metaphors entering and leaving the construction and use of a particular (first-level) metaphor might inspire greater awareness of how a metaphor can vary in meaning.

Another example of the use of the game metaphor for organization can further illustrate this point of considering potential metaphors behind an espoused metaphor. Frost (1987) uses the game metaphor in order to provide a general account of power and politics. He refers to Crozier and Friedberg (1980), which seems to be the major theoretical source behind his use of the concept. In terms of definition and general discussion of the concept, Frost indicates that he uses the game in exactly the same way as Crozier and Friedberg. He does not indicate any departures from their approach and says that: 'An organizational game thus involves social actors, payoffs, and a set of interpretive strategies that specify the rules, data, and successful outcomes in the game' (Frost, 1987: 527). Despite the apparently strong resemblance between Crozier/Friedberg's and Frost's positions, a close reading indicates differences in the view of the game metaphor. Crozier and Friedberg emphasize the positive functions of games; their relative innocence, and the relative equality of different players – compared with many other authors who, for example, downplay the extent to which leaders are constrained by games. Frost does not seem to fully share these assumptions. His presentation of games is divided into two parts, one on surface games and one on deep structure games. The former is described and discussed basically in the form of various strategies and tactics, for example impression management, gatekeeping, rule-citing, labelling, managing sanctions, covering up, budgeting, lines versus staff, rival camps, coalition, agenda controlling, using outside experts, selective use of objective criteria, and so on. On the whole it is not so much fully-fledged games which are described but individual (and group) tactics, moves and means for political action used against other individuals (or groups). It is not primarily the socially constrained aspects of power which are in focus, but all sorts of possible manifestations of political action. Nor are relations or interactive elements of games central in Frost's account. We learn about the possible moves of one agent, rather than the structured relations between various players. The account of the games is quite partial.

The deep structure games are of another character than are the surface games. While the latter are easier to pin-point, demarcate and describe, the former are more disguised, also for the players themselves: 'The primary deep structure game currently recognizable appears to be a systematic distortion of communication so as to maintain and enhance power relations that favour one social reality over other possible alternatives, that favor some interest groups at the expense of others' (Frost, 1987: 532). While the actors are very much present in the account of surface games, they play a much less clear and significant role in the case of deep structure games. In surface games, calculations and tactics are central, but in deep structure games the people involved have a limited understanding of the game. Instead ideologies, traditions and other distorting elements, at least partly existing beyond the consciousness of actors, are significant. Frost, referring to Deetz (1985), for example, writes about the political process of 'naturalization, through which "historically" chosen forms and privileges become defined as the way things are. Their "chosen" quality is no longer open to inspection and discussion, and change is not considered' (Frost, 1987: 533).

This emphasis on games as something which regulates relationships between players through constraints provided by organizational structures is not salient either in the surface or the deep structure games. The social relations as well as the regulatory (and thereby beneficial for the organizational whole) elements are not as central for Frost as they are for Crozier and Friedberg. Consequently, these authors employ the game concept in quite different ways.

In other words, Frost draws upon another second-level metaphor when he uses the game construct. Despite frequent references to game, play and players, his entire approach depicts games as being not that innocent. Instead of Crozier and Friedberg's functionalist idea of games as a kind of 'balance', Frost seems to understand games rather as a matter of domination. We can make sense of his approach by suggesting that organizational games are understood as *instruments of domination*. This is at least the case when he talks about the surface games. In the deep structure games the instrumental quality of the game is hardly salient. Here a metaphor of *frozen reality* may better reflect the idea of the game which is pursued. This does not mean that organizations are, simply and directly, understood as instruments of domination or frozen realities. Organizations are understood as games, but the conceptualization of games is partly structured through the instrument of domination and the frozen reality metaphors. The image of the organization as a (set of) game(s) receives a particular form and content. The central role of the game metaphor makes Frost's approach quite different from authors who view organizations as instruments of domination or frozen (naturalized) realities (as first-level metaphors).

Many Marxist and other radical authors use the instrument of domination metaphor for understanding organizations (Morgan, 1986) and some critical theory-inspired scholars proceed from a frozen reality view (for example Deetz, 1985). The appropriateness of understanding (parts of) Frost's work through the combination of the game and instrument of domination metaphors is illustrated by the following summary from his work:

> The political game construct . . . alerts us to the pluralistic nature of organizational life at all levels and to the inequality of that pluralism in many organizational activities. We are encouraged by this perspective to look for victories and losses, to explore the nature of both the victories and the losses, and to try to understand the alternative outcomes that might have emerged had the players been different in terms of the amount or use of their resources or had other players joined the game.' (Deetz, 1985: 536)

While the game concept mainly alerts people to the pluralistic nature of organizational life, in itself it hardly draws attention to inequalities, at least not in the case of Crozier and Friedberg. In order to provide that alertness, the game metaphor must be modified in a particular direction. The instrument of domination metaphor appears to illuminate this rather well. (The frozen reality metaphor to a lesser extent draws attention to precisely these features.)

In an effort to apply the surface and deep structure games notion on an empirical issue – how innovations are blocked by powerful groups – Egri and Frost (1989) clearly illustrate the socially negative aspects of political games and their role in subordinating people to a dominant order. The use of words such as game and play stand in contrast to the descriptions of the highly immoral political manoeuvring of the power elite and the weak positions of many innovators in relation to it. In a few cases, where actors from 'below' managed to successfully struggle against the dominating elite, games can instead be understood as resistance (defences against domination). This seems to be appropriate, for example, in the case of the introduction of numerical control in a factory, where 'workers effectively undermined ownership initiatives to deskill production work by engaging in political games of sabotage and insurgency' (Egri and Frost, 1989: 589).

Some Reasons for Paying Attention to Second-Level Metaphors

The reasons for taking an interest in second-level metaphors are similar to those raised for focusing on metaphors in general. These concern understanding, orientation, critique and the generation of new ideas.

Addressing second-level metaphors facilitates a more refined *understanding* of how metaphors inform conceptualizations of organizations and guide research. Instead of portraying the metaphor as a simple interaction between the principal subject (the organization) and a modifier, which is presumed to proceed from a metaphor-free base, a more complex view of the creation of metaphors is made possible. Especially when it comes to metaphors created by components which are very similar (such as culture and organization) or when a broad range of various perspectives are viewed as based upon the same metaphor (organism), it is vital to take into account what lies behind and structures the surface/explicit metaphor in order to understand how organization is metaphorically understood and the theoretical work and analysis that follows.

Another issue concerns the value of metaphors in providing *overviews* of the field. Metaphors facilitate people's orientation within the territory of organization studies. As this territory becomes larger and more difficult to get a good overview of, the need for landmarks is growing. Metaphors fit nicely into our cognitive maps and are therefore valuable as vehicles for orientation. This is well illustrated by Morgan (1986). A problem is that metaphors in themselves often give the impression of communicating a rather distinct image – 'the organization as a game' or 'the bureaucracy as an obsessive neurosis' – which can bring about a misleading certainty of what the metaphor really stands for in the case of different authors. A metaphor appeals to fantasy and triggers off associations which might lead to the forming of a certain picture which is not always easy to check against the 'true' meaning of the metaphor, that is the meaning of the author who uses it. The seductive nature of many metaphors covers their ambiguous nature. As a guideline for orientation, metaphors are often less reliable than they appear.

By drawing attention to second-level metaphors, this problem might be reduced. Of course, when looking closely at texts, a less imprecise understanding of what they express emerges. As an aid to closer reading, and to the process of orientating oneself before and after such readings, second-level metaphors might provide valuable clues. (In Alvesson, 1993, an overview of organizational culture research is based on second-level metaphors.) The point with metaphors is that they offer a picture for summarizing a particular understanding. As an important guideline to more complex understandings, second-level metaphors provide additional landmarks in the mapping of organization theory and often reveal that first-level metaphors are rough and ambiguous. Awareness of the concept of second-level metaphors might also lead to a more realistic appreciation of the relatively crude guidelines for orientation provided by first-level metaphors. Knowledge of the general 'existence' of second-level metaphors might provide a warning for over-reliance on the information provided by espoused metaphors.

Second-level metaphors might also serve as valuable foci in *critique and reflection.* Interpretation of the implicit, deeper thought structures of a text on this level might produce interesting critique as a complement to more detailed complaints or discussions about the deeper, paradigmatic roots and assumptions. To 'discover' or, rather suggest second-level metaphors as part of a critical scrutiny of theories and texts might provide critique and debate with some novel inputs, especially in cases where it is possible to identify discrepancies between surface/explicit metaphors on the one hand, and deep/implicit, second-level metaphors on the other. Also in order to find variations in the use of explicit metaphors – which might mean that there are actually different metaphors guiding analyses without being made explicit (often perhaps due to the author being unaware of this) – the second-level metaphor concept might be valuable. In this chapter the critique of Crozier's (1985) somewhat inconsistent use of his game metaphor indicates the benefits of using second-level metaphors as an entrance to critical examination.

Perhaps the most important aspect of paying attention to second-level metaphors, as with metaphors in general, concerns their *generative capacity.* Second-level metaphors are in this regard similar to first-level metaphors. One way of developing social science and organization theory might be to take new looks at established metaphors and create new metaphors for these. Instead of, or as a complement to, adding new metaphors to established ones, existing metaphors could be the targets of creative 'seeing-as'. How can we see organization as culture or organization as a political system in novel ways? There might be a risk of novelty here on a piecemeal level, but nothing prevents established metaphors from being re-seen in ways quite different from those indicated by established second-level metaphors. New second-level metaphors might, for example, emerge from paradigms other than those which have tended earlier to occupy a certain metaphor. (Some metaphors are probably paradigm-bound, but others, such as culture, theatre, neurosis and political system can be interpreted and re-interpreted from quite different angles.)

When considering second-level metaphors as a source of inspiration for creativity, it is important to consider the process aspect of metaphors. Schön (1979: 254) sees metaphor, apart from being a product, as 'a process by which new perspectives on the world come into existence'. As creative devices, metaphors do not 'live' for ever. Metaphors are often generative during a certain period after which they become parts of conventional knowledge (Czarniawska-Joerges, 1988). For example, after we have thoroughly learned that organizations are not self-contained and that they are dependent on, and interact with, an 'environment', the idea of seeing an organization as an organism is not very generative.

Second-level metaphors can also be viewed as a means for creating new generative powers for interpreting established metaphors through giving them new meaning. The re-seeing of a metaphor leads to a new way of seeing-as. Viewing organizational culture as, for example, a blindfold or male domination means that the culture metaphor can be generative in quite another way than its earlier dominating second-level metaphors such as social glue made possible.

This process aspect means that second-level metaphors for creative purposes must wait their turn. It is only when a new (first-level) metaphor has existed for some time, and its ability to throw new light on the research object has been established and utilized, that it becomes beneficial to address second-level metaphors for generating new ideas. Even though it can be argued that all metaphors from their very start involve second-level metaphors, it might complicate things too much to address that issue before the metaphor has reached a certain degree of maturity. When a new metaphor has emerged, it is probably best to direct energy to investigate its powers in guiding reasoning and observations, without getting caught in explorations of the metaphor behind the metaphor. The latter project belongs to a later phase in the history of a metaphor; but when the metaphor has matured, putting first-level metaphors into play with novel second-level metaphors might be an important part of creativity in research.

Second-Level Metaphors and Postmodernism

The argument of this chapter to some extent follows the path of post-modernist thinking, but stops short of accepting a view on language and texts as purely figurative, characterized by instability, difference, indeterminancy.

To some extent I have tried to 'deconstruct' metaphors used by authors to inform organizational analysis, and showed that they hardly achieve a specific, stable and fixed meaning, but when put in operation tend to drift away from such. The idea of a metaphor producing a singular meaning that functions like a robust starting point and guide for argumentation and analysis is then problematized. This approach parallels some postmodern scepticism about so-called 'grand narratives', that is overall frameworks aspiring to capture the essentials of a certain research area. In focus in my text are 'meso-narratives', that is the schools, theories and key concepts which aspire to guide studies of 'medium-level' phenomena such as organizational power games. When the various authors use metaphors as a key element in their research strategy they not only depart from a more formalistically rational procedure, trying to avoid or minimize metaphorically language to the benefit of a 'scientific' literal one, but also become caught in or – to stress a positive aspect – utilize metaphors for the (first-level) metaphors, thus ending quite far away from the more 'tightly structured' approach suggested by traditional epistemology.

Even though this chapter to a certain degree supports a postmodernist search for instabilities, the uncontrollable nature of metaphors in language and the contradictions lying behind claims on rationality, I am opposed to the idea of heavily stressing these elements. This chapter adopts a 'constructive' line in which the metaphor behind the metaphor supports more reflective forms of reasoning and analysis about research objects (theoretical as well as empirical) rather than an endless 'deconstructive' route in which one engages in an eternal unpacking of metaphors for metaphors for. . . . My text on the whole should be read as a contribution to increased sensitivity for and reflection on the metaphorical and 'meta-metaphorical' nature of theories and concepts, which may lead to a 'better' understanding of social research and more creative interpretations.

As Tsoukas (1991a) argues, it is not necessary to choose between a metaphor or a literal view on language and science. He proposes that the key question is 'how can metaphorical language be used in such a way as to contribute to the development of literatural language' (p. 582). Although I, in opposition to Tsoukas, am sceptical to the extent to which complex and interesting phenomena can be captured in a 'metaphor-free way', some space must be allowed for words and descriptions that represent phenomena in a non-problematical way (for example a reader is now perceiving this text). The reader may have noticed that I have discussed second-level metaphors only on the framework level, and have made no efforts to draw attention to language issues on a more specific level.

Given a constrained, or non-colonialistic, attitude to the metaphorical nature of research frameworks, issues raised by postmodernism may illuminate obstacles for a reflective social research rather than discourage aspirations in such a direction. The idea of focusing on the play of metaphors should also be understood as a suggestion for addressing one element (not *the* element) in research, which may contribute to the avoidance of some traps (such as a metaphor covering up very diverse ideas) and stimulate new ideas and conceptualizations. Through illuminating deviations or problems or complexities in relationship to research as a 'moderately rational' project, its sometimes fragile, but not necessarily illusionary, powers to illuminate human affairs and contribute to social and communicative reasoning are strengthened.

By drawing attention to second-level and possibly other levels of metaphors, we challenge the simplified assumption that the images of the research object which guide research are clear, distinct and well structured, and that the researcher completely masters his or her project through conscious choices of 'seeing as'. The idea of second-level metaphors suggests that ideas and frameworks are much more complex, ambiguous and inconsistent than the explicit metaphors often indicate. To understand the metaphorical nature of research becomes not only a process of finding or developing a metaphor, but rather a complicated struggle to provide partial understandings of the various combinations and interactions of different metaphors. The metaphors involved are only to a limited degree conscious to the researcher. A better metaphor for research than the development and application of a single metaphor might be a struggle with the ambiguous and slippery play of metaphors on various levels. Awareness of this dimension may alert up to certain traps in research, thus facilitating the options to reduce incoherence in theoretical frameworks and key concepts. It may also contribute to more creative uses of existing metaphors as targets of new forms of 'seeing-as'.

8

Organizational Discourse and the Gendering of Identity

Albert J. Mills

Postmodernism, Gender and Organization

The theoretical starting point for this chapter is the work of Michel Foucault, or more specifically a feminist reading of Foucault. From a feminist perspective the work of Foucault provides a valuable but angst-ridden framework for the analysis of the relationship between organization and gender. Of particular value is Foucault's notion of 'discourse' and its relationship to organization and to subjectivity. Foucault argues that human subjectivity is constructed within and as a result of given 'discursive practices' constituted as discourse, and that in the modern era those discursive practices have increasingly taken place within, and as an integral part of, organizational contexts. For Foucault, in the modern world social institutions influence discursive practices (Dreyfus and Rabinow, 1982: xx) and to the extent that 'the increasing organization of everything is the central issue of our time' (Dreyfus and Rabinow, 1982: xxii).

It is a world in which the pervasive organization of society can be characterized as 'bio-technical power' – the modern(ist) concern with control and focus upon the body and the contribution that those processes have made to human subjectivity. Foucault's major contribution is his 'unique emphasis on the body as the place in which the most minute and local social practices are linked up with the large scale organization of power' (Dreyfus and Rabinow, 1982: xxii).

For a number of feminists Foucault's work – with its explanation of the link between bio-power, subjectivity and organization – offers a new, yet problematic, way of understanding female oppression (Ferguson, 1984; Townley, 1990; Oseen, 1991; Calás and Smircich, 1992a, b). It is problematic in that Foucault manages to champion the underdog (Eribon, 1991) while rejecting any potential truth claims that would seek – à la *Animal Farm* – to justify a realignment of power in favour of the previously dispossessed. Despite positive references to the women's movement Foucault nonetheless would regard as illegitimate (or modernist) feminist attempts to re-create notions of female subjectivity.

One of the earliest feminist attempts to utilize Foucauldian analysis in an understanding of the relationship between organization and gender is the work of Kathy Ferguson (1984). Ferguson states that:

> I agree with . . . Foucault's major preoccupation; his belief that . . . 'the increasing organization of everything is the central issue of our time'. Foucault's discussions of modernity, particularly his insights into the production of individuals and relationships by the prevailing language and structures of power, provide a valuable means for comprehending the complexities of social control. (1984: xii)

Ferguson goes on to use Foucauldian 'insight' to analyse the nature of bureaucratic discourse and its implications for women. Ferguson's use of the term *insight* is intentional, meant to convey something more than a mere borrowing of Foucauldian terms yet less than a full-blown acceptance of Foucauldian methodology. A key departure from Foucault's methodological intent lies in Ferguson's concern to develop a feminist critique of bureaucratic discourse:

> Thus I conclude that Foucault would probably see my efforts to create a feminist discourse, grounding it on the concrete relations with others that shape female experience, as another misguided effort to create meaning and as another manifestation of the historical subjectivizing trends of modern culture. (Ferguson, 1984: xiii–xiv)

Rejecting Foucault as 'short-sighted' Ferguson goes on to argue that 'without a concept of human agency, the promise of resistance that the submerged discourse of outsiders can offer is rendered mechanistic, flat and empty':

> Foucault neglects to explicate a crucial aspect of our experience as both social and temporal beings . . . [and his] 'rejection of all recourse to the interiority of a conscious, individual, meaning-given subject' . . . renders much of our day-to-day experience incomprehensible. I see the creation of meaning both as unavoidable and as a potentially ennobling process, allowing us to order our collective lives in light of values we embrace and in a language we make our own. (Ferguson, 1984: xiv)

Indeed, without the possibility of a viable resistance the radical promise in Foucault's work is reduced to pessimistic voyeurism. Ferguson, in contrast, advocates resistance through the development of a 'feminist discourse'.

This chapter follows Ferguson in drawing upon Foucauldian 'insight' to explore the significance of the 'increasing organization of everything' for the construction of gender, but utilizes those insights to question the nature of gender itself, questions that Ferguson's critique of Foucault's notion of subjectivity leaves unanswered.

Valerie Walkerdine (1990) treats gender as a discourse, arguing that 'femininity and masculinity are fictions linked to fantasies deeply embedded in the social world which can take on the status of fact when inscribed with the powerful practices . . . through which we are regulated' (quoted in Ussher, 1991: 13). Yet this again raises the question of human agency. Jane Flax offers a way of reconciling postmodernism and feminism in proposing that 'a feminist deconstruction of the self . . . would point toward locating self and its experiences in concrete social relations, not only in fictive or purely textual conventions':

> A social self would come to be partially in and through powerful, affective relationships with other persons. These relations with others and our feelings and fantasies about them, along with experiences of embodiedness also mediated by such relations can come to constitute an 'inner' self that is neither fictive or 'natural'. Such a self is simultaneously embodied, gendered, social, and unique. It is capable of telling stories and of conceiving and experiencing itself in all these ways. (Flax, 1990: 232).

This approach offers a valuable framework with which to explore the relationship of the gendered self and organizational discourse.

The Discourse of Gender and the Development of Organizational Discourse

By *organizational discourse* I mean 'ways of thinking about organizing'; taken-for-granted, more-or-less unconscious meta-understandings about the way things are achieved in society. In particular that kind of thinking which unquestioningly accepts the fact that certain activities need to be structured, that contributes to 'the increasing organization of everything'. The act and art of organizing is a central part of our thinking that colours how we view ourselves and the world.

The modern organizational world – a world in which organizing is second nature – has been thousands of years in the making. Various studies suggest that the development of organizational forms arose out of a number of pre-existing gendered practices, values, and ideas. Weber's (1967) classic study of the rise of capitalist entrepreneurship, for example, argued that the 'spirit of capitalism' owes a lot to the practices and thought of the Calvinist Church, which in turn was enmeshed in a discourse of logical, calculative thought – 'rationality', that had spread from the narrow confines of science, through politics, to the new Protestant Church. Ironically Weber, noted elsewhere for his interest in 'patriarchy', is silent on the role of gender in the development of capitalism. As Joanne Martin (1990a) has pointed out, Weber's concept of rationality is remarkably gendered – it is a male notion of rationality, one that places emphasis on logic, calculability, and the absence of a certain type of emotionality. This raises interesting questions about the character of the gendered influences that came to form the development of the Protestant Church and, in turn, emergent capitalist organizations. At one level we have the influence of a set of dominant, male values (rationality); at another level we have the establishment of a set of male-dominated organizational practices (the Calvinist sects), and at a third level we have the establishment of male-owned businesses. The gendered links seem too intricate to ignore.

Numerous feminist studies – while not aimed at organizational analysis *per se* – provide various clues to the links between gender and the development of the modern form of organization. Rosaldo (1974) has detailed the links between the break-up of domestic-centred feudal production, the development of capitalist manufactories and the creation of 'domestic' (female) and 'public' (male) spheres of identity. Burrell's (1984) work has associated the development of a form of 'desexualized' bureaucracy with developments centred on an elite group of men in the ancient Catholic Church. Cynthia Cockburn's (1985) study of the development of technology has revealed the deep-seated masculine biases that came to shape notions of skill, technique and ability. And Marilyn French (1985) has suggested links between the harsh and competitive nature of early industrial work and changing forms of masculinity and notions of womanhood.

Masculinity, strength, aggression themselves have become linked to dominance and its micro forms – management and leadership. Organizational ownership and control, arising out of socio-legal structures of pre-industrial Europe (Brundage, 1987), was invariably in the hands of men. That the experiences of men shaped the development of organizational forms and realities is clear, but it is worth noting that male experiences differed according to their role in the operation of these organizations. Examination of the history of the modern corporation suggests that many early corporate forms (guilds, religious orders, universities) evolved from 'largely democratic organizations into closed corporations controlled by a few' (Hatton, 1990: 15). It was the elite few males who came to own and control organizations and put their rules, their stamp, and their model of behaviour on organizational expectations: a pattern extant in today's corporations (Jackall, 1988). As entrepreneurs and organizational leaders sought to replace themselves with functionaries it was almost to be expected that they would choose those who most resembled them in thinking and organizational commitment – not just other men, but men who appeared every bit as aggressive as they had been.

A key feature in the development of the modern corporation seems to have involved a striving for monopolistic control over an area of concern (for example a particular market, spiritual matters, degree-granting status) (Hatton, 1990). It is this peculiar form of control that has come to mark out how organizations are constructed and understood, and which has accorded organizations dominance *vis-à-vis* the domestic sphere of life. Over time dominance, organizational leadership and masculinity have become conflated.

Postmodernism and Organizational Discourse

Michel Foucault's work on power and knowledge provides us with an overview of how many of the various features of social life, of social practices, interact to create gendered organizational subjects. For Foucault a concern with knowledge of and control over the body characterizes the development of modern society and modernist thought. In the manufactories of the 18th century new forms of knowledge assisted the emerging class of entrepreneurs to regularize the extraction of time and labour from the bodies of their workforce. Increasingly entrepreneurs and government took an interest in the control and regulation of the body. The state became interested in the health, numbers and condition of the population, and this generated an array of new professionals – and new organizational types – concerned with translating and regulating the developing interest in the body. In the process particular concepts and practices of 'normalization' were produced:

> These practices are supported and exercised both by the state and by new bodies of knowledge, especially medicine and the human sciences. Under the humanistic rubric of the state's interest in and obligation to the creation and protection of the 'well-being' of its inhabitants, global surveillance of its members is increasingly instituted. The state needs experts to amass the knowledge it requires and to execute the policies said to effect and maximize this well-being and protection. Instances of such knowledge and associated practices include medicine, education, public health, prisons, and schools. (Flax, 1990: 207)

Foucault refers to these as 'disciplinary practices' – practices that are concerned with concrete and precise knowledge of the body, and as such constitute 'biopower' in their outcomes of control. A major outcome of the nature and widespread existence of disciplinary practices has been, according to Foucault, the creation of the individual self; a constant placing of individuals in situations where they are variously forced to think about their 'selves' and are simultaneously provided with the answers. Alongside these practices,

> the individual subject is also created through confessional practices. The primary exemplars of these practices are psychoanalysis and psychiatry. These discourses produce sexuality as a dangerous force within us that can be controlled only by the person exercising surveillance upon her- or himself. Such surveillance is said to lead to both 'self-knowledge' and freedom from the effects of these forces. However, in order to attain such self-knowledge and self-control, the individual must consult an expert whose knowledge provides privileged access to this dangerous aspect of the person's 'self'. (Flax, 1990: 208)

Thus, unlike any other, the modern(ist) era confronts us with a series of dominant discourses in which notions of the 'self' are primary and have helped to create various senses of 'self' in the image of the – largely organizational – practices from which they arise.

Jane Flax points out that the 'notion of biopower as a uniquely modern form of power runs contrary to many feminist accounts of history. According to these accounts, women's bodies have always . . . been "colonized" by the intersection of knowledge and power' (1990: 212).

Flax adds that, 'Perhaps what distinguishes modern culture is not the introduction of biopower *per se*, but rather the extensions of this power (in old and new forms) to different groups of men as well as women' (1990: 212). However, in exposing gendered notions of biopower Flax seems to have downplayed the significance of the 'new forms' of that power and what they may say for feminist understandings about the social construction of gender. What seems interesting about biopower is not its extension but its form. Unlike previous eras, the social construction of gender – as an integral part of disciplinary and confessional practices – in the modern day is a ubiquitous process, inherent in much, if not all, of what we do. Of particular interest to feminist organizational theorists is the relationship of new forms of biopower to organizational practices as pervasive forms of knowledge; that is how do our meta-understandings of organizing and organizations contribute to the way we view ourselves as gendered persons, and what are the peculiar outcomes?

Organization and the Gendered Self

Organizational discourse reaches into our understanding of self in a number of ways. The language of organizational relationships signifies our social worth and standing; informing us that we are pre- (preschooler) or post- (retiree) organizational, organizationally important (manager) or marginal (part-time employee), in organizational limbo (unemployed) or lacuna (housewife). Such classifications are rarely gender-neutral: we have a term for housewife rather than husband; we too often associate manager with maleness (Brenner et al., 1989), and we are more likely to associate part-time employment with females.

The language of organizational discourse is reinforced through a number of disciplinary practices through which youngsters are 'schooled' for their role as (gendered) organizational subjects. Schooling in the 20th century has largely been about the preparation of children for the world of work (Bowles and Gintis, 1976), and the process has been deeply gendered, involving not only discriminatory curricula (Spender and Sarah, 1980), counselling (Griffin, 1985), language (Evans, 1988), and technical training (Cockburn, 1985) but also in the way children are involved in play and team games (Mackie, 1987).

Gender socialization is particularly acute in adolescence. This crucial stage of identity formation takes place in the context of intersecting discourses concerning sexuality, domestic location and organizational destination: 'Developing a nature gender identity means coming to terms with these issues: physical sexual maturity; relationships with the other sex; future options with regard to vocation and marriage' (Mackie, 1987: 147). Mackie contends that male and female identities are shaped differently, with females being educated to 'be' and males educated to 'do': females are taught to *be* wives and mothers, males are taught that they have to *do* numerous things if they are to earn and re-earn masculinity – they have to strive for success, fight for what they want, initiate sex, stress their strength and toughness (Willis, 1977).

Disciplinary practices of this kind do not simply prepare males and females for different organizational roles but also prepare them to see themselves as males and females – to be gendered. The impact of gendered work practices on female opportunities is well known: women encounter widespread sexual harassment (DiTomasio, 1989) and in comparison with men and women are concentrated in fewer industries and occupations, occupy fewer positions of power and authority, and are lower paid (Peitchinis, 1989). What is less explored within the organizational and management literature is the psychological impact of organizational realities upon the self.

The Self

In the main, discussion of the 'self' has received limited attention and that of the gendered self even less attention within the literature: issues of 'personality' have received wider coverage but usually as an adjunct to concerns of leadership and motivation (Whyte, 1956; Argyris, 1987), and again gender has been neglected outside of the work of a few feminist theorists (cf. Kanter, 1979; Harriman, 1985).

In the last decade or so a number of psychoanalytical studies of organization have drawn attention to the links between self and organizational reality. These studies are striking in their sexist biases (for example linking narcissism with inadequate maternal care) and foci (an overconcentration on male leaders). Yet in the very focus upon organizational leaders and administrators they reveal valuable clues to aspects of the dominating organizational discourses within which male and female selves are constructed.

Christopher Lasch's (1983) study of narcissism in American life raises a number of interesting questions for organizational analysis. Lasch suggests that there is a strong relationship between the way we come to conceive of ourselves and of organization:

> Every age develops its own peculiar forms of pathology, which expresses in exaggerated form its underlying character. In Freud's time, hysteria and obsessional neurosis carried to extremes the personality traits associated with the capitalist order at an earlier stage in its development – acquisitiveness, fanatical devotion to work, and a fierce repression of sexuality. (Lasch, 1983: 87–8)

Our own time, according to Lasch, is characterized by a 'culture of narcissism', signified by the widespread evidence of 'borderline' personality disorders. In terms of clinical observations, patients who symptomize the malaise suffer from pervasive feelings of emptiness and a deep disturbance of self-esteem (1983: 89). Lasch's description of the general malaise of narcissism complements Foucault's notion of the construction of the self in suggesting that the end-product of discourses concerned with self-knowledge is the creation of individual self obsession:

> Medicine and psychiatry – more generally the therapeutic outlook and sensibility that pervade modern society – reinforce the pattern created by other cultural influences, in which the individual endlessly examines himself for signs of aging and ill health, for tell-tale symptoms of psychic stress, for blemishes and flaws that might diminish his attractiveness, or on the other hand for reassuring indications that his life is proceeding according to schedule. (Lasch, 1983: 99)

Drawing upon the work of Heinz Kohut, Lasch contends that narcissism arises out of the 'unavoidable shortcomings of maternal care' (Kohut, 1971) which results in the child coming to realize that s/he is not the centre of the universe, that the mother is ultimately separate from the child and not there solely for his/her total gratification. The resulting disappointment and frustration leads the child to strive to reverse the situation and 'involves either creating a tyrannical idealized self-image or the incorporation of tyrannical idealized parent image for the self' (Walter, 1983: 262).

Far from containing narcissistic disorders the structure of modern society both reflects and encourages them. As Joel Kovel expresses it:

> [The] stimulation of infantile cravings by advertising, the usurpation of parental authority by the media and the school, and the rationalization of inner life accompanied by the false promise of personal fulfillment, have created a new type of 'social individual'. The result is not the classical neurosis where an infantile impulse is suppression by patriarchal authority, but a modern version in which impulse is stimulated, perverted and given neither an adequate object upon which to satisfy itself nor coherent forms of control. . . . The entire complex, played out in a setting of alienation rather than direct control, loses the classical form of symptom – and the classical opportunity of simply restoring an impulse to consciousness. (Quoted in Lasch, 1983: 90)

Narcissism finds its expression in the modern organization in a number of ways:

> For all his inner suffering, the narcissist has many traits that make for success in bureaucratic institutions, which put a premium on the manipulation of interpersonal relations, discourage the formation of deep personal attachments, and at the same time provide the narcissist with the approval he needs in order to validate his self esteem. . . . The management of personal impressions comes naturally to him, and his mastery of its intricacies serves him well in political and business organizations where performance now counts for less than 'visibility,' 'momentum,' and a winning record. As the 'organization man' gives way to the bureaucratic 'gamesman' – the 'loyalty era' of American business to the age of the 'executive success game' – the narcissist comes into his own. (Lasch, 1983: 91–2)

In the organizational world the exteriors of buildings, the interiors of offices, and the presentation of self within offices have come to symbolize narcissism – symbols that not only reward but require narcissistic behaviour (Walter, 1983).

The narcissistic organizational culture gives rise to a type of leader who 'sees the world as a mirror of himself and has no interest in external events except as they throw back a reflection of his own image' (Lasch, 1983: 96). Such leaders are often more concerned with image than substance – advancing through the corporate ranks not by serving the organization but by convincing his associates that he possesses the attributes of a 'winner'. In getting to the top he manipulates people and symbols and, in an organizational culture created out of intersecting male values (Mills and Murgatroyd, 1991), many of those symbols utilize females and images of femininity:

> A graciously and perhaps even sumptuously decorated office reception of a company communicates opulence and self-assurance. . . . So too does the presence of a comely lady receptionist. These individuals are clearly not of goddess stature but are reminiscent of the nymphs who served as handmaidens to mythological gods in a variety of ways. (Walter, 1983: 259)

The organizational 'gamesman':

> avoids intimacy as a trap, preferring the 'exciting', sexy atmosphere with which the modern executive surrounds himself at work, 'where adoring, mini-skirted secretaries constantly flirt with him'. In all his personal relations, the gamesman depends on the admiration or fear he inspires in others to certify his credentials as a 'winner'. (Lasch, 1983: 93–4)

This type of leadership contributes to an organizational culture in which certain images of leadership and of masculinity are expected to be 'mirrored' (Kets de Vries, 1989a). For males the narcissistic organizational culture holds up images of certain types of male-associated behaviour that they are expected to mirror if they are to be deemed simultaneously successful and male. The process of mirroring is usually facilitated in such cultures by situations of excessive dependency between executives and subordinates: in these situations subordinates may come to overly identify with the leader (Kets de Vries 1989a, b, 1990). In its extreme form this may involve over-identification 'to the point of madness', as in the case of the relationship between Henry Ford and his lieutenants, Liebold, Sorensen, and Bennett, and the FBI under J. Edgar Hoover (Kets de Vries, 1984). On the other hand, failure to mirror the appropriate behaviour can result in organizational/sexual innuendo and rejection, as in the firing of an executive by Henry Ford II, who deemed that the man's tight trousers signified a lack of manliness and, *ergo*, managerial competence (Iacocca, 1984).

For females, organizational cultures hold out a whole different set of problems in relation to identity formation. Females are confronted with organizational discourses that not only shape notions of femininity (and of masculinity) but whose rules and practices are male dominated (Mills and Murgatroyd, 1991). From a feminist psychoanalytic perspective, Jane Flax argues that psychoanalytic theory – specifically object relations theory – 'lacks a critical, sustained account of gender formation and its costs to self and culture as a whole' (1990: 120). Contending that children have acquired a 'core identity' – of which gender is a central element – by the age of 3, Flax urges a reconsideration of the mother–child dyad and the mother's power in the unconscious lives of men and women:

> This is an important step in the process of doing justice to the subjectivity of women and undoing the repression of experiences of ourselves as mothers and as persons who have been mothered. (Flax, 1990: 123)

The significance of the mother–child dyad, however, should not be viewed separately from all the other social relations of which it is a part:

> Although part of a child's self is constituted through her or his internalization of the caretakers, in the process the child incorporates more than his or her experience of specific persons. . . . To some extent the parents' entire social histories become part of the child's self. An adequate theory of human development from an object relations perspective would have to include an account of all these different levels and types of social relations and their interactions, mutual determinations, and possible antagonisms. It would have to include an expanded concept of families – families not merely as a set of immediate relations among individuals but also as permeable structures located within and partially determined by other social structures, including those of production, culture, and race, class, and gender systems. (Flax, 1990: 124)

This perspective suggests that the influence of organizational discourse on the shaping of identity is significant, but more so in the early stages of core identity formation. Indeed, in supporting the postmodernist concern with undermining the notion of the essential or natural self, Flax nonetheless takes issues with the postmodernist·dichotomy of a 'false' essentialist self and a 'true' historically or textually constituted one (1990: 210). She argues that this 'confuses two different and logically distinct concepts of the self: a "unitary" and a "core" one' (Flax, 1990: 218).

In challenging the notion of an essential self Flax argues that essentialist notions of the self contribute to the idea of fixed gender categories. Embedded within disciplinary and confessional practices the idea of an essential self influences not only the way we categorize one another by gender but the way we view ourselves:

> These discourses create the idea that there is something 'deep inside' us, something bodily but at least partially knowable by consciousness, a source of both pleasure and danger. By transforming pleasure into 'sexuality,' these confessional discourses/practices in turn give rise to further practices/knowledges of self-control and self-knowledge. They teach us we have an individual 'self' about which knowledge is possible. This self is seen and experienced as deep and foundational. (Flax, 1990: 208)

What is not clear from Flax's analysis is the extent to which involvement in any number of disciplinary and confessional practices influences, shapes or modifies the core self and its gendered character. However, as pointed out above, she does offer the advice that a feminist deconstruction of the self would point to locating self and its experiences in concrete social relations.

Organizational Discourse as Gendered Experiences

Gender is not simply something that we carry around in a basically unalterable form and regardless of context. As Duveen and Lloyd argue, it is context that helps to generate and maintain a sense of gender:

> [I]ndividuals are so inextricably interwoven in a fabric of social relations within which their lives are lived that a representation of the 'individual' divorced from the 'social' is theoretically inadequate. There is no pure 'individuality' which can be apprehended independently of social relations. The complex inter-relations of the individual and the social mean that, in effect, an individual is inconceivable as a viable entity without a sustaining network of social relations. (Duveen and Lloyd, 1986: 219)

In a world dominated by organizational discourse 'networks of social relations' are likely to be embedded within organizational relationships. Within organizations and in our relationships to members of organizations we are almost certain to be confronted with practices that serve to confirm our sense of gendered self. For example, Rosemary Pringle's study of (female) secretary/(male) executive relations found that 'male managers use sexuality and family relations to establish their control over secretaries', treating them ' "narcissistically" as an extension of themselves'. Secretaries, on the other hand, are 'often able to get some power in relation to male bosses by occupying the position of "mother" ' (Pringle, 1989a: 173).

The individual at work is confronted at numerous levels by gendered relationships – relationships that require her/him to react in appropriately gendered ways (Cox, 1986; Collinson, 1988). It is through the 'doing' of gender that gender is reproduced:

> Gender is both something we do and something we think with, both a set of social practices and a system of cultural meanings. The social practices – the 'doing' of gender – and the cultural meanings – 'thinking the world' using the categories and experiences of gender – constitute us as women and men, organized into a particular configuration of social relations. . . . 'Being' a gender involves 'doing' a gender. But being and doing are not simple, and necessarily synonymous, activities. (Rakow, 1986: 21)

Gendered statements are embedded in almost every aspect of organizational life, be it joking, small talk, management policy or company advertisements (Cox, 1986), metaphors, formal letters, and organizational names (Meissner, 1986), space, ambience, use of time, body language, and face-to-face communication (Borisoff and Merrill, 1985).

Recent studies have indicated ways in which people's sense of gendered self becomes shaped by organizational discourse. Blustein et al., for example, found a relationship between 'the exploration and commitment processes that characterize one's identity formation . . . and an analogous set of career development tasks' (1989: 200). Specifically examining the gendered aspects of career development and identity Marshall and Wetherell (1989) interviewed a group of male and female law students about their perceptions of the characteristics required to be a lawyer. They found that there was a shared view about the masculine nature of the traits required to be a successful lawyer, and that this had different implications for male and female students:

> Effectively, the relation between women and occupational identity became problematized, whereas the relation between men and occupational identity became normalized. . . . Women and lawyers were portrayed as dissonant, the identity relationship became a site of struggle but, in contrast, the masculine and the law became synonymous, with the masculine personality portrayed as identical with the legal personality. (Marshall and Wetherell, 1989: 121)

For some of the female respondents this meant that part of the process of becoming a lawyer meant learning to overcome feminine traits. On the other hand, some of the other female respondents saw women as positive agents of change – improving the law through feminine characteristics. In either case women were faced with gender and occupational identity as 'conflict and a site of struggle' (Marshall and Wetherell, 1989: 123).

Pervasive gendered images of occupations and organizational realities are not simply reflected in the ideas of actors, reproduced by rote. It is through discourse that particular versions of reality and of self are produced/reproduced, modified and changed. As Marshall and Wetherell argue,

> [T]here is no one 'true' representation of self and identity. At any given moment there will be varying possibilities for self construction. . . . [I]dentities are actively negotiated and transformed in discourse and . . . language is the area where strategic construction and reconstruction of self occurs. (1989: 125)

Wetherell et al. (1987) argue that notions of career are imbued with intersecting and contradictory discourses concerning gender and employment opportunities. Their study of a group of final-year students found that:

> Two particular kinds of talk tended to dominate participants' discourse about women in the workplace, careers and children. These could be called the 'equal opportunities' and 'practical considerations' themes. (Wetherell et al., 1987: 61–2)

The equal opportunities theme was a form of talk which endorsed liberal values of egalitarianism, freedom of choice for the individual, equally shared responsibilities and so on. The practical considerations theme, on the other hand, combined notions of 'the reproductive role and maternal urges of females' with supposed understandable employer reluctance to risk hiring females over males. These themes did not represent differences of opinion between respondents but were often expressed by the same person. Wetherell et al. (1987) argue that 'these contradictions may be responsible for the force and continuity of the ideology' that continues to maintain discriminatory differences between men and women, contradictions which help people – men and women – to 'make sense' of a changing world in which gender notions remain strongly unchanged in the face of equity struggles and laws. Through the contradictions respondents were able to support the growing discourse of employment equity and yet, in a way that distanced them*selves*, explain why equity would not work.

From a different perspective, Ella Bell (1989) has shown how contrasting mythological images of black and white women in literature – respectively 'the mammy and the snow queen' – is negatively reflected in management expectations of the potential of women of colour to manage. Race and ethnicity, of course, add a whole different set of features to given organizational discourses and raise questions about the relationship between organization and sense of racial self.

Sexual preference is another area that needs to be explored, for it is clear that an important outcome of any stress on masculinity and femininity is the embedded notion of heterosexuality. As a consequence organizations have tended to seek to exclude signs of homosexuality (Hearn and Parkin, 1987), further encouraging particular shows of femininity or masculinity on the part of organizational members, and 'normalizing' heterosexuality (Hall, 1989).

Resistance, Contradiction and Discourse

People are not passive recipients of organizational images and expectations. As Wetherell and her colleagues suggest, organizational discourse is constructed out of a myriad of contradictory and conflicting views. Any given organizational discourse will reflect a stage in a number of intersecting relationships which involve power and power struggles, understandings and misunderstandings, acquiescence and resistance, complementary and contradictory elements.

Organizations over the last two or three centuries have been crucial sites for the construction of gender and self. Women have not always been rigidly excluded from the public domain in general and the organizational world in particular; they had to be excluded. As Marilyn French (1985) indicates, females for a long period of history occupied significant roles in the public life of their communities. Even in the latter stages of the Middle Ages women carried on a wide variety of trades and could be members in their own right of some guilds (Gies and Gies, 1980). During the early part of the Industrial Revolution women were extensively employed in the new factories (Struminger, 1979). But, for a variety of reasons – including the separation of work from home, the competitive character of capitalism, the concerns with biopower – a variety of struggles were waged to push women out of some trades and industries and into domestic life. It was a process that not only arose out of defined notions of sexual distinctions but which helped to create new distinctions. Lara Struminger (1979), for example, details how various forces – employers, guilds, the Church, fathers, husbands, the press – all came in to reinforce a certain view of womanhood as male workers strove to replace females in key aspects of the Lyon textile industry; these forces, no doubt, were engaged in large part due to the resistance of female textile workers and their willingness to strike and to take their struggle to the streets. Likewise the development of the modern army (Hacker, 1988) and the medical profession involved a purging and downgrading of women and their skills (Enrenreich and English, 1973).

There is little doubt that the current concern with employment equity in North America owes much to the women's liberation struggles of the last three decades, and that those struggles have helped to shape the form of the organizational discourse of our times. Wetherell et al. (1987) have indicated how this might be experienced as a series of contradictory notions. It is through resistance and struggle that new images of womenhood (and of manhood) have developed, but it has been a constant fight for women to resist male definitions of appropriate organizational and gender behaviour. Mackie puts it well when she says that,

> [H]umans retain some capacity to resist the societal script, to play things their way. All the world may well be a stage. Shakespeare to the contrary, men and women are not *merely* players. Nevertheless, the scriptwriters and stars tend to be men. (1987: 146)

In Conclusion: Implications for Employment Equity

Exploration of the relationship between organizations and the gendered self raises a number of questions in regard to the issue of sexual discrimination at work and how to deal with it. Postmodernist analysis provides several clues as to the generation of sexism, but at the same time discourages the potential for developing strategies for change.

The single most important thing we can learn from postmodernist analysis is that subjectivity is constructed in and through the processes of discourse generation, and that, in the modern world, 'the organization of everything' may have a disproportionate impact on how we view ourselves and the world. This suggests that feminists may need to rethink the strategy – central within the 'women-in-management' approach – of attempting change *within* organizations, while leaving unquestioned the impact of the (discriminatory) construction of persons into 'women' and 'men'. Organizations are not simply spaces into which people enter but, rather, networks of relationships which are deeply gendered. As Ferguson puts it, 'the argument that organizations will somehow be altered simply by virtue of recruiting women into them is . . . fallacious' (1984: ix), particularly given that organizational discourse contributes not only to sexual discrimination but to the construction of gendered selves: 'public discourse today is not the language of women even when women speak it' (Ferguson, 1984).

That is not to say that strategies of change within organizations are wrong, or need to be rejected in favour of a broader strategy of widespread social change. But it does raise some crucial problems for feminists. On the one hand, women are fundamentally discriminated against in the workplace. This is real in that it is experienced by women in numerous ways. As such discriminatory practices *cannot* go unchallenged. Indeed, postmodernist analysis suggests that challenges are a way of altering discourse and changing the practices which support it. The dangers, on the other hand, lie in a stress on 'women' rights in ways which may contribute to the essentialist notion of woman:

> Feminists also depend partially on Enlightenment ideals in the way claims to and visions of gender justice have been formulated. Concepts like natural rights, due process, and equality are grounded in part in certain ideas about innate or essential human properties. (Flax, 1990: 230)

The potential for mixed messages or contradictory discourses, as noted by Wetherell et al. (1987), may contribute to 'the force and continuity of sexist ideology'.

This problem may be alleviated to some extent by encouraging parallel processes of questioning political, personal and organizational agendas. That is, to develop change strategies that challenge sexist political biases and organizational practices, while at the same time encouraging people to periodically interrogate their sense of gendered selves and to ask how they got there, how do they sustain it, and what are the potential outcomes? In the latter regard, postmodernist analysis may prove valuable in indicating how 'men' can be won over to the fight against sexism at work. Discourse analysis suggests that many men may be the unwitting players of a way of viewing reality, a strategy 'with no one directing it and everyone enmeshed in it, whose only end is the increase of power and order itself' (Dreyfus and Rabinow, 1982: xxii). Exposure to this idea may help to free some men from the perceived need to go along with sexist archetypes (of management/leadership) and practices that, in any case, do not fit in with their own experiences and image of 'manhood'.

Alongside this it is important to encourage a questioning of the way we think of organizing – to deconstruct, as far as possible, our understandings of organization and our commitment to organizing as a way of life. To that end, postmodernism provides a valuable insight into the nature of management and organization theory – as discursive practices that serve particular, narrow truth claims and which, in the process, contribute to the production of limited and gendered subjectivity (Mills and Tancred, 1992).

Ultimately, however, postmodernist 'insights' fall far short of providing an alternative strategy to the problem of gendered discourse. The 'way forward' may lie in the development of a feminist discourse which centrally seeks to expose thinking and practices that contribute to the oppression of women while, nonetheless, remaining sceptical about alternative truth claims. In the words of Calás and Smircich:

'From a post-structuralist feminist approach the work is never done; you have to keep on questioning who you can be, as you are today' (1992b: 232).

Note

I would like to thank Julie Mills, Martin Parker, John Hassard, Sue Jones and Pushkala Prashad for comments on an early draft of this chapter.

9

Organizations, Multiple Oppressions and Postmodernism

Jeff Hearn and Wendy Parkin

Kinds of Monolith

Ideology is partly about, attempts to simplify, to obscure or erase contradictions, to invert reality, to produce monoliths. These are all major themes in Marxian theories of ideology. Related but different theories have been elucidated by and through feminism, as, for example, in constructing femininity as alienation (Foreman, 1977). Feminist appreciation of ideology is also about the very construction of knowledge and theory.

> when a theory is transformed into an ideology, it begins to destroy itself and self-knowledge. Originally born of feeling, it pretends to float above and around feeling. Above sensation. It organizes experience according to itself, it is supposed to know. To invoke the name of this ideology is to confer truthfulness. No one can tell it anything new. Experience ceases to surprise it, inform it, transform it. It is annoyed by any detail which does not fit into its world view. Begun as a cry against the denial of truth, now it denies any truth which does not fit into its scheme. Begun as a way to restore one's sense of reality, now it attempts to discipline real people, to remake natural beings after its own image. All that it fails to explain it records as dangerous. All that makes it question, it regards as its enemy. Begun as a theory of liberation, it is threatened by new theories of liberation; slowly it builds a prison for the mind. (Griffin, 1982: 280)

This imperative to(wards) ideology has been particularly important in the historical development of organization and management theory and practice – most obviously in the various strands of modernism, and indeed the grand narrative of *modernism itself* as a social phenomenon. Though some elements of the general form of modernism are identifiable in post-Enlightenment rationalism, it is not until the development of the mass-production machine technology that organization and management theory become more clearly articulated. The strands of modernism that have most explicitly represented these different kinds of monolith include the Weberian rationalization thesis and the 'bureaucratization of the world' (Jacoby, 1973), Michels's (1968) iron law of oligarchy, the 'one best way' of Taylorism (1947), the machine metaphor itself (Morgan, 1986), managerialism as both a prescription and object of critique

(Burnham, 1942), the universalizing assumptions of systems theory (Emery, 1969), Marxism as the grand narrative of history and thus of social and organizational analysis (Allen, 1975), the analysis of power as a technical matter of uncertainties (Crozier, 1964) and contingencies (Hickson et al., 1971).

Additionally, within and counter to these modernist strands have lurked various romanticist monoliths, represented in the search for and rhetorical creation of the 'deep interior'. While romanticism is a historical precedent of modernism, what is especially interesting is how romanticist(ic) themes have been resurrected and promoted within the modernist project(s). This is most clearly seen in the attempts to re-create 'community' within organizational theory and practice – as in the work of the Tavistock Institute, human needs theorists in human relations, human resource management and elsewhere, personal resource approaches to leadership, theories of organizational commitment, empathy and dialogue (see Gergen, 1992: 209–10). In all these cases romanticist *gemeinschaft* is sought within or counter to modernist *gesellschaft*. And furthermore, such romanticism can itself become reified in analyses and prescriptions of organizational cultures, which may be liable to become dominating monocultures, gendered and dominated by men (Mills, Chapter 8 this volume; Cockburn, 1991; Hearn, 1992). The incorporation of such 'humanistic' and 'communalistic' values can be a means of further 'rational' social control.

This complex variety (a variety that is itself a contradiction with the universalizing of each) of grand and not-so-grand narratives is inter-mingled with yet one further grand narrative – the (his)tory of man/men. In this sense, they are all subplots of men's story. 'Man' (previously a male God) is set at the centre of all these discourses. And what a laugh that would all be if it were not for the material and painful effects they have had – on others and each other, on women and young people and men, throughout time and space.

Paradigms, Feminisms, Oppression and Postmodernism

Mainstream, that is malestream, organization theory has generally and traditionally been constructed as non-gendered. Written through a male perspective, culture and discourse, it has espoused theories of empiricism, rationality, hierarchy, leadership, management and other masculinized concepts. In this way mainstream organization theory has been implicitly gendered. Through the 1970s and into the 1980s there was a growing cri-tique within and around organization theory. This came from several directions: from 'critical perspectives' on organization theory, influenced by a combination of Marxism, Critical Theory, and ethnomethodology (for example Clegg and Dunkerley, 1977); from identification of multiple sociological paradigms, influenced by Kuhnian and related theorizing on science and social science (for example Burrell and Morgan, 1979); and from feminist work on women and paid work, women's domestic work, and women's politics and organizing (for example Martin, 1981). It was from this last body of theory and practice that there developed explicitly gendered critiques of organization theory (see Hearn and Parkin, 1983). Even so most mainstream, 'critical', and paradigmatic organization theory remained immune from explicitly gendered analysis.

The multiple-paradigm approach to organizational analysis (Burrell and Morgan, 1979) has certainly been useful in opening up more possibilities and perspectives on organizations. Subsequent debates have considered how far Burrell and Morgan could call their frameworks 'paradigms', how mutually exclusive each was, and how far they were just a 'mass' of theories or means of critiques of mainstream (malestream) theory (Cox, 1979; Harvey, 1982). To some limited extent it was possible to relate feminist critiques and prescriptions for change to each of the four paradigms (Hearn and Parkin, 1983): liberal feminist, Marxist feminism, radical feminism, phenomenological feminism. Each of these perspectives could be seen in a way of analysing gender in organizations with eman-cipatory outcomes from each paradigm and associated prescriptions for change. At the same time paradigms and the paradigmatic approach were limiting in the sense that feminism did not easily fit into this framework, which itself could be seen as a further edition of the various malestream grand narratives. Paradigmatic approaches provided some potential for analysing gender but the subtleties and powers of the discourse of feminisms and their relation to the male discourse of organization were not addressed: feminism was being reduced.

Following on the paradigmatic approach an image (Morgan, 1986) or metaphor-based (Morgan, 1980) analysis of organizations looks at the various images of and metaphors for 'organization', as a way of under-standing organizational life. There is no explicit metaphor for gender and it is only addressed implicitly by it being introduced as in paradigms, through feminist critiques of organization as, for example, 'machine', organism or political system. Alternatively, gender could be introduced as an issue into all the metaphors. However, both of these approaches miss the fundamental issue around gender: namely that mainstream organiza-tion theory is premised upon a malestream discourse in which organiza-tions supposedly adjust to the appearance of women (and other groups/people) who are presumed not to really belong there. This misses the fundamental nature of gender divisions, and the relationship between the public and the private, production and reproduction (Hearn, 1987). Gender is not just an issue or an image, metaphor, paradigm, factor or 'problem': gender *is*. Or gender historically is. Gender has *always* been there but has come to be translated *into* an issue, when women have pushed for change: but this way of looking at gender is itself a reduction to an issue and to women; gender *is*. In this sense, most of the ways in which gender is still talked about in, and in relation to, organization and organization theory are (')male('). Paradoxically, part of the way in which gender is (defined in a) male (sense), is by the dominant equation of gender with femaleness/women, and hence the avoidance of seeing men/male as gendered.

In contrast, feminist analyses have seen organizational analysis and the analysis of gender as more pervasive and more problematic. Organizations and gender have been approached through a variety of different perspectives and concepts. These include the enduring significance of essentialism; the relationships of the public and the private, production and reproduction, the personal and the political; the domination of gender power and indeed gender class; and the power and paradox of sexuality.

Feminism and the analysis of gender issues have also opened up the debates around organizations as an arena of exploitation of various groups of people, with a growing recognition of the various oppressions which operate in organizations around 'race', age, (dis)abilities, class and sexuality. Many of these have been recognized initially as discrete 'isms', and later in this chapter we shall attempt to begin to develop an organizational analysis which recognizes both that actuality and the fundamental role of 'organization' in their creation and re-creation. The previous multiplication of paradigms has thus to some extent been superseded by the multiplication of oppressions. Meanwhile these sets of multiplicities have been met by another set, namely that of postmodernism.

In speaking of the interrelation of feminism and postmodernism there is inevitably the question of how that relationship is to be constructed and understood. Is 'the feminism' to be placed within postmodernism, as implied in the phrase 'feminist postmodernism'? Or is 'the postmodernism' to be located within feminism, as implied by postmodernist feminism? Indeed there are strong arguments that to place either 'inside' the other is to contradict the differentiations of postmodernism, and perhaps of feminism too. Alternatively, the basic object of examination and thus of this chapter could be understood as 'organization' and 'organizational analysis'. In this case there is a danger of incorporating feminism and postmodernism into the pre-set traditions of organizational analysis.

Whilst postmodernism attempts to take organization theory beyond the application of grand narratives, issues of gender, feminism and organization have only recently entered into the debates around paradigms, metaphors and other narratives on and around organization theory (Hearn and Parkin, 1983). As gender issues have sought a location within (a-gendered) paradigmatic theorizing, that theorizing has moved on to other (postmodernist) concerns before issues of gender, let alone sexuality, have established their theoretical location, political analysis or practical critique.

There Is No One Postmodernism

Just as postmodernism can be summarized or even 'unified' as assault on unity (Power, 1990), so quite understandably there is and can be no one postmodernism. At the very least there is the tension between post*modernism* and *postmodern*-ism. The term is used in a plurality of ways, often drawing on and citing one or more of the several 'key figures'/'male heroes', usually from the shortlist (for the interview panel) of Foucault, Lyotard, Baudrillard, Derrida, Eco. Expositions of postmodernism, usually by men, usually fail to mention the (possible) interrelations of postmodernism and feminism. In this sense, the only 'real' postmodernists are men!

Some authors do attempt the task of clarifying, codifying and classifying what postmodernism is. One of the most useful examples is White's (1987/88: 306) focus upon four major characterizing features: the 'increasing unpersuasiveness of metanarratives'; the 'rise of new informational technologies'; an awareness of new social problems associated with 'societal rationalization'; and the emergence of new social movements. This is, however, only a beginning. Indeed what is distinctive about debates on postmodernism is their diversity. Postmodernism is also variously characterized in terms of the succession to modernism (Lyotard, 1984), the end of aesthetics/the anti-aesthetic (Foster, 1985), the realm of signification (Lash, 1988), the reinforcement of the logic of consumer capitalism (Jameson, 1985), 'the crisis of cultural authority' the ubiquity of difference, *différance*, and de-differentiation (whether socially, or between signifier and referent) (Lash, 1988), the movements to globalization (Friedmann, 1988), the pluralization of realities and perspectives, and the interrogation of poststructuralist theories in social analysis, *amongst many others*.

As such, it is not really clear what it might mean to be either *for* or *against* postmodernism. It depends, at least in part, which one, which element, and to an extent to what extent. This point is made especially clearly by Wickham in showing that there is no necessary unity between 'protagonists' and 'antagonists' in the object of their concern. He writes:

> For the protagonists consider Foster, who sees postmodernism as 'a practice of resistance', 'a new strategy of interference' (Foster, 1985: xvi) and Stanley Aronowitz, who sees it as 'marked by the renunciation of foundational thought, of rules governing art; and of the "ideological discourses" liberalism and marxism' (Aronowitz, 1987/88: 99). While for the antagonists consider Rita Felski, who sees postmodernism as an occasional tool used to 'smooth . . . over diverse and often non-synchronous political interests (Felski, 1988: 1) and Phillipe Lacoue-Labarthe: 'I define the postmodern quite simply as the *failure* of [the] movement of resistance'. (Lacoue-Labarthe, 1986: 8, (emphasis in original) in Wickham, 1990: 126)

Furthermore, postmodernism can be directed towards either certain (postmodernist) social forms or certain (postmodernist) forms of analysis (Bauman, 1988a). On the other hand, there are certain things that can more easily be agreed upon in relation to postmodernism: the use of 'careless generalization' (Wickham, 1990), the diverse meanings, and the neglect and/or ambiguity in relation to structural power, and *oppressions* more generally.

There Is No One Oppression

When we say oppression(s) what we mean is the multiplicity of ways in which certain people(s) within and as social categories are excluded from organizations or discriminated against within them. These include marginalization, domination and subordination, degradation, ignoring, harassment, invisibilizing, silencing, punishment, discipline and violence. These processes may be directed towards staff, members, employees, residents, patients and clients, amongst others. For example, sexual abuse of children in a children's home was compounded by the intimidation of female staff so preventing their complaints from being heard. Accordingly, in this situation both staff and vulnerable children were silenced and degraded (Parkin, 1989: 114).

Thus there are a number of different specific categories of both oppression and people subject to oppression. We have already introduced gender as one form and arena of oppression. Increasingly the shorthand term of 'sexism' is becoming recognized as part of organizational life to refer to the numerous practices in the subordination of women. Another form and arena of oppression is sexuality. This is clearly linked with gender, but deserves separate and specific attention, as clearly illustrated in sexual harassment studies and the harassment of people because of their sexualities (for example Taylor, 1986; Hall, 1989). Perhaps it would be more accurate to refer to genderism and sexualism in speaking of these two sets of processes (Hearn and Parkin, 1987: 163-4).

There is an increasing debate both around 'race' as a concept and racism as a process of oppression (for example Cashmore and Troyna, 1983). In this way 'race' is a form and arena of oppression even though the concept itself is problematic and questionable. This is not least because the concept of 'race' has been and continues to be used to justify social discrimination of the false premise that physiological differences dictate social differences.

Economic class is a form and arena of oppression that has been the focus of certain kinds of (class) politics and has been massively theorized, and indeed has been the basis of one particular grand narrative. Despite this, and the activities of trade unions, class and classism do not seem to feature strongly in most of the current debates around equal opportunities (Arber, 1989; Nelson, 1990; Cockburn, 1991). Having said that, it is possible to reconceptualize much of the debates around labour process theory as a commentary on economic class and equal opportunities.

Age as a form and arena of oppression remains relatively unnoticed and untheorized. Yet ageism is strongly entrenched in this society and culture, though gradually becoming more recognized as a practice and concept (MacDonald and Rich, 1983; Fennell et al., 1988). It rarely figures in equal opportunity debates.

Disability is a further major form and arena of oppression; accordingly disabilism is rife but seldom recognized, and seldom on organizational agendas. Despite and because of this we consider that disabilism should be a key concept in analysing organizations in developing policies and theories. The politics of disability and disabilism (Oliver, 1990; Morris, 1989, 1991; Hahn, 1988) is changing from a focus on 'deservingness' and 'gratitude' towards a focus on 'rights' and 'action'. These political changes are increasingly bringing these issues into paid work organization in terms of law and regulation around discrimination.

For all of these oppressions and their associated '-isms', the oppressed category are often constructed as a/the problem/issue. This avoids a/the problem/issue of those who are the oppressors, for example, men and white people. In our view we have come to recognize that assumptions around 'able-bodiedness'; and 'mobility' are fundamental to the reproduction of power in most organizations.

Postmodernism without Oppression

Much postmodernism ignores or plays down oppression. Typically in the movement towards representation, signification and fragmentation, oppression, power and pain are not the prime object of attention. Less generously, postmodernism is just one more device of the powerful to deflect attention from attention to power. Oppression is characteristically reduced to difference (Middleton, 1989). However, while much of postmodernist theorizing is negligent of power and oppression, this is not so in all cases. The social theorist who has been most obviously influential in this respect is Michael Foucault. His work frequently returns to the question of the pervasiveness of power and the further complex interrelation of power, knowledge and transgression. But even Foucault's perspective is lacking when it comes to the *specific* explorations of oppression in their material experience. For example, even in *The History of Sexuality*, we are left wondering what if anything happens (in discourse?) between gendered/sexual/sexualized subjects, say, in the material experience of sexual violence. This kind of poststructuralist writing, typified by Foucault, has been elaborated at length within the discourses of postmodernism – that is, writing on representation, signification and discourses without resort to material experience, power or oppression.

Postmodernism with Oppression

Having recognized the frequent avoidance of oppression within postmodernism, there are several ways in which the connection of postmodernism and oppression has been made: through theorizing postmodernism as a relation of late capitalism and capitalist consumer exploitation; through postmodernist feminism; and through the exploration of the intersection of 'race', colonialism, imperialism, and indeed gender relations.

To illustrate these possibilities we shall focus on the second of these developments. The most influential theorists in connecting feminism and postmodernism have often been strongly psychoanalytic in orientation, including Kristeva (1980a), Irigaray (1985), Moi (1985) in Europe; Harding (1986) and Flax (1987) in North America; and Morris (1988) and Felski (1989) in Australia. Most are at pains to deconstruct the dominant malestream (Nicholson, 1990); all can happily critique the Enlightenment and much more besides. Some, particularly following Irigaray, see the need to seek new forms of women's language and communication outside and separate from men's media. In this search the sensual experience of woman's body/bodies may be involved. Some wish to go on to deconstruct not just the taken-for-granted empty centre of 'man' and men's language but also 'woman' too. Thus for Kristeva, for example, there is no essential woman. Some favour 'gender-scepticism' – that is a new scepticism within feminism about the use of gender as an analytical category (Bordo, 1991: 135). These debates attend, in different ways, to uncertainties around the social construction of woman. If that social construction is deeply embedded and contingent, then the very ideas of the 'bonds of womanhood' or 'of sisterhood', or of 'woman' herself are 'essentially' problematic – as Denise Riley (1988) asks, 'Am I that name [woman]?'

These struggles – and they are clearly personal, political and intellectual struggles – are complex, contradictory and anti-dualist: they operate in the middle-ground between subject and object (Grosz, 1987). The deconstruction of woman's experience in feminism/postmodernism frequently involves a double-take on reality, itself dominantly defined by/in the malestream. This speaks not just against male grand narratives, gender injustices and inequalities, but also against the internalization of oppression by women and other oppressed people. You can intellectually abolish/demolish the malestream, and still feel oppressed. Reapprehending oppression is characteristically a personal, psychodynamic and multifaceted process (cf. Bartky, 1977).

For the purposes of this chapter the obvious next question is – how do these debates relate to organization and organization theory.

Postmodernist Organization Theory without Oppression

Postmodernist organization theory is a slight development relative to the discipline of organization theory as a whole. To label something as postmodernist organization theory could refer to the implications of postmodernist theorizing of Baudrillard or Jameson or Foster for organization theory, or it could refer to those more conscious to link the concerns of postmodernism with the traditions of organization theory. Accordingly, there are two major ways in which postmodernist organization theory can be developed without adequate attention to oppression. The first is represented by those attempts to 'translate' the writings of postmodernist (or poststructuralist) theorists into organization theory. For example, Robert Cooper and Gibson Burrell's series of articles in *Organization Studies* on this theme is relatively generous to the social theorists in question (for example, Derrida), presumably for the purposes of demonstrating to the organizational audience the potential (usefulness?) of these theorists' work. The second alternative is also illustrated by those attempts by organization theorists to produce a more integrated account of what postmodernist organization theory might look like. For example, Power (1990) characterizes postmodernist organization theory in terms of 'an irreducible plurality of language games'; and Linstead (Chapter 3 in this volume) approaches postmodernism organizations as paradox, otherness, seduction and discourse. Gergen's (1992) focus on the postmodern transformation in terms of the five emblematic themes of indeterminate rationalities, social supplementarity, power as social coordination, power as self-destructive, heteroglossia and the recovery of efficacy is more ambiguous. Though citing power as one (self-destructive) theme, this is (de)constructed as producing its own undoing. Be this as it may, this insight does seem to be liable to diminish the power of interpersonal, institutional, structural oppressions.

Postmodernist Organization Theory with Oppression

The major development of what might be called postmodernist organization theory that does recognize oppression has come from the interaction of poststructuralism and feminisms. These conjunctions are inevitably diverse, influenced as they are by discourse analysis, semiotics, linguistics and psychoanalysis. The path-breaking text that has attended to the deconstruction of gender and organization is Ferguson's (1984) *The Feminist Case Against Bureaucracy*. This has been followed by studies on organization theory and epistemology (Calás and Smircich, 1992a, b); organizational conflict (Martin, 1990b); organizational power (Czarniawska-Joerges, 1990, 1991); organizational forms (Ferguson, 1987), and managers and secretaries (Game, 1989; Pringle, 1989b). There are also a number of texts that have been written collaboratively by women and men, such as those on management theory (Jacobson and Jacques, 1990; Calás et al., 1991), rationality (Mumby and Putnam, 1992), and sexuality (Hearn and Parkin, 1987; Hearn et al., 1989), or by men alone such as those on shopfloor humour (Collinson, 1988), communication (Mills and Chiaramonte, 1991) men and masculinities (Hearn, 1991, 1992; Collinson, 1992; Collinson and Hearn, 1992), that are influenced by poststructuralist feminism. This emerging tradition is thus important as a powerful and positive approach to gender, organizations and management. It helps to provide greater recognition of the diversity, fragmentation and gendering of people's lives in and around organizations, and as such promotes postmodernist organization theory with oppression.

Multiple Oppressions and their Relation to Postmodernism

Furthermore, particular social divisions and social oppressions appear to highlight special issues in relation to postmodernism and organization. This is partly a consequence of the dichotomous (gender), temporally shifting (age) culture relative (ethnicity); partly as a consequence of their relation to *organizations*, for example, created *in* organizations (social class), created in the life course (age); and partly a consequence of the particular *substantive content* of different oppressions, for example existing in appearance (gender), existing in relation to production (social class), existing in relation to body and mind (disability).

We will now briefly consider each of six major arenas of oppression in relation to postmodernism and organizational realities. So far we have focused mainly on gender and partly on sexuality, as underpinning gender, and recognize how, through feminist analyses, the construction of the public/private relation is fundamental. Although public/private divisions may have arisen from gender and sexual relations and divisions, they are also applicable to an analysis of other oppressed groups and their locations, for example organizations are often based on the exclusion of people with disabilities and thus their location in the private realm. Similarly, with age, older and younger people are excluded from power and power structures in organizations and are constructed as consumers, clients, patients, pupils or residents. By contrast, social class is defined in relation to organization position; for example owners, managers and workers and the hierarchical gradings within them. When in private people are still defined according to organizational position, either their own or that of the nominated person (usually the 'head of the household'). As regards 'race' and ethnicity, there are parallels with both age and economic class, as in the exclusion of black and ethnic minority people from many organizations as well as the formation of organization with their own hierarchies but seen as subordinate to white organizations.

These processes of exclusion from organization, social construction by organization and relation to the public/private are both reinforced and underpinned by general ideologies and more specific stereotypes. For example, gender can be seen as essentialist with women stereotyped as 'hysterical' and men as 'rational'. Sexuality is seen as 'natural' with men as uncontrollable and women as passive or seductive. Dominant ideologies of age are around not being seen and not having a voice, with stereotypes of young people as irresponsible and older people being seen as in a 'second childhood'. For class, there is an ideology of meritocracy, hierarchy and rewards for the stereotypes of 'captains of industry'. Ideologies of race are characteristically founded in superiority and inferiority, with stereotypes of black people having a culture and white people not.

Disability has been the most marginalized and least present in organization or organizational analyses of all the oppressions. The prevailing ideology is that of medicine and medication, with people's disabilities being seen as sickness or illness and able-bodied people being seen as able and well, rather the environment being disabling. For example, a woman in a wheelchair was not at all disabled in her adapted flat but became disabled when elsewhere. We are increasingly recognizing that fundamental to organizations and the way they oppress is an unquestioned assumption around possession of abilities, particularly the possession of intact senses and mobility. Indeed, we see disability as more fundamentally important than has been recognized in organizational analysis at least. This is for several reasons, such as the absence of people with disabilities; their visibility through organizational location even if their disability is not visible (for example people with heart conditions being lift attendants); the diversity of what is meant by disability and the different kinds of disability. This also highlights the need, as with other oppressions, to focus on the oppressors, in this case those who are able-bodied or constructed as such. Apart from a very small number of non-medicalized organizations, in most organizations the 'fit' and 'able-bodied' dominate the workplace, and hence disability becomes the most prevailing form of oppression in terms of numerical over-representation and lack of research and recognition. In addition, to consider the construction of disability and ability raises the yet more fundamental issue around organizational construction of the perceptions of the senses, their possession and their differential valuing – hence the very basis of knowledge and its construction.

Interrelationships of Multiple Oppressions

In the developing literature and analysis on oppression and discrimination within organizations, besides staying within discrete theoretical frameworks, the group of people discriminated against are often researched and analysed in discrete ways and in terms of various '-isms'. It is useful to look at ideologies, stereotypes and discourses around categories to see the differences and similarities in terms of the structural features around disadvantage. However, often the next part of the process is an 'add-on' (O'Brien, 1984) in terms of 'what if' this woman were also black and disabled. This could lead to an adding up of factors of disadvantage, or even a multiplication. We feel it more useful to explore interconnectedness and locate this within the organizational context. This can be difficult, for emphasis in practice and theory is focused more on some categories than others, with increasing research and literature and theorizing around gender and race and class and less on issues of age, (dis)ability, sexualities/sexuality.

In the initial recognition of the interconnectedness of oppressions it is difficult to give examples without over-simplifying the issues or continuing to just 'add on' various '-isms', for example, the links between age and class in premature exiting from the workforce (Arber, 1989).

Another starting point could be to look explicitly at organizational hierarchies and see how often the assumption is that 'management' equates with white middle-class able-bodied men whereas low-paid domestic posts are frequently occupied by working-class women, in many localities black, working-class women. Increasingly recognized is the power of sexuality in terms of 'hidden hierarchies' and as a powerful underpinning of gender powers. Often invisible are older people, though this has a class gradient (Arber, 1989). Frequently invisible are people with disabilities leading to the formulation of the possibility that the most oppressive powers are those exercised by the able-bodied in setting organizational mores and agendas. It is then taken for granted that possession of the senses and mobility are key necessities to function as an organization person, whether high or low in the hierarchy. People will attempt to hide illness and weakness as, in organizational terms, illness, disability, grief and upset are confined to the private domestic realm and constructed as if they should be dealt with there. Most organizations emphasize 'fitness' and abilities even though the organization may be the cause of illness and disability. Thus, underpinning the variety of oppressions around gender, age, class, sexualities, race, etc. is a more fundamental oppression which underpins all of them, that of ability. In this way organization is not the arena for oppression but organization is oppression by its very structures and composition.

Multiple Oppressions and Postmodernism

An analysis of the interrelations of multiple oppressions (or the multiple interrelations of oppressions) has interesting, and probably contradictory, connections with postmodernism and postmodernist perspectives. Both kinds of analysis are fundamentally at odds with single or even prime dominant causal explanations of organizations, whether that be the historical grand narrative of economic class within Marxism or the local grand narrative of system or goal in particular organizations. In this way both kinds of analysis can be understood as responses and reactions to and against monocausal (malestream) modernism. In this sense, at least, the analysis of multiple oppressions is compatible with the 'directions' of attention of postmodernism.

More specifically, both the analysis of multiple oppressions and postmodernism show up the inadequacy of organizational analyses that rely on either (a) a single dominant set of social categories, be they those of economic class, occupational status, institutional hierarchy, gender, etc. or (b) fixed, unproblematic versions of such social categories.

Instead both the analysis of multiple oppression and postmodernism rely on assumptions of the *complexity and interrelations* of social categories and social categorizations, and the changing nature of such categories and categorizations. Thus social categorizations are at the very

least *relational* within discourses. This relationship applies in the construction of specific discourses; for example, the way in which 'women' and
'men' 'femininity' and 'masculinity' are constructed relationally to each
other. It also applies in a much more complex way in terms of the rela-
tionality of different oppressions to each other. By this we mean that
specific oppressions – for example, age – are maintained as such not in
any isolation but only through their interrelations with other oppressions.
This mutual reproduction and reinforcement of oppressions thus occurs in
all cases. All oppressions contribute to the reproduction and reinforcement of all others. They are all bound in systems of difference and
differance. More particularly, social divisions and oppressions are
continually reproduced through organizational hierarchies and interrelations with such hierarchies. Organizational hierarchies are the routine,
formal means of reproducing the variety of social divisions and oppressions in patterns of mutual reinforcement.

For this reason, among others, the concept of difference is a central one
in both the analysis of multiple oppressions and postmodernism.
However, in saying this, it is necessary to acknowledge that there are
different and sometimes mutually incompatible concepts of difference
(Barrett, 1987; Halbert, 1989; Hearn, 1992). On the one hand, there is the
relatively categorical, and sometimes essentialist notion of difference, in
which its proponents argue for the importance and recognition of current
differences as in 'sexual difference' between females and males, or
differences of perspective between black people and white people. On the
other, there is the paradoxical, and sometimes Derridean, notion of
différance, in which difference implies its own relationship to its opposite,
its own self-reference, and its own reversal. All differences are constructed
within social processes of deferral: there is no basic or unmediated
difference. This latter version may be linked to the globalizing processes
of redifferentiation – in which former and present 'differences' are
reduced and overridden by/in systems of signification.

Both these, and other, concepts of difference can be seen to be valid
within postmodernism, though also open to critique. The more categorical
or essentialist view of difference opens up the possibility of different
realities for different people and social categories. The more paradoxical
view (apparently) denies modernist explanation, opens up the possibility
of reducing difference and seeks to transcend dualism. Both these
categorical and paradoxical processes/analyses operate and permeate
through organizations, for example, in the creation of separate organizations, and in the dominance of organizational systems of signification
throughout people's lives.

The understanding of these issues has recently been furthered by
Cynthia Cockburn's (1991) research into multiple oppressions in four
organizations, reported in her book *In the Way of Women*. Not only does
she describe the variety of ways in which oppressions are reproduced and
interrelated in the four locations, but she also shows how dominant

definitions of difference are inadequate for such an analysis. Though she is working in the context of feminist/modernist traditions she is raising issues of great relevance that should be, though rarely are, on the agenda of postmodernism.

Concluding Remarks

Organizations can be viewed from the bottom, the middle or the top, from the inside or the outside. Those who view from the outside may not be organizational members but may often be consumers of organizations, such as children or patients or clients of services. They usually have policy made for them and have often been viewed as *outside* organization theory and politics. This is especially evident, as we have discussed, with issues of disability. Cockburn's (1991) analysis of working from the position of the most disadvantaged in an organization could be widened to those who are also consumers of organizations and not participants in organizational life, including unemployed people, older people, disabled people, unpaid carers. Categories of people are created within organizations for people outside organizations as well as within. Theory should thus encompass the most disadvantaged of those outside organizations. Any analysis of organization theory within postmodernism is limited if only applied to participants in organizational life. On the other hand, when broadened out in this way, postmodernism can be seen as a trap for those who are disadvantaged by neutralizing attempts to politicize themselves within the grand narratives of modernist theoretical frameworks.

The debates around the move from modernism to a postmodernist view of the world of organizations seem to be an epistemological leap over issues such as those around feminism and other oppressions, still not accommodated and analysed within the grand narratives of modernism. It is as if the small amount of progress made can now be leapt over by stating we are in a postfeminist, poststructuralist, postmodernist era which can assume that theorizing and political change has been accomplished for and by various categories of people suffering oppression. A further dimension of power over oppressed groups is the power to control theory.

If the abolition of structural analyses leads to the apparent abolition of categories of people it also de-politicizes issues which have not yet been fully politicized. 'Category politics' have been criticized not in terms of the need for political action but in terms of their tendency towards separateness (that is, the separation of oppressions), an issue we have tried to address in the recognition of the interrelations of oppressions. There are theoretical affinities between postmodernism and the interrelations of multiple oppressions in the attempt to go beyond category politics. The danger is in assuming these issues of oppression have been dealt with rather than ignored or leapt over as theory moves on. In the postmodernist era of no reality except from one's own definition, there is the possibility for everyone's category to be taken seriously. This view, however, ignores issues of power, especially the power to relegate certain categories of reality to a political situation of disadvantage. Power was the central focus for theorizing on oppressions in organizations in the modernist tradition. When power is focused upon and recognized in organizations as oppression then those in power have the ability to shift the debate. Cockburn (1991) saw this process as she researched equal opportunities and the various resistances to its implementation. In the context of this debate the move from modernism to postmodernism could be the ultimate in the 'mobilization of bias' of those in power. For as Schattschneider (1960) said, 'organization is the mobilization of bias', and therefore is oppression.

Despite the theoretical affinities of the analysis of multiple oppressions and postmodernism, in practice there remains a major divergence between them. In particular postmodernism has been used to diffuse critiques of the powerful and to play down and undermine feminism and other emerging analyses of oppressions. Postmodernism has typically, though not always, embodied a fundamental contradiction: between the context of the message and the medium of the message. (The medium is the *real* message.) While the message is that of postmodernism, the medium remains firmly modernist, typically malestream, using existing power structure and hierarchies, so that reality continues to be defined through the same modes as before. Postmodernism in action would be different ways of writing, theorizing, practice, structuring and organizing. Through opening up realities rather than closing them down, organization would no longer equal oppression.

Note

We are grateful to Helen Meekosha and David Collinson for discussion on these issues, and to participants at the conferences on 'Gender, sexuality and power in organizations', Newcastle Polytechnic, March 1991, and 'Towards a new theory of organizations', Keele University, April 1991, for comments on our papers there.

10

Organizations and Modernity: Continuity and Discontinuity in Organization Theory

Michael I. Reed

Discontinuity has been the dominating theme or problematic in organization theory over the past two decades. This period has been characterized by a discourse which lays overwhelming emphasis on theoretical and structural discontinuity. Both in terms of the intellectual constructions through which organizations and organizing are analysed, and in relation to the emerging institutional forms that the latter attempts to capture, the recurring theme is one of the deep-seated, fundamental transformations – a veritable 'paradigm shift' which breaks with the past and its accumulated intellectual heritage (Reed, 1991a).

The most obvious example of this 'celebration of discontinuity' in organization theory is the relatively recent intrusion of postmodernist thinking with contemporary discourse. But this is merely one – if the most conspicuous and dramatic – example of a continuing series of interventions in organization theory over the past 20 years or so which have either entailed or demanded a fundamental 'break with the past' in terms of preferred analytical frameworks and projected institutional forms. Ethnomethodology, labour process theory, poststructuralist analysis, symbolic and cultural analysis, to name but a few, have all vied for our attention as perspectives or approaches which signify the intellectual exhaustion of functionalist orthodoxy and the explosion of alternative languages and problematics which this has facilitated.

This proliferation of theoretical perspectives and approaches has been matched by growing interest in and support for analyses of changing organizational forms which undermine evolutionary theories of institutional development that assume as inexorable drive in the direction of formal rationalization and bureaucratic centralization. While mainstream organization theory assumed that the underlying trajectory of institutional development in industrial and postindustrial societies necessarily produced more highly 'organized' socioeconomic systems, recent debate and analysis has focused on the 'disorganizing dynamic' inherent in long-term structural change. Post-Fordism, Disorganized capitalism and post-modernism have – in very different ways and anticipating very different kinds of socio-economic, political and cultural outcomes – all challenged the orthodox view that modern societies are necessarily structured around organizational principles based on the integrative and regulative mechanisms provided by rational bureaucracy. Indeed, the emergence of a 'new orthodoxy' that emphasizes the unavoidable necessity for much more flexible organizational forms, and the fragmenting impact which this exerts on established structures and practices, has set the agenda for debate over the dynamics and direction of organizational change during the previous decade (Thompson, 1989; Reed, 1991b).

Thus, the decay, not to say decomposition, of the 'grand' or 'meta' narratives which are assumed to have structured the development of organization theory as a meaningful and relevant area of social scientific endeavour has become a taken-for-granted assumption (Burrell, 1990). A conception of organizations as the institutional embodiment of the diffu-sion of instrumental or functional rationality within modern societies – and the benefits which were expected to spring from this process in terms of sustained material advance and social progress – has been superseded by a conception that stresses the innate capriciousness and uncertainty of organizational life in all its multifarious forms (Cooper, 1990a). In particular, the totalizing impulse which was assumed to have underlain so much of 'modern' organization theory – the drive towards an all-encompassing general theory – has been replaced by a fragmenting dynamic that inexorably pushes in the direction of plurality, ambiguity, contingency and arbitrariness. The totalizing embrace of modernism has given way to the intoxicating promise of the postmodernist demiurge.

A number of recent attempts have been made to resist these 'subversive' intellectual movements and to recover 'the world we have lost' (Donaldson, 1985; Hinings, 1988). Yet the prevailing intellectual ethos and direction in contemporary organization theory are largely sympathetic to and supportive of the 'celebration of discontinuity' and the putative transformation in conceptual frameworks and substantive agendas which this has made possible. A grand narrative shaped by an underlying faith in reason, progress and scientific objectivity has given way to a cacophony of voices that no longer share any sense of collective intellectual engage-ment, much less identify with a common theoretical project and tradition. Plurality, relativity and incommensurability – rather than consensus, objectivity and rationality – are taken as the defining characteristics of the intellectual world which organization theorists inhabit.

The purpose of this chapter is to provide an overview of these develop-ments and a critique of the arguments of those who have been most vociferous in articulating the 'discontinuity thesis' in contemporary organization theory. It will also suggest that there are very definite continuities in analytical forms and substantive concerns between the 'old' and the 'new' organization theory. These have to be understood in terms of the collective criteria and practices which the latter makes available as a community of inquiry. These continuities – and their implications for assessing the current condition of, and future prospects for, organization theory – can only be recovered and evaluated if contemporary debates and trends are located within a broader problematic focused on the strategic role of modern organizations in facilitating the globalization and radicalization of 'modernity'. In addition, the chapter will argue that the 'modernist project' which informed the rise of organization theory needs to be interpreted and assessed in rather different terms than those proposed by advocates of the 'postmodernist' turn in organization theory (Gergen, 1992). Rather than emphasizing the totalizing or universalizing embrace endemic to modernist thinking and analysis, this chapter will stress the underlying contradictions and tensions *inherent* within the modernist project and their continued relevance for assessing the future development of organization theory.

In these respects the chapter is intended to challenge conceptions of organizational analysis which ignore the meaning and impact of its intellectual and institutional history or interpret the latter in such a way that they automatically legitimate a preferred theoretical stance and strategy. As a result, theoretical debate and development have tended to proceed in a socio-historical vacuum; that is, disengaged and separated from the recurring 'master themes' in which they are located. Alternatively, theoretical discourse has been subordinated to a predetermined theoretical position that establishes the conceptual prism through which the past is refracted and the ideological resources by means of which the future can be projected and controlled. Both of these tendencies must be counteracted if organizational analysis and its practitioners are to develop a more informed and sensitive appreciation of the socio-historical roots of their practice and the intellectual sustenance which they continue to provide for contemporary work and its future promise.

The Modernist Project

In general terms, the 'modernist project' can be characterized as entailing a long-term movement in ideas dating from the 18th century onwards which strove to establish:

> objective science, universal morality and law and autonomous art, according to their *inner logic*. At the same time, this project intended to release the cognitive potentials of each of these domains to set them free from their esoteric forms. The Enlightenment philosophers wanted to utilize this accumulation of specialized culture for the enrichment of everyday life, that is to say, for the *rational organization* of everyday social life. (Habermas, 1981: 9, quoted in Kellner, 1988b, emphasis in original)

Considered in these terms, the modernist project simultaneously entails the liberation from pre-Enlightenment tradition and conservatism, as well as the mobilization of systems of thought and the initiation of ways of life which prove to be as constraining as the traditional restraints from which they had escaped (Bauman, 1988a). What Habermas is emphasizing here is the paradoxical, not to say contradictory, impetus of the modernist project which at one and the same time releases us from the confines of the past but also imprisons us in a new intellectual and institutional edifice that is virtually impossible to deny. A sustained intellectual movement in Western European societies, developing over a period of three centuries or so, provided the theoretical foundations and methodological apparatus for successive waves of institutional transition which eventually culminated in the cultural domination of instrumental or technical reason and the coming to socio-political power of those groups most closely associated with it. In this respect Habermas is attempting to understand and explain the process of 'creative destruction' whereby transformations in culture norms and values impacted on the social and institutional structures that made possible the transition to modern industrialized societies. Thus, the social organization and administrative coordination of industrial life came to express the culture norms of rationality, efficiency and progress most closely associated with the 'operationalization' of modernist thinking within reasonably unified social practices associated with factory production, bureaucratic coordination and the market economy (Poole, 1991).

Within sociology it is Weber's work on the inexorable advance of bureaucratic rationality and imperatively coordinated institutions within modern societies which most closely presages the cultural and intellectual upheavals integral to the process of 'modernization'. Indeed, it is Weber, more than anyone else, who is regarded as *the* theorist of modernity. He articulates and analyses the deeply embedded processes of socio-cultural change through which premodern societies are transformed into modern societies, based on a set of relatively well-integrated and coordinated social practices operationalizing the *principles* or instrumental rationality into the appropriate organizational forms:

> Although Weber is often narrowly associated with a debate about the origins of capitalism in the famous Protestant Ethics thesis, it is more appropriate to interpret him as a theorist of modernization, of which the key component can be identified as rationalization. Modernity is thus the consequences of a process of modernization, by which the social world comes under the domination of asceticism, secularization, the universalistic claims of instrumental rationality, the differentiation of the various spheres of the life-world, the bureaucratization of economic, political and military practices and the growing monetarization of values. (Turner, B. 1990: 6)

For Weber, bureaucratic organization constituted the paradigmatic institutional expression of an institutional form which clinically expresses and exploits the cultural principles and technical norms entailed in the 'modernist project'. As Callinicos argues:

Weber's theory of rationalization – perhaps the centrepiece of non-Marxist social theory – provided the most important single account of the constitution of modernity. Modernization involves, in the first place, the differentiation of originally unified social practices, in particular, of the capitalist economy and the modern state. . . . Secondly, this process of differentiation involves the institutionalization of a specific kind of action, what Weber called purposive-rational (Zweckrational), or instrumentally rational action, which is oriented to selecting the most effective means to achieving some predetermined goal. The rationalization of social life consists for Weber in the increasing regulation of conduct by instrumental rationality rather than by traditional norms and values, a process which is accompanied by the ever more widespread use of the methods of post-Galilean science to determine the most efficacious course of action available to individuals in pursuit of their goals. . . . The key to understanding the process of modernization is the transposition of cultural rationalization into societal rationalization; for example, the process whereby the Calvinist conception of life as a vocation encouraged the institutionalization of instrumentally rational economic action. (1989: 33)

Both the cultural ethos of the modernist project and Weber's seminal contribution to its intellectual advance and institutional expression have been interpreted in terms of a 'totalizing' drive or momentum; that is, the aspiration to contain the understanding and practice of modernization within a structured narrative exemplifying the inevitable historical advance of reason, progress and order (Kellner, 1988a). This reading emphasizes the distinctive character of the modernist project as entailing a dramatic break from or rupture with premodernist forms. Interpreted in this manner the modernist project, and Weber's particular formulation of its strategic cultural and institutional components, constitutes an attempt at intellectual imperialism to which any prospective counter-discourse will be subordinated. It is the 'authoritarian' thrust of the meta-narratives constructed and promulgated by modernist thinkers which constitutes the overwhelming intellectual and social impact of such an ethos or intellectual movement for all those who wish to resist its restric-tive and cloying embrace (Carter and Jackson, 1991). By attempting to construct and promulgate totalizing theories of society and history that claim universal validity and a privileged epistemological status as scien-tifically legitimated 'objective truth', modernist thinkers are seen to impose an unacceptable and unrealistic set of expectations on social scien-tific discourse:

In philosophy and social theory a concept of 'postmodernism' has been invoked to signify that the limits of the modern have been reached, that the pursuit of unshakeable foundations for analytic truth constitutes a fruitless project, one that will continue to remain incomplete in so far as the metaphysical pre-suppositions at the heart of western philosophy are themselves problematic. . . . In addition, it has been argued that the promise of modernity to achieve the emancipation of humanity from poverty, ignorance, prejudice, and the absence of enjoyment is no longer considered to be feasible. Such grand hopes associated with global or totalizing forms of social theory and a politics of 'revolution' have been diminished by the realization that forms of knowledge, social conditions, human experiences and subjectivities are not as they were once thought to be . . . the grand old narratives of modern social theory and philosophy have been rendered inoperative, they have lost their credibility. (Smart, 1990: 24)

Yet, the overriding emphasis which the postmodernist critique of the modernist project gives to the dissolution of the meta-narratives of reason, science and progress, and the corresponding 'loss of unity and integration' which this produces, may be guilty of grossly overestimating the totalizing momentum of modernist thinking and underestimating the fragmenting and localizing consequences of its chequered history as an integrating narrative. The tendency to overstate the intellectual imperialism and institutional authoritarianism inherent within the modernist project, and the 'disciplinary regimes' that it fostered, produces a narrative drive every bit as 'totalizing' in its aspirations as the tradition from which it wishes to escape (Kellner, 1988a).

More perceptive intellectual historians have shown us that the 'modernist project', such as it was, forced social theorists to recognize that the study of society was a 'vastly *more complicated* matter than one of merely fitting observed data into a structure of human thought that was presumed to be universal' (Stuart-Hughes, 1958: 16). Indeed, modernist thinkers encouraged an enormous heightening of intellectual self-consciousness and self-examination of the key presuppositions or 'domain assumptions' (Gouldner, 1971) which underpinned social thought and analysis. As Stuart-Hughes has argued:

The dominant theme of the re-orientation of European social thought between 1890 and 1930 was the *critique* of all *universalizing* philosophies and social theories – such as Positivism or Marxism – and a corresponding *undermining* of the rationalistic, empiricist, materialist epistemologies on which they rested. (1958: 16)

This view contrasts sharply with that articulated by postmodern commentators and their consistent focus on the coherence of the discursive formations of modernity – the intellectual and organizational practices which produce knowledge claims and administrative mechanisms which 'systems of power' find useful – and the 'totalizing' achievements of the disciplinary regimes or technologies which they generate. As Wolin says of Foucault:

In a curious way, therefore, Foucault seems to have repeated the same classic error of totalizing thinking with which he taxed classic theory. . . . Not only does he give us a vision of the world in which humans are caught within imprisoning structures of knowledge and practice, but he offers no hope of escape . . . . Foucault has *overstated* the coherence and ambiguities of discursive formations. They never attain the monolithic unity ascribed to them. . . . Discursive formations seem to have acquired the occult qualities that the ancients ascribed to circles: they reproduce themselves to infinity (1988: 185–97; also see Garland, 1991 for a further development of this point).

In this respect much of the postmodernist critique of the modernist project and its insinuation into various specialized branches of the social sciences, such as organization theory, may be based upon a very narrow reading of the meta-narratives of modernity and their pervasive influence on the development of social analysis. The modernist project and its narrative account of social development may be much more internally fragmented, ambivalent and inherently self-reflexive than postmodernist commentators suggest. The 'totalizing' interpretation which the latter provide of the former may, unintentionally, establish intellectual legitimation and institutional support for a reading of organization theory's past history, current state and future prospects that is even more authoritarian and imperialistic that the discourse which it has played a central role in challenging.

The Modernist Project and Organization Theory

Modernism has been interpreted as consisting of three interrelated components; a theory of knowledge, a substantive sociopolitical theory and the disciplinary technologies arising out of, and reinforcing, both the epistemological position and its theoretical correlates (Cooper and Burrell, 1988). As such, it is seen to constitute a discursive formation which

> unites thought and practice in a seamless and circular web: Practices set the conditions for discourse and discourse feeds back statements that will facilitate practice. Discourse appears completely incorporated into practice. It has no autonomous identity of distance. (Wolin, 1988: 184)

At the epistemological level, modernist thinking is based on the assumption that rational principles and practices of knowledge production and evaluation will lead to social progress and personal growth. Thus, modernism is based on a belief 'in the essential capacity of humanity to perfect itself through the power of rational thought' (Cooper and Burrell, 1988: 92). At the level of substantive social theory, modernism is seen to produce and sustain a meta-narrative that emphasizes the rationalization and objectification of social life through the imposition of an instrumental or technical rationality that subsumes all forms of social interaction within a means–ends calculus (Habermas, 1981). The latter is geared to the problem of extending effective control over a recalcitrant physical and social environment through the development and implementation of various disciplinary practices and mechanisms which ensure close surveillance over, and incorporation of, a docile and subject population (O'Neill, 1986; Burrell, 1988). A therapeutic, rather than coercive, technology of power becomes established, initially in carceral institutions, and is gradually diffused within other sites of social and political struggle (Rose, 1989; Dandeker, 1990; Garland, 1991). Modernism is the social theory which constructs and legitimates the 'disciplinary society' by forging and reinforcing the control technologies and practices on which it depends for its continuation.

Within organization theory, modernist thinking is seen to find its clearest expression in the intellectual dominance and ideological power of systems analysis (Cooper and Burrell, 1988; Power, 1990; Parker, 1992a; Gergen, 1992). The latter is aligned with the control needs of large-scale technological systems; that is, the need for discursive formations, such as a theory of organizations based on the logic of systems analysis, which establish the knowledge claims and related disciplinary practices through which the rational management of complex activities can be routinely achieved (Bell, 1974). Whatever critical impulse or potential which may once have been offered by modernist thinking has been completely sublimated within a 'conservative' narrative of technological determinism for extending rational control over large-scale, complex organizations and the highly ordered and routinized forms of social life which they make available:

> The object of orthodox organizational analysis is *the* organization: a bounded social system with specific structures and goals which acts more or less rationally and more of less coherently. Within this context, the concept of organization itself functions as a meta-discourse to legitimate the idea that organization is a social tool and an extension of the human agent . . . the subject of organizational analysis is *formal* organization. It is not organization as such that demands analysis but its 'formal' character . . . what is formally organized takes on the virtue of a moral order. Hence the emphasis in modernism on the search for 'rational authority' as the basis of the *good* social order. (Cooper and Burrell, 1988: 102–8)

However, postmodernist writers have argued that the dominance of modernist thought in organizational analysis has been challenged and undermined by 'counter-movements' that have striven to expose the limitations of systems-driven theories of formalization which censor the grotesque side of organizational life: 'Postmodernism reveals formal organization to be the ever-present expression of an autonomous power that masquerades as the supposedly rational constructions of modern institutions' (Cooper and Burrell, 1988: 110). Thus, the 'control' model of organization which provided the intellectual foundations for the rise and development of modern systems theory in organizational analysis has been questioned by alternative approaches that centre on

> the indeterminacy of organizational systematic unity. Methodologically, this directs us towards boundaries of 'surface' or organizations as scenes of potential instability. The organization is permeable rather than closed. The communicative processes within are localized and have no underlying rational basis. What is crucial is to set up the 'free play' of discursive processes both as a researcher and within the domain of organizational action. (Power, 1990: 117)

Increasingly, modernist forms of thinking and analysis within organization theory are being criticized for their

> intellectual imperialism that ignores the fundamental uncontrollability of meaning . . . we are advised to stop attempting to 'systematize', 'define' or impose a logic on events and instead recognize the limitations of all our projects. The

role of language in *constituting* 'reality' is therefore central and all our attempts to discover 'truth' should be seen for what they are – forms of discourse. (Parker, 1992a: 3)

The waning intellectual power and prestige of modernist discourse within organizational analysis is seen as one part of a wider movement against totalizing narratives within the social sciences in general (Gergen, 1992). As Kellner puts it:

There is a sense in many disciplines of an end of an era and there are equally compelling searches for new paradigms, new politics and new theories. . . . The postmodern debate poses in a dramatic way the issue of competing paradigms for social theory and the need to choose paradigms that are most theoretically and practically applicable to social conditions of the present era. (Kellner, 1988a: 267)

In this way, the postmodernist critique of conventional organizational analysis as a discursive formation which closely reflects the central features of modernist discourse in its epistemology, theory and practice gives overwhelming emphasis to 'the break, rupture and alleged novelty in the contemporary socio-historical epoch and is downplaying, and even occluding, the continuities' (Kellner, 1988a: 267).

However, before we can be in a position to offer a better grounded appreciation of the postmodernist critique and the response which it might receive, we need to achieve a better understanding of the processes of theoretical change and development which organizational analysis has undergone since the break-up of the 'orthodox consensus' from the late 1960s onwards (Reed, 1985, 1992; Thompson and McHugh, 1990; Mills and Murgatroyd, 1991).

Organization Theory in Postmodern Times

There are a number of respects in which Silverman's *The Theory of Organizations*, published in 1970, can be regarded as a pivotal book in the recent intellectual history of organization theory. In broad terms, it seemed to open the intellectual floodgates for a virtual torrent of publications which offered an often bewildering array of novel and innovative problematics, perspectives and programmes which broke with the dominant systems orthodoxy. In this way the book provided intellectual legitimacy for the development and strengthening of theoretical approaches and research strategies that rejected the 'systems paradigm' as their primary point of analytical and ideological reference.

It can also be viewed as a characteristically 'postmodern' publication in three other respects. First, it privileged 'theory' over 'history' in the sense that its critique of the systems frame of reference and its advocacy of an action perspective were based on the presupposition of a Kuhnian-type epistemological break or rupture between an outmoded and obsolete dominant paradigm and a rising, but still fragile, challenger (Silverman,

1970: 4). This epistemological break was *assumed*, rather than being demonstrated through a detailed analysis and assessment of the intellectual trajectories that organization theory had followed since the early decades of the 20th century. Kuhn was invoked to legitimate the presumed epistemological shift from one dominant paradigm to another, without following through on a Kuhnian-type analysis of the internal *development* of organizational thought in its encompassing socio-historical context. Analytical assessment and theoretical innovation were preferred over historical excavation and narrative development (I am grateful to Martin Parker for highlighting this point in a personal communication).

Second, Silverman strongly expressed a commitment to theoretical incommensurability, not to say polarization, between the conflicting paradigms which found it very difficult, if not impossible, to live with each other within the same field. The action paradigm entailed a fundamentally opposed conception of ontology, epistemology and theory for organizational analysis to that offered by the systems paradigm; they were not to be considered as two different sides to the same analytical coin as advocated by Cohen (1968), but were radically opposed perspectives on 'the nature of the social order that sociologists study and of the major characteristics of the social reality thereby implied' (Silverman, 1970: 5). This commitment to a strong version of paradigm incommensurability – 'we are so locked into these frameworks that we cannot communicate with those encased in radically different frameworks or paradigms' (Bernstein, 1983: 45) – set the tone for subsequent advocacy of paradigm closure (Burrell and Morgan, 1979) or for weaker versions which permitted some degree of theoretical overlap and interparadigmatic communication, but still insisted on distinctive separation between opposed frameworks (Benson, 1977; Carter and Jackson, 1991). The fact that some of the strongest advocates of incommensurability and closure placed Silverman on the leading edge of the functionalist paradigm (Burrell and Morgan, 1979) can only be regarded as a prime example of the difficulties, not to say silliness, which such forms of thinking can produce. He suffered at the hands of 'paradigm warriors' who were determined to locate him in one camp or another and keep him there. At the same time he provided an indirect justification for this categorization fetish.

Third, Silverman's book simultaneously anticipated and reinforced the incipient fragmentation of organizational studies into querulous and squabbling factions during the subsequent decade, as had been projected in Mayntz's seminal article – and on which Silverman drew for much inspiration – in 1964 (Mayntz, 1964). Mayntz identified a drive towards convergence, if not consensus, around a systems-based approach, but she also anticipates with some prescience – particularly in regard of the widening split between administrative science and the sociology of the organizations – a theoretical and methodological bifurcation between 'a prescriptive theory focusing on efficiency on the one hand, and towards the systematic linkage with problems on the societal level on the other hand' (Mayntz, 1964: 118). Silverman's book, and the intellectual productions of many who were to follow in his theoretical wake, demonstrated the truth of Mayntz's overall assessment that the integration and unity which systems theory had provided were extremely fragile and tendentious: 'contrary to the promise of the theoretical approach, the unity and coherence of the field of organizational research is highly precarious' (Mayntz, 1964: 111). Consequently, Silverman's book set a tone and fashioned an agenda dominated by the themes of discontinuity and fragmentation which were to prove to be very evocative and powerful within organizational studies in the 1970s and 1980s.

By the late 1970s the perception that there was a 'crisis' in organization theory had almost become 'passé' in the sense that talk of crisis merely reinforced a growing perception of a field of study that had outgrown the intellectual tutelage of orthodoxy without discovering an alternative formulation or formulations that could provide a reinvigorated sense of direction and purpose. By this time the established rational/systems orthodoxy was perceived to have no answer to the mounting clamour for approaches that could deal with:

> the social production of organizational reality, including the reality – constructing activity of the organizational scientist; the political bases of organizational realities, including the ties of theorists to power structures; the connection of organizations to the larger set of structural arrangements in the society; and the continuously emergent character of organizational patterns. (Benson, 1977: 16).

There were various attempts to downplay the impact and significance of these developments in the mid to late- 1980s (Donaldson, 1985; Hinings, 1988) – in other words, to suggest that beneath the swirling eddy of intellectual introspection and disputation all was basically well in terms of an emerging policy science that had established its credentials as a legitimate and relevant area of socio-technical knowledge. But the sense that organizational analysis had lost its 'age of innocence' and would never be quite the same again was difficult to deny. In other words, nearly two decades after the publication of *The Theory of Organizations*, organizational studies seemed to have reached a stage of intellectual development (maturation?) where its ability to see or sell itself as an integrated, totalizing narrative account of 'organization' had been damaged beyond repair. It found itself in a position where it was virtually impossible to rediscover and retrieve a sense of intellectual and historical continuity which had been scattered to the four winds in the maelstrom of critique that had descended in the ensuing decades.

Yet this interpretation was based upon an assessment that had relatively little feel for, much less knowledge of, the *actual* intellectual history of organizational studies as a worthwhile and relevant intellectual practice. It also coincided with something of a reaction against the emphasis on discontinuity and fragmentation that had structured the engagement in and development of 'organizational discourse' over a period of two decades or more. By the end of the 1980s one was witnessing the reformulation and redevelopment of organizational analysis as a field of study based on a shared intellectual heritage and recognizable historical continuity.

Beyond the Fragments

A growing perception that the postmodernist critique of organization theory has been pushed to its logical limits, if not absurdities, is evident in recent commentaries on the 'state of play' in the field that attempt to recover a sense of historical continuity and the way in which it continues to inform the lines of debate opening up between different perspectives. The need to construct intelligible narratives that continue to speak to concerns and dilemmas that have shaped the historical development of the field as a reasonably coherent and significant intellectual practice has re-emerged as a major concern within contemporary discourse. What one might term the 'discontinuity thesis' is increasingly seen to obscure the underlying continuities in focus and analysis which shape the current condition of and future prospects for a field of study that has survived the uncertainties and doubts of an extended period of intellectual self-doubt and re-appraisal. Indeed, the desire to avoid the worst excesses of epistemological relativism and theoretical polarization, as well as the inclination to identify and reoccupy the common ground on which coherent dialogue and debate can ensue, are very potent intellectual influences within organizational studies at the present time. The fragmenting momentum felt so strongly and vividly in recent years has gradually been superseded by an awareness of the need for shared focus, intelligibility and pattern, without a return to the constraints and distortions imposed by an unreflective fealty to an intellectually bankrupt orthodoxy.

The perceived need to re-establish a collective sense of historical continuity and narrative pattern – not to say 'drive' – in contemporary organizational analysis is reflected in a number of developments. They suggest that the fragmenting tendencies released by a single-minded focus on paradigm incommensurability and 'culture conflict' between competing factions have been gradually receding. They have been superseded by the renewed quest for a sustained dialogue which has direction and gives the field an identifiable coherence (Burrell, 1992b). The latter recognizes the force of continuing disagreement over epistemological principles and ideological commitments, but suggests that their polarizing proclivities can be contained within a search for the making and re-making of intelligible narratives concerning organization theory's historical development and its significance for present-day concerns. This, it is anticipated, will extricate organizational studies from the intellectual paralysis and 'collective amnesia' which came to pervade it as a result of the 'triumphalism' of systems orthodoxy or the 'forgetfulness' of postmodernist thinking in regard of the social struggles that inevitably structure the growth and transformation of modern or postmodern organizational forms (Clarke, 1988; Clegg, 1990).

This general movement in organizational analysis away from paradigm incommensurability and polarization between competing groups or factions and towards a renewed search for narrative patterns and forms which are flexible enough to accommodate a plurality of divergent views is reflected in a range of more specific transitions within the field.

First, the determination to locate intellectual developments within organization theory in their wider socio-historical context – including the academic organization of organization theory itself (Brown, 1992; Perry, 1992) – as opposed to the decontextualized and depoliticized interpretations offered by previous accounts. As Thompson and McHugh have argued:

> A great weakness of much organizational writing is the failure to locate theory in its historical context. . . . Organizational theory and practice can only be understood as something *in process,* otherwise the search for general propositions and instant prescriptions becomes disconnected from reality as it has done in conventional historical approaches. (Thompson and McHugh, 1990: 3–32).

Second, a growing realization that epistemological uncertainty, theoretical plurality and methodological diversity do not necessarily entail a terminal drift towards a disordered field of study characterized by total disarray over philosophical fundamentals, substantive problematics and conceptual frameworks. Indeed, it is the lines of debate that are initiated and developed by different modes of inquiry that hold the field together as a reasonably coherent intellectual practice. They provide the problematics, frameworks and explanations that, together with the institutional arrangements within which 'organizational analysis' is actively carried on, link together epistemological claims and disciplinary practices in such a way that a coherent field of study can be sustained (Reed, 1992).

Third, the relationship between 'discourse' and 'practice' in organizational studies is now subjected to non-deterministic and non-reductionist forms of analysis that contrast sharply with the previous emphasis on the material and structural factors which were thought to direct intellectual change and development (Reed, 1992). There is very strong resistance to collapsing discourse into practice – that is, assuming that debates about ideas can be simply rendered down to power struggles between conflicting ideologies and the material interests which they observed protect – or to treating discourse as an autonomous activity independent of its social base. Instead, there is an attempt to trace out the dialectic interaction between intellectual development and changing control practices over time as it moulds the organizational forms through which social order is managed in advanced industrial societies (Morgan, 1990).

Finally, one can detect a reaction against the 'extreme relativism' symptomatic of the 'paradigm mentality' that tended to dominate reflection and debate over theory development in organizational analysis during the 1970s and early 1980s. In its place the inclination to tease out the practical epistemologies or 'epistemologies in use' (Mulkay, 1990) and social networks (Latour, 1990) through which debates are conducted between different theory groups or research communities has emerged as a central concern. This work takes its cue from Cohen's argument that:

> one of the most important results of post-empiricism has been to overturn the Cartesian duality of objectivism and relativism. While no neutral alogrithim exists for the choice between theories, this does not imply that science is an irrational enterprise. Rather scientists are obligated to submit good reasons for the acceptance of their programme in preference to competing schools of thought. The criteria to which these reasons refer are established as a result of the *historical development* of the community of inquiry within which justificatory arguments are made. This implies a rejection of the thesis of incommensurability of meaning between theories. . . . On this basis, the rational appeal to scientific criteria involves a limited degree of rational persuasion. (Cohen, 1986: 129)

Organization Theory as a Practice

Cohen's stress on the historical and social context in and through which 'theory choice' can be subject to a degree of rational evaluation and progression normally denied by postmodernist writers (Lyotard, 1984) can be developed further into a more considered appreciation of the nature and status of organizational analysis as a social practice. Building on recent work on the concept of 'practice' (MacIntyre, 1981; Poole, 1991), it is possible to regard organization theory as a field of study constituted by three interrelated elements. First, as an intellectual practice which necessarily involves its participants in social established cooperative activity that expresses and develops significant human activities through the realization of 'goods' internal to that practice. Second, as a tradition of historically generated norms, rules, conventions and standards of excellence through which the practice can be subjected to critical evaluation and transformation over time. Third, as a narrative structure and context through which we make sense of and give meaning to 'our' participation within the practices and traditions which provide the substantive and critical resources that allow us to engage in 'organizational analysis'.

Taken together, these three interrelated elements of practice, tradition and narrative provide a framework for thinking about and engaging in organizational analysis which resists the relativistic tendencies inherent within postmodernist critique. This framework establishes a robust notion of 'grounded rationality' through which critical judgements and assessments can be formulated. It also offers a coherent alternative to the postmodernist inclination to argue that all social scientists, including organizational analysts, are so tightly imprisoned within their own linguistic conceptual worlds that it is 'impossible to create even relatively independent knowledge about the actions and intentions of those outside one's cultural group' (Alexander, 1992: 333).

A conception of organizational analysis as an intellectual practice drawing on a range of theoretical traditions to produce accounts of organizational life that can be located and evaluated within a narrative structure of context (Reed, 1992) provides for a negotiated and dynamic set of standards through which rational debate and argumentation between proponents of rival perspectives or approaches is possible. These standards are historically embedded within social practices, traditions and narratives which provide 'embedded reasons' (Bernstein, 1983) for judging an argument true or false or an action right or wrong. They do not provide decontextualized, universal and objective axioms for making critical evaluations, but rather shared criteria for assessing the knowledge claims of competing interpretations which have accumulated and sedimented within the practices, traditions and narratives constitutive of the discipline or field of study. As Alexander argues:

> the disciplines of the human sciences are organized theoretically around broad and competing traditions and empirically around competing research programmes. . . . In periods of fission, the existence of such cleavages often leads to scepticism and discouragement. . . . These traditions and programmes are not just sources of disagreement but powerful means of intertwining impersonal theoretical controls with disciplinary practice. . . . The objectivity of such practices is conditional but not ephemeral. Dominant and mature research programmes often create an entirely new realism of observational statements; they also set standards of explanatory scope and internal coherence that competing programmes must meet. In the competition between such programmes and traditions is found whatever progress the human sciences can provide. (Alexander, 1992: 358–9)

By assuming a 'Hobson's choice' between foundationalism and relativism, postmodernist thinking has ignored – or at the very least radically underestimated – the modest, but nonetheless significant, grounded rationality inherent within those intellectual practices, traditions and histories through which the study of organizations has been conducted and developed. This negotiated or embedded rationality has been deposited within the theoretical arteries through which the latter has been sustained as a viable and coherent intellectual practice over time. It has also been secreted through the programmes, traditions and stories by means of which organizational analysis has been given a shared sense of theoretical direction and meaningful substantive focus. When arguments are advanced or interpretations developed concerning any aspect of social life within complex organizations they have to be defended and supported by reference to a rich body of accumulated knowledge and procedures which make organizational analysis a coherent discipline or field of study rather than 'a babble of alternative ideological assertions: procedures which provide for their own relevant discourse about proof' (Thompson,

1978: 205–6; quoted in Alexander, 1992: 36). While postmodernist analysis is correct in its rejection of an ultimate cognitive or epistemological basis for justifying our knowledge claims, it is profoundly mistaken in the logical inference that it draws from this truth; that a rejection of foundationalism or universalism must inevitably entail an acceptance – even a celebration of – an extreme form of epistemological and political relativism in which social scientific knowledge is totally absorbed within 'power discourse' and the control practices which it legitimates (Burrell, 1988; Carter and Jackson, 1991).

This irrational leap from foundationalism to relativism is blind to the ways in which organizational researchers are bound to collective standards and traditions of rationality through which a coherent and sustainable narrative emerges. A clearer recognition of the narrative drive and momentum implicit within the practice of organizational analysis provides an appropriate reminder of the extent to which the search for shared understanding and explanation is a, perhaps the, essential characteristic of any engagement with the sociological – or for that matter social scientific – vision (Mills, 1959). The latter does not demand fealty to the quest for narrative unity or epistemological and theoretical monism. Indeed, it abjures these unattainable and unattractive goals. Instead, it calls for a much more realistic and useful commitment to the involvement within a historically bounded and contextually grounded set of procedures and standards which permit and facilitate participation within a critical dialogue over the organizational equipment through which the quality of human life is enhanced (Burns, 1970). These procedures and standards will change over time as the wider traditions and programmes in which they are imbedded also develop in new directions and incorporate novel problematics. Organizational analysis may indeed lack the strong disciplinary controls operative in the natural – and some of the social – sciences, given its relatively fragmented and loosely coupled academic structures and negotiated quality control mechanisms (Whitley, 1984). Yet it does possess a reasonably robust framework of collective understandings and conventions through which the conflicting claims of incompatible, but comparable (Gioia and Pitre, 1989), perspectives or paradigms can be subject to a process of sifting, assessment and adjudication. While the results of the latter process are always conditional, and can be revised at a future date, it provides a general scheme of procedural referents and criteria – that is, a disciplinary matrix (Toulmin, 1972) – through which conjectures, hypotheses and theories can be continuously compared and critically evaluated.

Towards a New/Old Organization Theory

The cumulative impact of the shifts in theoretical focus and direction outlined in previous sections provides a context in which a different kind of research agenda for organizational analysis is beginning to emerge in the 1990s. The construction and development of this agenda has undoubtedly been influenced by the impact of postmodernist thinking – most obviously in regard of the renewed interest in organizational culture and symbolism. Yet both its substantive content and analytical focus connect with older, well-established traditions of thought and mature research programmes as they are reflected through the community of inquiry constituted by organization theory as an intellectual practice (Reed, 1992). Rather than presume irreparable ruptures with the past and the fundamental discontinuities in orientation and approach which they seem to presage, contemporary organizational theory seems set to rediscover and renew its connections with forms of analysis which have their roots in a coherently articulated intellectual narrative and research programme that continues to speak to recurring themes and problematics. The rhetoric of paradigm incommensurability and closure – though still heard, admittedly in a more muted voice and diluted form, in certain quarters (Carter and Jackson, 1991) – has given way to a more realistic and sober assessment of the pressing need for mediation between competing perspectives and paradigms as a theoretical precondition for understanding and explaining the organizational dynamics of modernity (Child, 1988; Clark and Starkey, 1988; Bryman, 1989; Gioia and Pitre, 1989; Whittington, 1989; Ahrne, 1990; Hassard and Pym, 1990).

This emerging agenda can be specified in terms of six major research themes or problematics. First, the growing sophistication and reach of surveillance and control processes or techniques within complex organizations and the wider social formations of which they are a part (Miller and O'Leary, 1987; Dandeker, 1990). Second, the strategic role of professionals and other expert groups or 'knowledge workers' in constructing and implementing the more advanced disciplinary regimes through which surveillance and control is routinized in modern organizations (Crompton, 1990; Morgan, 1990; Reich, 1991; Reed and Anthony, 1992). Third, the construction of power/knowledge discourses within various institutional settings – and particularly in regard of 'corporate management strategy' – through which 'normalized' organizational subjectivities or identities are produced and reproduced (Thompson and McHugh, 1990; Mills and Murgatroyd, 1991; Knights and Morgan, 1991; Rose, 1989). Fourth, the process of long-term transitions in organizational designs and the repertoires of structural poses and institutional myths through which they are enacted (Child, 1984; Pettigrew, 1985; Clark and Starkey, 1988; Smith et al., 1990). Fifth, the putative development of different forms of 'flexible Fordism' in a wide range of organizational settings and the emphasis which they give to combining flexibility and rigidity within an integrated institutional framework (Dore, 1989; Harvey, 1989; Littler, 1990; Starkey et al., 1991; Whitaker, 1992). Finally, the impact of more sophisticated types of information technology on established systems of corporate governance and organizational management (Zuboff, 1988; Lammers and Szell, 1989; Faulk and Stein-field, 1990; Poster, 1990; Reed, 1991b).

Each of these specific themes can be contextualized within a larger leit-motif concerned with the strategic contribution that contemporary organization theory has to play in accounting for the globalization and radicalization of 'high' or 'late' modernity (Giddens, 1985, 1987a, 1990, 1991). Giddens argues that the peculiarly dynamic character of modern social life has to be accounted for in terms of three interrelated elements: the separation of time and space; the disembedding mechanisms through which this separation is facilitated; and the institutional reflexivity which these disembedding mechanisms both depend on and generate (Giddens, 1991: 16–21). Complex organizations – of various types and forms – play a central role in constituting and reinforcing these three interrelated processes through which 'modernity' is globalized as a radicalizing move-ment or dynamic throughout the world. This is so to the extent that they provide the strategic mechanisms and related practices which facilitate the 'reflexively monitored system reproduction' and change integral to the institutional fabrication of modern societies.

These mechanisms, and their related practices, are crucial to any understanding of the role of complex organizations as *the* strategic social units through which 'modernity' is globalized as a radicalizing dynamic on a world-system scale. First, the various administrative devices and resources – such as timetables, maps, schedules and technologies – through which time and space can be separated, emptied, stretched and then recombined to coordinate the multitude of actions and interactions of many human beings who are physically absent from one another. Second, the abstract systems – such as money, expertise and trust rela-tions – through which social institutions become 'disembedded' as units 'lifted out' of their local contexts and re-articulated across indefinite tracts of time–space. Third, the practices through which institutional reflexivity becomes *constitutive* of modern societies by providing the formalized and codified information or knowledge systems through which 'performance' can be continually monitored and modified. In each of these respects – time/space distancing, disembedding mechanisms and institutional reflexivity – modern organizations provide the key resources, structures and practices through which 'modernity' is globalized as a ubiquitous and pervasive institutional dynamic that inevitably radicalizes established or customary ways of life. As strategic mechanisms for the institutionalization of reflexively monitored system reproduction and change, modern organizations thus provide one of the most important sites or arenas in which the conflicts and power struggles to control the future are fought out.

It is in these broader theoretical terms that the specific thematic components of the current and projected research agenda in contem-porary analysis can be most fruitfully interpreted. Within each of these research sites one can detect an aspiration to develop *'analytically structured narratives*' that link agency, structure and process as they interweave with 'structural inertia', random events, contextual discontinuities and significant changes in trajectories' (Clark and Starkey, 1988: 195). These analytically structured narratives must focus on the 'new' power struggles between different groups, classes and movements to control the political agenda for socio-technical change and transformation in modern societies. They must also connect these 'new' tensions and conflicts to the 'older' struggles out of which they emerged, rather than indulge in the historical forgetfulness often encountered in postmodernist discourse:

> From within this model (post-modernism), it is possible to 'forget' the struggles which have taken place over the politics of data control and access; to 'forget' the struggles over the introduction and use of new technology; to 'forget' the struggles which take place at the chip-producing and assembling ends of the Imperial communicating chain . . . the development and integration of new technologies . . . are enmeshed in, *not separate from*, the complex of economic, cultural and political struggles. . . . What remains striking about this process (for all the post-modern conceptions of arbitrariness, indifference and fragmentation) is how narrow the range of meanings has remained in the dominant media of communication. (Clarke, 1988: 395–8).

Underpinning the research themes constituting the agenda for a 'new' organization theory outlined above lies a continuing debate that has shaped its intellectual development since the latter half of the 19th century; that is, the extent to which modern organizations can be regarded as the primary institutional carriers for the pervasive diffusion of technical or instrumental rationality in Western industrialized societies. From its inception in late 19th-century social thought over the dynamics and trajectories of institutional change in industrial capitalist societies, organization theory has struggled to provide a better understanding of and explanation for the rise of rational bureaucracy as *the* strategic social mechanism embodying technical or instrumental reason as a legitimizing principle and as an operational norm (Clegg, 1990; Reed, 1992).

However, the overall tendency exhibited by organizational studies in recent years has been expressed, in both theoretical and practical terms, as entailing a 'retreat from rationality' as the dominant feature of intellectual discourse and research-based analysis (Bryman, 1984; Brunnson, 1989; Butler, 1991). The proliferation of alternative perspectives that reject the rationalistic bias of mainstream writing seems to have left the field in a state of comparative disarray, not to say dissolution. The theoretical glue once provided by an assumed epistemological commitment to rational analysis of 'organized rationality' has given way under the pressure exerted by a cacophony of voices which celebrate the reality of multiple and contested organizational *rationalities* which cannot be assessed or evaluated in any coherent way.

However, current evocations of multiple rationalities constructed and communicated through a plethora of 'language-games' have traded on a very constricted, not to say misleading, view of the past. They have tended to ignore the strong theoretical connections that Weber originally forged between the analysis of bureaucracy as a technical device and the wider struggles for political control and cultural hegemony in which it was developed and operationalized (Beetham, 1985, 1987). This 'Weberian tradition' has been sustained in organization studies (McNeil, 1978) and presents a very different view of organized rationality to that expressed by either the defenders of the positivist faith or by the high priests of postmodernism. The current renewal of that tradition within contemporary organizational analysis would seem to provide a much more fruitful basis for exploring the dynamics of organizational change and institutional transition in advanced capitalist societies to that offered by either of the latter alternatives. In this way we may be much better placed to explore:

> The enduring importance[1] of Weber's analysis of rationalization and the bureaucratization which is its ubiquitous concomitant. Disembodied, the very forms our sociality turn against us, and within them there is no place for humane values. The soulful corporation or the compassionate state are, by virtue of the very constitution of these social forms, contradictions in terms. (Sayer, 1991: 154)

Conclusion

The overall thrust of this chapter has been to argue a case for the continued need for the construction of, and debate between, intelligible narratives within organizational studies as a, perhaps the, vital process which sustains the continued search for collective understanding of such a complex and ambiguous phenomenon as 'modern organization'. It has also been contended that this activity can only be maintained if the shared sense of long-term historical and intellectual continuities between current concerns and past achievements is retrieved from the selective amnesia or forgetfulness encouraged by recently fashionable modes of discourse and analysis.

Organizational analysis has a vital role to play in furthering our understanding of 'organization' as constituting the strategic institutional site or setting in and through which the interplay between the micro-politics of control and the macro-politics of order is worked through to prosecute the radicalization of globalization of modernity. It will only be in a position to fulfil this role adequately if it begins to tell a new story that critically engages with older narratives which will be in need of radical overhaul, but continue to speak to present problems and projected futures.

11

Postmodernism: Fatal Distraction

Paul Thompson

The chapters in this book are further indicators that the relentless march of postmodernism has reached the distant shores of organization theory. It has travelled a long way from its origins in architecture, art and literature. But what has a rejection of universal standards of beauty or a preference for pastiche got to do with organizations? In one sense it could be simply argued that the cultural shifts attendant to this epoch of postmodernism are having significant effects on patterns of work and management, and therefore we need to analyse them.

Clegg (1990: 2) goes further. 'Organization theory is a creature of modernity', because it is based on notions of a bureaucratic division of labour that is no longer dominant. For Carter and Jackson (Chapter 5 in this volume) management is also an 'essentially modernist activity' rooted in the application of formal logic to problem-solving. Others (Gergen, 1992) stress that organization theory has committed the modernist sin of belief in the 'narrative of progress', within which rational design of organizations to minimize uncertainty and maximize efficiency play a central role. The sinners therefore include scientific management, systems approaches, exchange theory, trait methodology and cognitive accounts of individual behaviour.

However, theorists are not homogeneous in their approach. Running like a fault-line through the growth of postmodernism in organization theory, as elsewhere, is a difference between an emphasis on ontology and epistemology. The former camp, such as Clegg, concentrate on the material changes in society and work organization. He endorses Bauman's view that it is possible to use the conventional tools of rational discourse to analyse postmodern*ity*. Postmodern*ism*, however, is first and foremost a way of seeing the world. For the adherents of this view (see the articles in *Organisation Studies* by Cooper and Burrell) modernism is primarily a form of knowledge and acquiring knowledge which has to be replaced by alternative forms of enquiry that recognize the 'fundamental uncontrollability of meaning' (Parker, 1992a).

In principle it is hard to see how these two 'sides' can meet on the same terrain. Those concerned with forms of knowledge normally refuse any notion that it is possible to have an empirically verifiable picture of social structure. Those who do embrace the latter are violating that epistemology. But in practice the waters are muddier. A softer epistemology may be utilized that acknowledges a self-limiting social science concerned with local narratives and rationalities, reflecting the surrounding culture of fragmentation and pluralism. More significantly reference to the 'postmodern condition' can include issues of culture, knowledge and socioeconomic trends. As I will show later, postmodern*ist* writers such as Baudrillard and Lyotard draw on a specific set of assumptions about social structure, albeit sometimes implicitly. This chapter will focus on three levels of analysis: macro, societal notions of post-modernity which underpin thinking on organizations; work organizations themselves; and issues of epistemology and methodology. In doing so I am aware of the dangers of 'lumping together' diverse issues and perspectives. Differences will of course be examined, but there is little doubt that a series of overlapping themes have emerged in the postmodern literature that does create considerable common ground. It is appropriate to start by examining the claims made concerning organizations.

The Postbureaucratic Organization?

Parker (1992a: 4) asks how do we recognize a postmodernist organization? The general answer *appears* to be to identify the characteristics of modernism, then look for the opposite. Clegg helps us on both counts. Modernist organization 'may be thought of in terms of Weber's typification of bureaucratised, mechanistic structures of control, as these were subsequently erected upon a fully rationalised base of divided and deskilled labour (1990: 177). For contrast he quotes extensively from Heydebrand:

> it would tend to be small or located in small subunits of larger organisations; its object is typically service or information, if not automated production; its technology is computerised; its division of labour is informal or flexible; and its management structure is functionally decentralised, eclectic and participative, overlapping in many ways with nonmanagerial functions. (Clegg, 1990: 17)

The new diversity is held together by a combination of strong cultures and information networks. As for detailed examples – Benneton, the survival of master bakers in France and East Asian business; only the familiar one of Benneton is substantially consistent with the above description. Japan and Sweden are held by Clegg to offer the main contrasting postmodern futures, so it is appropriate that supportive arguments concerning new forms of management are put forward by Berg:

> Scandinavian companies also seem to have a predilection for loosely coupled corporate structures, such as the matrix form with built-in contradictions . . . ad hocracies in the knowledge industry . . ., organisations as 'tents' rather than palaces . . ., or in organisations with double or even triple authority structures and reporting systems as in the public sector. (1989: 207)

Back to the UK, and we find similar imagery in Mulgan's (1989) account of new organizational forms that manifest a shift from 'strong' to 'weak' power. The former are embodied in a Fordist, bureaucratic regime of rules, hierarchies, predictability and centralization; to be replaced by decentralized, self-regulating, fluid and flexible structures. In Parker's (1992a: 4) words, this world of flexibility has 'no clear centre of power or spatial location'.

This view of organizations is of course consistent with the more general portrait of a postmodernist culture expressing paradox, indeterminacy, heterogeneity and disorganization: a 'general impression of disorientation and chaos', as Bauman notes (1988a: 793). More importantly for the purposes of this chapter, it is also entirely consistent with current thinking in pop-management. Clegg's (1990: 203) diagram of the organizational dimensions of modernity/postmodernity, with its opposites of specialization vs diffusion, bureaucracy vs democracy, mistrust vs trust, disempowerment vs empowerment; could have come straight from the pages of UK gurus such as Handy (1987, 1989) or US equivalents (Naisbett, 1982).

What do we find in such books? Basically the message that large companies can no longer afford to be burdened with bureaucratic structures and procedures and are in the process of eliminating them. Decentralization is a key theme. Handy (1989) in fact claims that it goes further towards the *'federal* organization', whereby central business functions are 'disaggregated' to small or independent units. Modern organizations are in reverse thrust, with initiative, drive and energy coming from the parts, not the centre. This is held to be particularly appropriate to multinationals who are now only concerned with 'keeping watch' on long-term policy and finance. Benneton, of course, is given a lead role, but honourable mentions go to UK companies such as Plessey and British Telecom, new corporate structures based on autonomous profit centres which devolve decision-making and responsibility.

The message is also firmly anti-hierarchical. Flat organizations with no more than four layers are facilitated by a range of factors including 'downsizing' and the 'shrinkage' of the middle layers. The benefit is not only narrowing of status differences, but more effective and direct means of two-way communication. Alternatives to hierarchy come in the form of networking. For Naisbett (1982: 219) networks promote informality and equality and, 'offer what bureaucracies can never deliver – the horizontal link'.

For Handy, the federal organization is also likely to be the *contractual* organization: 'At the extreme the core of an organization need contain no more than a design function, a quality-control function, a costing and estimating function, as well as some co-ordinating management' (1987: 80). We get the usual menu of core and periphery, subcontracting, telecommuting, franchises and small firms. The latter are the result of de-mergers and new initiatives, and exist in loose federations and cooperative relationships with large companies. All are said to be indications of the breakdown of bureaucracy. The new structures are based on professional autonomy and cultures of consent.

A further link with pop-management is the emphasis on *dis*organization. The supposed fact that firms 'seem to be more prepared to live with structural chaos and ambiguity today' (Berg, 1989: 207), is reflected in new titles from old gurus, such as Tom Peters' (1987) *Thriving on Chaos*. This parallels similar themes in the work of Mintzberg (1983) for whom 'tomorrow's organization' is an ad-hocracy, without standardization, rule-bound behaviour, formalization and centralized authority.

With the exception of Mintzberg, such writers are not overly concerned with the consequences for organizational theory. But the postmodernists are. New developments constitute a decisive break with Weber (Clegg, 1990: 2–5, 73–4). The iron cage is no longer required by the drive for efficiency. Neither are organizations any longer dominated by the concern for rationality and planning. Instead they are fundamentally reactive, remedial moves triggered by the inherent uncertainty and disorder in local situations (Cooper and Burrell, 1988). Such behaviour is supposedly characteristic of all organized human activity, Berg (1989: 207) refers to 'the final rejection of the grand narrative of organisations as tightly coupled rational machines run by conscious and mature men in full control of operations and proactive strategic choices'.

If organizations and managers are no longer concerned with bureaucratic rationality, what are they? For many, the answer is a strategic shift to the management of culture, explored in detail within what Cooper (1989: 487) calls organization studies' 'symbolic turn'. This encompasses the well-trodden path of the corporate culture literature (Peters and Waterman, 1982; Deal and Kennedy, 1982); the more academic interest in language and symbolism (Turner, 1989); to the linguistic applications of poststructuralists such as Derrida (Cooper, 1989). Postmodernists are particularly interested in deconstructing the taken-for-granted aspects of images, signs and symbols, as it is through those that we construct and interpret the world. However, the postmodern perspective, though not named as such, has been popularized through the best-selling *Images of Organisation* (1986), in which Morgan presents organizational practices through a series of contrasting metaphors which are supposed to help us 'read' workplace life.

Postmodernity as Context

Why are organizations postbureaucratic? For Clegg (1990) postmodern corporations are an *organizational response* to broader changes in the socioeconomic environment. In his analysis, as with many other writers, modernism is represented by Fordism at the level of work organization. To square the circle of argument Fordist bureaucracy and Taylorist task specialization are said to decline under the impact of flexible accumulation as a new stage of capitalism (Harvey, 1989). Hence postmodernism is linked to and underpinned by a family of theories including post-Fordism (Hall and Jacques, 1989), flexible specialization (Piore and Sabel, 1984) and disorganized capitalism (Lash and Urry, 1987). Indeed, though he emphasizes elements of continuity to the past, Harvey manages to put both together under the common label 'flexible postmodernism' (Smart, 1992: 192). The themes of flexibility and disorganization are particularly supportive of the broader postmodern themes of disaggregation and diversity of capital, culture and political management.

For other theorists the equation modernism = industrialism still holds sway. As indicated earlier, Lyotard (1984) and Baudrillard (1983b) are primarily concerned with attacking the grand scientific discourses of Western modernism. But their focus on the conditions of knowledge rests easily with comments on the condition of society. In particular they draw uncritically on notions of postindustrialism, with all its end of ideology baggage (Boyne and Rattsani, 1990). The imagery of postmodern society is particularly dependent upon the primacy of information, computerization and knowledge (Best and Kellner, 1991: 166).

Whatever the label, new forms of information and technology are held to be a driving force of social and organizational change. Generally the assumed consequences are optimistic. Production and services can improve efficiency and flexibility; organizations can devolve responsibility and spread power, consistent with postmodern images of plurality and communication through language-games. The 'dark side' of information society is represented in the analysis of Poster (1984). He stresses the surveillance and control potential, which in turn is used by Burrell (1988) to justify the relevance of an updated version of Foucault, with computer architecture rather than the Panoptican playing the starring role.

If society is postindustrial, culture is postmodern and that culture is expressed through *consumption* and driven by the logic of the market. At least that is the line taken by some commentators on postmodernity (Jameson, 1984; Bauman, 1988a). Unafraid to totalize, Jameson gives 'consumer society' a Marxist tag by referring to postmodernism as the cultural logic of late capitalism. As capital seeks new and global territories to commodify, it establishes both a different socioeconomic order based on consumerism, advertising, information and reconstruction of the city; and an appropriate cultural dominant expressed through postmodernism. Joining Jameson in the periodization stakes, Bauman also charts the shift from work, wage labour and production to consumption: 'in the present-day society, consumer conduct (consumer freedom geared to the consumer market) moves steadily into the position of simultaneously, the cognitive and moral focus of life, integrative bond of the society, and the focus of systemic management' (1988a: 807). Consumerism enables Bauman to utilize themes from Durkheim (integrative bonds), Weber (purposeful rationality through systemic management) and Marx (new stage of capitalism) in an ever more bizarre combination. Whereas Bell

was afraid that the hedonistic excesses of consumer culture would undermine the stability of postindustrial capitalism (O'Neill, 1988: 494);
Bauman sees it as sweeping away the system's problems. The market
brings with it the pressures and pleasures of seduction by the symbolism
of spending power. So effective is this seduction that capital can dispense
with repression and much of its apparatus of control, the need for
political legitimation and ideological domination (O'Neill, 1988: 809–10).
Of course there are differences between the three on issues of scope and
content. But the core focus on and account of the changing relations
between production, consumption and political regulation contains
substantial similarities. We meet once again an economic logic as the
stable markets, large corporations, mass production and interventionist
state characteristic of Fordism is replaced by sovereign consumers seeking
specialized goods in niche markets, served by decentralized companies
with flexible products, technologies and manpower; with the state
retreating to take a back seat. And, as Reed (1989: 14) notes, 'underlying
each of these perspectives one can identify a shared logic of explanation
relating to the process of disorganisation and its longer term institutional
impact'.

Critique

We have to start with evidence, the quality and quantity of which is
signally deficient for the perspectives outlined above. My main concern is
with challenging the picture of organizations, but I will make some brief
remarks about the macro-underpinnings first.

Society

Callinicos (1989: 122–3) begins a detailed and effective critique by observing that 'The idea of post-industrial society is, of course, nonsense', based
on a misreading of economic trends and their consequences. Though the
employment figures show a shift to services, manufacturing remains the
core activity of capitalist societies; its decline in countries such as the UK
is in part a result of contingent national economic strategies. Some
services have been replaced by manufacturing, for example public
transport services; and many services are either connected to manufacturing or increasingly resemble highly controlled, standardized and
fragmented industrial work. The last point is particularly important in
that the impression given of this postindustrial or information society is
of an ever-growing number of professional and white-collar 'knowledge
workers'. This is a nonsensical category given that information-handling
is an aspect of virtually all jobs, and ignores the army of low-paid,
deskilled service workers.

Postmodernism is particularly dependent in its imagery on this notion
of an information age that has broken with industrialism or the mode of

production. But the 'reproduction' of information is not separate from capitalism. This overlooks:

> the fact the information that most corporations rely on has to do with such things as accounting, which is to say, with the tracking of the efficiency in wages paid and prices extracted, with in other words the very material world of production that informationalism supposedly replaces. (Ryan, 1988: 567)

Writers such as Lyotard simply do not know enough about the relations between technology, capital and social development to sustain their claims. Lacking a macro-theory of their own, they simply have to trade on others (Kellner, 1988a: 250). Postmodernists are only the latest in a long line of academics infatuated with technology. Whether regarded as liberatory or ushering a Foucauldian nightmare of total surveillance, we are still getting a technical determinist vision. When Cooper (1992) says that 'More than anything else, it's technology which gives the modern organisation its special character', it is as if the whole debate on the social construction of technology never happened.

When reading the accounts of the new consumerism from Bauman, Jameson and others, the feeling again grows that we have been down this way before. The end of work as a focal interest and the workplace as a source of social conflict was a recurrent theme of postwar sociology (Kerr et al., 1963). It is now dressed up in new language, so we talk of the 'decentring of work' (Bauman, 1988a: 808), but the claims are even more excessive and misguided. For example, the claim that, 'capitalism has won the struggle for control over production' (Bauman, 1988a: 808), is hardly consistent with the wealth of literature on worker resistance in labour process and industrial relations literature. Even Clegg (1990: 17) is moved to note that the failure to recognize developments in the world of work is Bauman's 'one blind spot'. Jameson is not as bad, and provides some sensitive readings of cultural trends, but the account of the underpinnings of a new stage of 'multinational capitalism' lacks detail and is again largely borrowed (Kellner, 1988a: 258–9, Callinicos, 1989: 133).

Such borrowings also reinforce the capacity of postmodernists to exaggerate the breaks and ruptures of historical development. But an even more depressing aspect of the interrelationship is that labels and concepts frequently become interchangeable, as if modernism, capitalism, industrialism and Fordism are minor variations on the same phenomenon. Is there really any such thing as 'modernist regimes of mass consumption?' (Clegg, 1990: 135). Though accounts of post-modernity stress the goal of explaining the *connections* between the cultural, economic, social and political, much of it is based on a highly reductionist appeal to socioeconomic developments (Crook, 1990: 55; Callinicos, 1989: 135). We see this particularly in Jameson's analysis of cultural logics of late capitalism. Best and Kellner (1991: 188) comment: 'Like extreme postmodernists, Jameson tends to inflate insights that apply to limited sectors of contemporary social life into overly general concepts representing all social spheres, thereby failing to analyse each sphere in its specificity.'

The final set of borrowings from the flexibility and post-Fordism literature is particularly unfortunate given that it has 'attracted a veritable torrent of criticism' (Reed, 1991a). Setting aside the more specific issue of flexibility of labour, the main thrust of the critiques (Williams et al., 1987; Murray, 1987; Meegan, 1988; Pollert, 1988; Hyman, 1988; Thompson and McHugh, 1990) is that Fordism as a way of organizing work and the economy has never fitted most sectors of industry in the UK; that mass production and mass consumption are far from dead; and conversely that there is little evidence that customized niche markets are the main trend, even on 'home territory' such as Emilia Romagna. Unfortunately most of these points are largely ignored or treated as if they never existed in the literature of postmodernity, which is happy to use theories which lack any substantial empirical basis.

Bureaucracy: A Premature Burial

This is not the first time that bureaucracy has been declared dead, and the evidence is not much better on this occasion, as we can see if some of the basic features of bureaucratic work organization are re-examined.

Centralization and Hierarchy

Organizations *are* frequently becoming leaner and more decentralized, but these trends can be interpreted very differently than the fundamental break with centralized bureaucracy present in postmodern imagery. Essentially what we are seeing is a duality in which the decentralization of the labour process and production decisions (through mechanisms as diverse as profit centres, subcontracting and quality circles); is combined with increased centralization of power and control over the spatially dispersed, but interdependent units. These processes can and do operate on an international level, as Hyman notes: 'Advances in computerisation and telecommunications facilitate the concentration of "conception" (research, planning, directive and strategic management) at corporate headquarters, while "execution" is dispersed around the globe' (1988: 13). We can see that an enhanced technological capacity is crucial, but as a facilitator, not an independent driving force. New forms of IT software and hardware – such as management information systems or decision-support systems – put knowledge in the hands of senior decision-makers, which aids long-term strategic planning, as well as detailed monitoring of schedules, inventories and costs lower down the corporate structure. Local and lower management may have increased operational autonomy and delegated responsibilities, but mostly within a more tightly controlled framework. Take British Telecom: their system of profit centres relies on accounting structures and marketing forecasts to allocate and control costs. Decentralization is therefore accompanied by strengthened financial controls which tie district managers even more tightly to central budgets imposed from above (Hallet, 1988: 35). Information thus wraps itself around existing power structures unless a political struggle in the organization dictates otherwise.

Extensive opportunities exist on the shop and office floor to electronically monitor and reintegrate decentralized tasks and locations. Supervisors and managers can keep track of caseloads and set new targets in the insurance industry (Baran, 1988), or use computerized data to monitor workers' productivity status and check labour costs against other plants (Giordano, 1988). The very process of dispersal to decentralized production sites in advanced and developing countries requires considerably more complex coordination and tighter control mechanisms. For example, to complement its 'world car' that can be sold in all major markets, General Motors bought a company called Electronic Data Systems. This will allow instant global communications so that a highly centralized management can run its operations around the world as one factory (*International Labour Reports*, 1986).

A similar trend towards a combination of centralization and devolved structures can be observed in the process of merger and acquisition (Thompson et al., 1991). The large predators, faced with complex problems of coordination, may necessarily allow degrees of operational autonomy. But they also have at their disposal an increasingly sophisticated range of financial and strategic controls, monitoring devices, targets and reward systems that can regulate the management of subsidiaries. These are potentially more powerful than the older and more direct methods.

The merger and acquisition process highlights another important weakness of the postmodern perspective. To argue that contemporary forms of organization are essentially reactive, chaotic and put little emphasis on planning and control is particularly foolish when many spend a considerable proportion of their time and resources rationally calculating which firm to swallow up, which market to move into and what to spend their cash mountain on. In other words any decline in instrumental rationality is strictly in the minds of postmodernists, who must have some difficulty coming to terms with the dominant position of accountants in the apex of modern corporations.

Postbureaucratic arguments not only wrongly interpret changes in the structure of modern organizations, they vastly overestimate the extent of the challenge to the domination of the large firm itself arising from small firms, subcontracting, franchises and the like. In fact the power of large firms is at its strongest over the smaller units, disaggregated or otherwise. We already know from Japan that parent corporations can exercise 'hegemonic power' over the satellite firms that supply them (Kumazawa and Yamada, 1988). But in the UK also Rainnie (1988) shows that the much-vaunted partnership between the two is largely a myth, and dependency rather than interdependence is the norm. As with the more general process of decentralization, it allows corporations to transfer costs and uncertainties on to the small firm who may be treated as a servicing unit for uneconomic activities. Many retailers use exclusivity clauses to control suppliers. For example, in the clothing industry a huge network caters for the needs of the major high-street retail chains who are able to dictate methods and profit margins. In turn this creates less-than-benign pressures towards a low-pay, low-skill sweatshop economy based on small workshops and homeworking (Mitter, 1985).

An equally clear example can be seen in the rapidly growing number of *franchises*. Felstead shows that the business format imposed by the central company lays down precise procedures, criteria and often performance targets governing the operations of franchisees. Agreements, such as those imposed by MacDonalds, frequently contain clauses that stipulate that contracts can be unilaterally modified by the franchisor, or that restrain ex-franchisees from engaging in similar types of business. By restricting the transference of 'know-how' and accumulated business experience to its franchisees alone, a dependent relationship is developed. Ironically, given the postmodern emphasis on language, the original French meaning 'freedom from servitude or restraint' bears little relationship to a situation which, 'Both in terms of the day-to-day operation and in terms of longer-term trajectory, franchisors are armed with a whole battery of control mechanisms designed to induce franchisees into their service' (Felstead, 1991: 47).

What about *hierarchy*? Decentralized, yet highly structured organizations indicate a 'constriction rather than elimination of managerial hierarchy' (Giordano, 1988: 181). Companies such as MacDonalds and Coloroll claim 'no-boss' structures, yet there are elaborate hierarchies based on incentives, badges and grades. Removing some of the middle layers of organizations is not the same as altering the basic power structure. For example, special management teams can cut across existing hierarchies and strengthen overall corporate goals at the expense of the potentially conflicting demands from rival departments. By cutting out intermediary levels and getting project teams to report directly to senior management, the power resources of those at the top can be increased. The increasingly popular anti-bureaucracy device of removing 'time-wasting' committees removes the main base for the formation of coalitions that have traditionally been a source of countervailing power in organizations.

Accepting that there is a trend towards more flexible firms, albeit exaggerated, means that we have to widen our conception of hierarchy beyond the internal structures and labour market to include the activities dispersed to those indirectly employed to provide services or labour by the large firm. This makes Benneton, though innovative in its own right, not quite the epitome of postbureaucracy it appears. For the extended hierarchy of decentralized, subcontracted production work inside Italy and franchised sales throughout Europe, is held firmly together by a centralized marketing function and complete managerial control over the design, cutting, and finishing of garments.

Changing the Rules

Rules are at the heart of bureaucratic organization. The continual focus on the ending of 'inflexible' work rules has given the impression of organizational life based on much looser informal arrangements or rules. We have already, however, observed that managerial use of information technology can add to financial control and monitoring of activities. The 'integrative logic' of such systems creates *decision-rules*. That is: 'operating procedures are designed into the computer programs by a small group of managers, systems analysts, and programmers, users have little comprehension of the system's overall function or the normative criteria on which it was based' (Baran, 1988: 698–9). Flexibility and interchangeability of functions is entirely compatible with extremely tight job and task specifications, as experience at companies as diverse as Nissan and MacDonald indicates. At the latter total flexibility among crew members is combined with standardized products and precise planning of subdivided tasks, underwritten by 'the book' – a 385-page operations manual crammed with detail such as 'Cooks must turn, never flip, hamburgers one, never two at a time . . . cashiers must make eye contact and smile at every customer' (Silver, 1987: 109). The tools of industrial bureaucracy and their uses to time, classify and record work are, if anything, becoming more sophisticated in nature.

This is not to deny that traditional task-based rules have declined in some sectors of the economy. However, that does not mean that the *overall* amount of bureaucratic regulation has lessened. One important trend is a shift from task to *behavioural* rules. Indeed the two processes are linked. Flexibility and QWL-type initiatives rely heavily on the performance of workers who are technically unskilled or semi-skilled, but behaviourally highly skilled. Such skills include cooperativeness, adaptability and self-discipline. This shift has a number of consequences for managerial policies and practices.

Recruitment and selection is receiving more prominence in relation to routine manual or clerical workers. Though Japanese companies in the UK are predictably leading the way some Western firms are catching up. Even franchisors are using lengthening waiting lists to develop more sophisticated vetting procedures. A major purpose of the new practices is the *screening-out* of those with 'undesirable' attitudes and an early start to continuous socialization. The latter can be followed through by an extended role for training and employee development programmes.

An increased role for behavioural skills leads to a requirement for assessment of the 'responsible worker', beyond the narrow task sphere. Criteria may include positive attitudes such as loyalty to the company or participation in quality circles. Again this means an important role for the supervisor, who may have added duties for monitoring of attendance and timekeeping in the absence of 'clocking on'. This is an integral feature of the growing number of individual appraisal and performance-related pay schemes. Indeed many professional employees are being incorporated into rule-governed bureaucratic regulation for the first time through a variety of performance review measures.

Though it sometimes masquerades as part of the trend away from bureaucracy, corporate culture is very much part of the orientation towards behavioural rules. As Deal and Kennedy (1988: 15) admit, 'Strong culture companies go into the trouble of spelling out, often in copious detail, the routine behavioural rituals they expect their employees to carry out.' Postmodernists also agree that culture is the glue that holds the decentralized parts of the new organization together, but seem to miss the point about the bureaucratic consequences. This is well put by Weick:

> whenever you have what appears to be a successful decentralisation, if you look more closely, you will discover that it was always preceded by a period of intense centralisation where a set of core values were hammered out and socialised into people before the people were turned loose to go their own 'independent' ways. (Quoted in Alvesson, 1990b: 42)

Even Reed (Chapter 10 in this volume) gets this process wrong, counterposing cultural–normative forms of control to technical–bureaucratic ones.

Overall then the postbureaucratic position can be seen more as symbol than reality. Specific trends such as decentralization or smaller organizations are either misinterpreted or their significance is overestimated. Too much emphasis has been given to either a small range of unrepresentative examples, or 'leading edge' sectors and companies. With some exceptions the whole concept of bureaucracy has become devalued through its lazy and stereotypical usage. Changes in the form and content of hierarchies, plus shifts in rule-governed behaviour, indicate that we have to constantly renew our understanding of bureaucratic processes. The 'break with bureaucracy' fits nicely into an era when entrepreneurial activities are a highly valued part of the cultural and political climate. It is a pity that postmodernism has seen fit to endorse the sweeping statements and global prophecies so characteristic of pop-management. Having made this critique, we now turn to examining the 'safer' ground of epistemology.

Postmodernism and Epistemology

The epistemological path of postmodernism was established by poststructuralist writers such as Deleuze, Derrida and Foucault in the 1970s; all stressing the fragmentary and plural character of reality (Callinicos, 1989: 2). This concern with multiple viewpoints is strongly influenced by Nietzsche and his 'perspectivism' in which constructs of individuals or groups replace facts or objective truths. Given that discourses cannot escape the mark of their producers, who in turn bear the mark of their social identity and interests, 'epistemic suspicion is at the core of postmodernism' (Seidman, 1992: 68). Objectivity is thus not the only game in town, and not even desirable given that rationalistic methodology suppresses a multitude of alternative voices (Gergen, 1992). There are, of course, a variety of positions within the poststructuralist and postmodern spectrum.

The extreme of the anti-science position is taken to be Baudrillard with his concept of *hyperreality*. In a world of MTV and Disneyland information dissolves meaning and everything is a spectacle in which it is no longer possible to distinguish between real and fictive, or to recognize distortion of reality, as there is nothing left to measure it against. But the inseparability of reality and representation is a constant theme of postmodernism. The consequences can be seen in the following quote from Hebdige: 'It is no longer possible for us to see through the appearance of, for instance, a "free market" to the structuring "real relations" beneath (e.g. class conflict and the expropriation by capital of surplus value)' (1989: 51).

As for truth, it may be seen as a product of *language-games* in which we need not assume a reasoning agent or mind. Reality is constituted through shared language and we can only know it through discourse. Not surprisingly this leads to the equally famous – nothing exists outside the text. The real is governed wholly by the process of *calling* (Gergen, 1992), and Parker (1992a: 6) notes that 'things "out there" like the market, employees and customers are called into being by language'.

But not all postmodernists reduce everything to textuality (Best and Kellner, 1991: 27). Following Nietzsche, Foucault and others see truth as linked to a will to power, though still part of discursive techniques and practices. They prefer to talk of 'truth effects', a position supported by a number of contributors to this volume (see Chapter 2, by Jeffcutt, and Chapter 3 by Linstead). Berg (1989: 214) spells out the consequences with commendable honesty; 'In organisation and management science today it is not important whether a statement is true or false, but whether the fact or statement is accepted, saleable or valid for a larger audience.' Similarly Gergen (1992) argues that whether something is true or accurate is unimportant; an orientation seemingly reproduced in Chapter 5 of this volume, by Carter and Jackson: 'We are not particularly concerned with validity of any theory of motivation to work, but with their logics and contradictions.' Any capacity to agree on truth or validity is undermined by the incommensurability of perspectives and language-games. Theories thus operate self-referentially or in respect of local 'communities', building on ideas of self-enclosed discourse established by structuralists and poststructuralists (Callinicos, 1989; Crook, 1990).

Much of this is argued in a way that is largely incidental to organizational analysis. Though Gergen (1992) argues that managerial functions are constituted discursively; while Cooper (1989: 25–6) distinguishes between organization by representation and enactment; and we have

Morgan's (1986) attempt to persuade us that we are living in an organizational world constituted by images of what is real.

However, to return to more general themes, what about the practice that accompanies such epistemology? Deconstruction of all forms of representation and signification is the favoured route. Existing systems of knowledge can be 'unravelled, until their origin in human praxis is exposed' (Murphy, 1988: 602). The search is for differences, gaps and instabilities in time, space and text (Cooper, 1989). This process is consistent with Foucault's genealogical method which seeks to uncover the social processes in the making of totalizing narratives or essentialist discourses.

Critique

I shall not deal extensively with the scientific riposte to this, as has been well-rehearsed elsewhere (Dews, 1986). Instead I will focus on the contradictions and negative consequences for theorizing in general, and for organizational theory in particular, that arise from treating the world as a text.

The idea that there is nothing beneath the surface of representation is absurd and dangerous. As Norris observes:

> The response to all this could take various forms, among them the flat rejoinder that there are real and present facts of experience – inequality, deprivation, urban squalor, unemployment, massive and increasing differentials of wealth and power – which make nonsense of Baudrillard's sophistical case that nothing exists outside the endless circulation of ungrounded arbitrary signs. (1990: 147)

As Norris goes on to argue, Baudrillard makes an unjustifiable move from a description of certain trends in contemporary social life, to an epistemological stance that denies any claims of validity or truth. Uncovering the difference between appearance and essence, as Marx put it, is still the prime purpose of intellectual enquiry. Such activity cannot stop at language. Gergen (1992) poses the rhetorical question, 'abandon all talk of profit and loss and what happens to economic enterprise?' My answer would be – *nothing* necessarily happens. After all, the managerial revolution discourse was built entirely round such 'talk'. Though the way that managers *understood* it changed, capitalism went on regardless.

As for deconstruction, we can all agree with the need to break down taken-for-granted assumptions in texts. The issue is *how*? Once again, proceeding through the 'minutiae of language-games' (Reed, 1990b: 38), or the 'prison house of discourse' (Norris, 1990: 143) can be very limited. While it may allow us to spot inconsistencies and metaphors, it does not enable us to reveal the interests and power structures that underpin texts. Take the example of 'mission statements' which have become the order of the day in many organizations. We could have a very interesting time deconstructing them, but the priority should be to investigate the gap between rhetoric and substance in areas such as equal opportunity.

Keeping these points in mind, the need to theorize through creating pictures of reality is inescapable. We can see this again and again in the work of the epistemological postmodernists such as Foucault, Baudrillard and Lyotard. They rely implicitly or explicitly on periodization to establish breaks with the modern and totalization to capture the characteristics of a given era or society. As has been widely noted (Boyne and Rattansi, 1990: 39–40), postmodernism is itself a meta-narrative, and one that is greatly undertheorized. The issue, then, is what *kind* of narrative and generalization, avoiding teleological explanation or forms of totalization that impairs much theorizing. Arguments that it is impossible to grasp the whole of reality within a single analytical framework are well taken. But that does not invalidate social theory that seeks to generalize and make truth claims across more limited territories. That is different from purely 'local' narratives that remain locked in self-limited space and time, and are fragmentary in focusing on the perceptions and experiences of particular groupings. The limitations can be seen in Seidman's (1992: 72) argument that postmodern local narratives would not be transnational in their focus, but centred on particular nations or social units. Not very useful in an increasingly globalized economy. Best and Kellner (1991: 260) put the alternative well: 'Our position is that while it is impossible to produce a fixed and exhaustive knowledge of a constantly changing complex of social processes, it is possible to map the fundamental domains, structures, practices and discourses of a society, and how they are constituted and interact.'

If the above is correct then the distinction between postmodernism and postmodernity collapses. Those working within the latter sphere, such as Jameson and Bauman, are happy to theorize in such a manner. Others persist in pursuing the pretence that they are not making ontological claims and are thus able to avoid specifying the elements of societal analysis or have it subject to adjudication. The last point is important. For if such intellectual activity is inevitable then there must be rules of analysis and evidence through which it is judged. Postmodernists fail to 'distinguish between the frameworks within which sociological theorising must proceed from the knowledge generated by employing those frameworks' (Seidman and Wagner, 1992: 8–9). It is not enough to evaluate theory 'in terms of its challenge to the taken for granted and its simultaneous capacity to open new departures for action' (Gergen, 1992: 48). Nor is there anything inherently useful in a multitude of voices or 'carnivalesque discourses' (Jeffcutt, Chapter 2 in this volume), if any sense of organizational reality is lost in the babble. Aside from the need to establish accuracy within competing claims, it is sometimes better to seek common languages of communication, action and analysis in order to understand and change the world.

One of the consequences of this epistemological failure can be seen in the extreme relativism of Morgan's *Images of Organisation*. As Reed shows in his brilliant critique, there is no way of adjudicating which metaphors or combination of them actually describe the reality of organizations: 'Organisation theory is transformed into a supermarket of metaphors which its customers can visit to purchase and consume its conceptual wares according to their brand preferences and purchasing power (1990b: 38). So myopically is Morgan's gaze fixed on the text and language-games, he is unable to explain the actual historical and social processes of knowledge production, dissemination and evolution. This highlights the dangers of self-enclosed discourse raised earlier. We see the same sort of problems arising in the attempt by Cooper (1989) to apply the work of Derrida. Writing is held to be fundamental to the division of labour, but because the two divisions of labour are collapsed into one another we never get any real sense of the organizational or social context. So, though Cooper rightly notes that organization always harbours disorganization, the countermovements are conceived as solely textual. The problems with research such as the Aston Studies are presented not as innacuracy about the structuring process, but as a product of the methods through which they are represented.

This reinforces the point about self-enclosed discourses raised earlier, the effects of which are again seen in this volume. Organizational issues are frequently reduced to 'paradoxes of textuality' (Jeffcutt), 'inter-textuality' (Linstead), or 'second level metaphors' are used to explain the meaning of the original metaphors used by other authors (Alvesson).

Enclosed discourse and self-referentiality also tend to legitimize the obscurantism of much of postmodern writing. Some wonderfully inventive excuses are made for Derrida (Cooper, 1989: 481) and Foucault (Burrell, 1988: 222), but if intelligibility is a criterion, it is a test many would fail. Even worse is when obscurity is introduced through *renaming* original concepts. A clear example can be seen in Townley's (1990) attempt to marry Foucault to the personnel manager. Determined to find the operation of 'disciplinary practices' centring on the creation of order and knowledge, she utilizes his three dividing practices – enclosure, partitioning and ranking. The problem is that all the examples, labels and descriptive material come from existing theory and research. Foucauldian terminology adds nothing to the process. However, Townley's allied purpose is to convince us of the relevance of the approach to an analysis of organizational power. As this has been one of the few areas of direct application of postmodernism and poststructuralism to organizational theory, it is to this that we now turn.

An Example – Power

There are two dimensions of current applications of postmodernism to power which I want to briefly discuss, not so much as a discussion of power in its own right, but as further illustration of the problems of postmodern epistemology. Both derive in part from Foucault and refer to the location of power and to the role of language and knowledge.

On the issue of location, poststructuralism presents power as everywhere and nowhere; 'ubiquitous, but ultimately uncentred power relations' (Boyne and Rattansi, 1990: 18). Postmodern imagery of social life as fragmented and pluralistic is echoed in analyses of power as diverse, shifting, unstable, and with no originating source of action, but rather an endless series of contingencies (Clegg, 1989: 9). Above all it is stressed that power is not *possessed* by individuals, groups or functions, but is always a *relationship*, implying positive-sum rather than zero-sum outcomes. In this sense, such analysis is limited to the decentring of the subject. That is, power is understood without reference to agency, its mechanisms impersonal and independent of conscious subjects.

Turning to language, this is seen as the central feature of the discursive constitution of power. Townley invokes Foucault to explain personnel practices as a power/knowledge discourse: 'Personnel may in this sense be understood as the provision of language or knowledge, in order to reduce the "space" resulting from the unspecified nature of contract' (1990: 7). She restates his argument that there is no power relationship or change in power without a correlative constitution of language or field of knowledge.

The two elements of plurality and language are briefly brought together by Gergen. Professions or functional divisions in organizations attempt to achieve power through developing 'local definitions of the real and the good and coordinate their actions around such definitions' (1992: 221). Their languages of power create localized worlds, insulating them from each other, while the multiple fields of power disenable the organization as a whole. Equally Townley (1990: 23) remarks that 'A Foucauldian conception of power does not imply the domination of one group over another, but rather illustrates how all are implicated.'

There are important themes raised in the Foucauldian analysis of power appropriated by postmodernists. An emphasis on the relations between power and knowledge can generate critical interpretations of professions such as accounting (Burchell et al., 1985). It is also perfectly reasonable to recognize diverse forms and locations of power, as well as the role of language in their constitution. But the flaws vastly outweigh any benefits.

It is one thing to claim that language is an important resource for the way that power is identified, shaped and fought out, and another to say that *of necessity* it is brought into being by, and is indissolubly linked to, language. Let me give two examples. Gergen (1992: 219) deconstructs the meaning of the statement 'Let's be logical about this: the bottom line would be the closing of the Portsmouth division.' There may indeed be multiple meanings to words such as logical or bottom line but the *outcome* may be the same, as management power to close the plant is not dependent on them.

The second example is drawn from my own previous research on industrial relations at Plessey plants on Merseyside, and is directed against Townley's account of personnel practice. There had been a long-standing toleration by management of senior stewards spending time in the pub. Then one day in 1983 the key union officer was called from the pub and sacked. There is no evidence whatsoever that management action was premised on or required any change in language or field of knowledge. Of course over a period of time the linguistic resources used by management will change and develop dialectically in relation to their social context. But in this example the shift in power relations was primarily a result of labour market circumstances. As one worker commented, making comparisons to the rosier 1970s; 'the order books were full and labour was in short supply. The attitude from the company now is, if you don't like it, go. There are three million on the dole, so who needs you?' (Thompson and Bannon, 1985: 93). In the context of accounting controls Armstrong (1991: 28–9) makes a similar point that Foucauldian analyses tend to idealize disciplinary power and present it without reference to material sanctions or rewards.

On the issue of the location of power we can return to Gergen's reference to relations between professions or functional divisions. Unfortunately there is no sense of what each 'power of functioning' can be measured against. Such groups do not just develop local rationalities and fight linguistic battles. A far more persuasive account can be found in Armstrong's (1984) work on interprofessional competition. Here personnel, engineering and accountancy are shown to be competing agencies to carry out functions on behalf of capital in the enterprise. Given that each profession has a core of specialist knowledge and activities that can form of the basis of its collective power, language is a resource in that struggle. But more importantly they are frequently competing in the same space, so that such struggles result in winners and losers, in this case accountants, not just a plurality of ever-shifting localized powers.

With reference to management and their agents, power is therefore *somewhere*. Though Foucault and Baudrillard both fail to identify any actual power structures or dominant groups (Best and Kellner, 1991), it remains legitimate to speak of power 'holders'. That is, power is both a relationship and controlled and administered by individuals or collectivities. Paradoxically because Foucault and other writers see power as everywhere and nowhere, it can equally wrongly be presented as omnipresent. And while it is not also omnipotent, the dice are loaded against resistance, because 'only power is positive and productive, while resistance is simply a reaction to its productions' (Dews, 1986: 99). Burrell (1988) typifies how such frameworks are incorporated into organizational analysis. Interpreting Foucault's analysis of the movement from traditional to disciplinary modes of domination, he explains that disciplinary techniques are hidden within all forms of organization. Hospitals, factories and anything else are presented as paler versions of carceral institutions, with prisons as the model. As an example, Burrell refers to the control of sexuality, 'Organizations such as the prison, or the ship at sea or the commercial enterprise are all-alike in their attempts to suppress sexuality and are all-alike in the failure to do so' (1988: 233). Furthermore as individuals we are all incarcerated within an organizational world and the arm of discipline reaches so far that we are even imprisoned as we sit alone at our desks (1988: 228). With this kind of 'power everywhere' thinking, it is hard to disagree with Dew's (1986: 166) judgement that the concept 'loses its explanatory content and becomes a ubiquitous metaphysical principle'.

Conclusion

To conclude we need to return to more general themes and the main body of postmodernist analysis. I have tried to demonstrate both the limited relevance and the distorted applications to an understanding of organizations. Much of the problem arises from trying to apply concepts and approaches designed for literary and cultural purposes. I have long believed that the further a body of knowledge travels from its origins, the worse and more vulnerable it gets. Away from that context, modernism and postmodernism become conceptual catch-alls, conflating quite distinct social processes. In her attack on the applications of post-modernism to architecture, G. Rose (1988: 364) notes that 'Architecture, social theory and philosophy seem to be complicit in exchanging each other's most undifferentiated and general concepts and theses.' A particularly horrible instance of the broader problem is Hebdige's exposition of postmodernism for readers of *Marxism Today*:

> The violence that can flow from the fusion of centralised power structures, Fordist production models, aggressive modernisation and a debased version of Modern Movement architectural principles is nowhere more apparent than in Romania today where the 70 year old Ceausescu is engaged in a village-levelling exercise. (1989: 49)

When not obliterating differences, postmodernists are busy demonizing their opponents. So science and grand narratives are out because Auschwitz commanders used bureaucratic methods and listened to Beethoven whilst carrying out mass murder (Clegg, 1990: 12). Or how about this for original sin? 'The collapse of "really existing socialism" is the result of taking the promises of the enlightenment too seriously' (Tester, 1990: 161).

It may be true that 'Literary critics are producing some of the most exciting theory currently available' (Murphy, 1988: 602). But that does not mean that analysis of organizations, social structure, and that of art in the broadest sense share the same rules. If I dislike postmodern architecture or the films of David Lynch, or reject absolute standards against which to judge pop-art or Bruce Springsteen, then that is a matter of *preference*. But if I argue that organizations *are* postbureaucratic, then it is not a matter of preference but of *proof*.

In what sense, then, is postmodernism a distraction? I believe it represents a retreat from engagement by sections of the intelligentsia. This can be viewed *politically*. Commentators have certainly made a good case that the abandonment of rationality and progress frequently involves a worship of the new and uncritical presentation of capital as innovator (Shusterman, 1988); a new form of irrationalism and neo-conservatism (Habermas, 1985); or a product of the disillusioned turn inwards and rightwards of the 1968 generation (Callinicos, 1989). Sympathetic though I am to such critiques, it is impossible to demonstrate that postmodernism is *inherently reactionary*. Multiple realities and readings of the text mean that it can be all things to all people, or as Boyne and Rattansi (1990: 28) put it, 'Textual politics depend in part upon the modes of appropriation adopted by other actors, by activists, writers, artists and so on.' Some uses can be progressive, such as the emphasis on decentring the sovereign subject, the exploration of multiple identities, and the challenge to traditional hierarchies of knowledge.

The mode of appropriation adopted by the postmodern*ists*, as opposed to the advocates of postmodern*ity*, does represent a backward step in our field of studies. For years those from a radical perspective have criticized mainstream theories for viewing organizations in a largely self-contained world and for neglecting the relationship with societal structures of power and domination. Just when organizational analysis was beginning to discover the relationships between its traditional domain and the wider world, we are encouraged to retreat into the text.

Once there, we can sit back, switch into ironic detachment mode and engage in 'serious play' with Gergen who, however, is not above suggesting a few uses of postmodern insights to those which run organizations. For example, 'The ideal of the organisation as a smoothly running machine, clean and austerely effective becomes dangerous. Rather from the present perspective, organisational survival depends ultimately on the insinuation of polyglot, immersion in metaphor, and the prevalence of creative confusion' (1991: 26). Elsewhere Blackler (1992) argues that postmodern insights are important to the management of 'disjunctive' organizational changes. We are back on the pop-management terrain of 'thriving on chaos'.

Even when not playing with words, we are often back to a concern with *process*, rather than content, or 'the production of organisation rather than the organisation of production' (Cooper and Burrell, quoted in Parker, 1992a: 5). There are parallels here with the 'progress' of Silverman and action theory which also became gradually disconnected from wider issues, and 'buried in an obsessive concern for the minutiae of "everyday life" as exemplified in the intricacies of organisational routines' (Reed, 1985: 48). Indeed the presentation of the benefits of postmodern epistemology by some writers (Murphy, 1988, Platt, 1989) sounds remarkably like symbolic interactionism and the work of Garfinkel, Schutz and Mead; but with the added miracle ingredient of language games.

Never having thought of myself as such, it is disconcerting to have the epithet 'modernist' flung at me. I have never regarded science as neutral, and long ago stopped believing in the inevitability of progress, whether through the working class or any other agency. But I obstinately cling to the idea that knowledge and rational inquiry can be modest aids to illuminating and changing society. Postmodernists have got away with reifying 'science' as if it has a life independent of the purposes to which it is put (as in Seidman, 1992: 51), presenting rationality as if it necessarily depends on meta-narrative or teleology. As Mike Reed points out in this volume (Chapter 10) there are and always have been tensions in modernism. Critical and instrumental rationalities have done battle in a whole tradition from Weber and Marx, through to Habermas. The intellectual tools of the critical tradition of modern theory remain an indispensable means to 'recognise the differentiation and fragmentation within modernity, while also providing a language that addresses its integrative and macroscopic features' (Best and Kellner, 1991: 258).

12

Life After Jean-François

Martin Parker

Problems with the Reader

If you have read this book from beginning to end, in the manner prescribed in the introduction, you will have engaged in the linear narrative that I, as one of the editors, intended you to. You will have moved from a state of ignorance to one of knowledge as each of the authors convinced you of one thing and then another. The chapters are arranged so that I can close the book with some judicious balancing and weighing of issues. I will demonstrate, with suitable quotes and references, that the postmodernists have certain problems and that the modernists also have other problems. I, on the other hand, have answers to all these problems which is why my chapter comes last. I stand humbly on the shoulders of giants and can therefore see much further. Consequently I will have the final word and conclude with some general reflections on the implications of the foregoing chapters for the practice of those who study organizations.

However, you might not have read this book in the way that you were intended to. You may be the kind of reader who already has ideas about postmodernism, postmodernity, organizations and life in general. You might have missed paragraphs, pages, even chapters in your haste to get to what you think is the substance of the book. You might already agree with one author and obstinately refuse to be persuaded by others. If you are an academic, you might only like those chapters where your own work is cited. It is even possible that you might understand what we have written in a different way to that which the authors intended. How can I write an essay for a reader who refuses to play by the rules and doesn't accept that I am allowed to have the last word? I don't know who you are and I don't know what you want, so how can I write for you at all?

You are all, of course, the second type of reader, I have never met one of the first. The author has always been dead despite the fact that many do not recognize it, and I can no more control the meanings of this text than I can control what you think. Any act of representation may be an attempt at closure, but it can never be a final closure since other voices will always continue the conversation. In that sense meaning is always inter-subjective, is always deferred. But for me, now, I am the author and I am going to write as if you were the first type of reader. This is because

I do not believe that I can, or should, evade the responsibility that this involves, and if I have something to say I should attempt to say it in a way that I believe will be as clear, and as convincing, as possible. The authorial 'I' is the stylistic and political point of this chapter – I will not speak for myself in the third person – and I will try to convince you through rhetoric because that is all the authority I have. I might not be able to control your interpretations of this text but I do have closure over mine – for now at least.

The broader question that this authorial diversion points to is, 'how can we know the other?' If you can't really know me by my writing then how can you know me at all? Furthermore, is this a project which is really worth attempting, or are we all merely flickering phantoms of language who melt away from the analyst's crude tools? Put like this, I think that the issues raised in this volume boil down to one simple question. Do you ever want to claim that you (or we) can ever have all the answers about organizations and organizing? If you say yes then you are a comprehensive or systematic modernist, a species given a fairly thorough critique by all the authors in this book as well as much of 20th-century philosophy and social science. If you say no then you are either a critical modernist or a postmodernist – neither claim that truth is a grail that can be reached – though they differ about whether the quest is worthwhile. In this short and final chapter I am going to argue that you don't need postmodernism to be humble about your truth claims – versions of modernism will do fine. Further to this I am going to argue that critical modernism provides a far more powerful reason to write about organizations at all, a political intent that seeks to continually interrogate the means and ends of organizing for defined ethical–political purposes. Postmodernists might be correct about the dangers of assuming that I write the truth but they do not give me a clear reason for wanting to write at all – and I do.

One caveat is necessary before I continue. My targets in this piece are Lyotard, Baudrillard and the postmodernists, and not poststructuralist writers such as Derrida and Foucault. This is an important point to make because, as I note below, postmodernists have a tendency to appropriate other thinkers who might better be appreciated under other categories. The conflation of poststructuralism and postmodernism is just one example of this, and one that tends to conceal the sophisticated defence of critical affirmation contained within Derrida's writings in particular (see Norris, 1990 and Bernstein, 1991 on this point). My critique is aimed at those writers who express incredulity towards any narratives and not those who simply seek to make our critique more reflexive.

The Ontological Distraction

Before moving to the above argument I wish to dispose of the issue of a postmodern ontology. As several authors have pointed out, in this volume and elsewhere (Bauman, 1988a, b; Parker, 1992a), the post-modern periodization and the postmodern epistemology need to be analytically distinguished. The former makes ontological assertions about organizational and social change (Clegg, 1990; Crook et al., 1992), the latter makes claims about the nature of knowledge about organizations (Jeffcutt (Chapter 2) and Linstead (Chapter 3) in this volume). That this book is not titled 'Postmodernity and Organizations' indicates a fair degree of scepticism about claims that flexibility, decentralization, cultural control and so on indicate the rise of a postbureaucratic organizational form. It seems to me that these claims are unpersuasive. Certainly organizations are changing, that is an essential element in the process of organization, but there appears to be little evidence that these changes are not still centrally related to changes in global capitalism and management fashion. In other words, I see little or no evidence that modernism is on the wane. The assumption that these changes are indications that a broader shift is taking place remains to be proven. Indeed it can be argued that the addition of the 'post' simply distracts attention from key continuities in management control strategies (see Reed (Chapter 10) and Thompson (Chapter 11) in this volume).

Against this rise of a new postindustrialism thesis I tend to agree with authors as diverse as Habermas (1987), Giddens (1990) and Jameson (1991) in asserting that the period of modernity, if we wish to call it that, is still dominant. Terms such as capitalism and industrialism are still appropriate, and I don't yet see how we can do without the legacy of Durkheim's insights on the division of labour, Weber's writings on bureaucracy and Marxist political economy. They are not, of course, all beyond question but seem to provide a framework for thinking about organizations that has not yet been transcended or superseded. Perhaps the 'postmodern organization' is nothing more than a new phrase to capture the imagination of the jaded reader because it seems to add little else that is new. The modern/postmodern couplet echoes many of the other dichotomies of control versus commitment, Taylor versus Mayo, formal versus informal, mechanistic versus organic and so on. There seems no reason then, apart from academic fashion, to introduce a term which appears to have little empirical foundation and provides no convincing theoretical reasons for adopting a periodization of organizational forms. As Barry Smart notes, the assumption that the millennium is upon us is a common theme in human thought, our time is always a time like no other (1992: 5). In that sense the difference between Kerr et al. (1963), Bell (1974), Lyotard (1984) and Fukuyama (1992) is of decade and terminology – not substance.

My rejection of these periodizing ontologies of course requires that I explain the philosophical grounds from which I claim to be able to do this. If I were an epistemological postmodernist such a rejection would not be possible since the postmodernist, postindustrialist or postcapitalist account of organizations would be just as valid and convincing as anything I might want to put forward to counter it. I would have denied myself the grounds from which to disagree. In addition I would have given myself no reasons for wishing to assert that society is like this, or like anything else for that matter. So, back to the question raised in the first section, how and what can we know of organizations?

Knowledge

The contributors to this volume have established that uncritical positivism has clear limits where organizations are concerned. We can never know all there is to know, we cannot predict with any accuracy and we have no special claims to knowledge over and above that of the participants themselves. As Rorty puts it, the mind is not the mirror of nature, there are no privileged representations and what we call truth is no more than a name for a historically located practice of justification (1979). So much for Auguste Comte, Emile Durkheim and Talcott Parsons, but surely these are straw targets already tattered from decades of critique. Any student of interpretive social science from the 1970s onwards learnt the critique of naive empiricism and the game of exposing the hidden meta-narrative. But what is the point of this highly sophisticated unmasking and where does it take us? As I have suggested elsewhere (Parker, 1992a) once we have acknowledged that progress and rationality are relative it seems incumbent on us to either give up, on the grounds that nothing we say matters, or re-establish new grounds from which to pursue our practice if we still believe it to be valuable.

Firstly, however, it seems necessary to briefly assess the claim that nothing but language, metaphor and discourse shapes the organizational world – a central element in postmodern epistemologies. Unlike postmodernists I believe that there *are* limits to human action – just because someone claims that the moon is made of green cheese does not mean that, to all intents and purposes, it is. This is, of course, an assertion that I cannot support. I simply state it because, to me, it seems a sensible reflection of my own beliefs and experience. I do not believe that the world is infinitely pliable and would want to assert that physical, biological and social constraints exist in a real sense outside of whether I want them to or not. Samuel Johnson's response to Bishop Berkeley's subjectivism was to kick a stone and exclaim 'I refute it thus' (Hospers, 1967: 510), and I am attracted to such brazen dismissals of subjectivism even if they are full of philosophical holes. Whilst solipsism is rarely explicitly argued it clearly underwrites much of postmodernism and seems to me to be counter-intuitive. However, we must also accept that there are lots of different ways of describing stones, depending on where you are standing, who you are describing them for and why you are doing it in the first place. Whilst the choice between these descriptions can never be absolute, the final word is never possible, that does not disqualify us from attempting to argue for the most convincing explanation for a particular purpose or from suggesting that the stone exists in some meta-observational sense.

However, organizations are not like stones. As every critic of Frederick Taylor knows the organizational world is not like the natural world and cannot be kicked, tested or measured in an uncomplicated way. Yet to suggest that organizations exist only as shifting and indeterminate webs of meaning also seems counter-intuitive. The organization that I work for has a physical and temporal solidity for me and, I would assert, all those who come into contact with it. While each of my co-employees' perceptions of this solidity will be different there are clear patterns. Cooks, teachers, administrators, managers, porters and students do not all agree on everything about this organization but they agree on some things and differ on others in a fairly systematic way. To argue otherwise would be to deny the possibility of social organization at all. My male academic story about the University of Staffordshire will clearly be different from that of the woman who cleans my office, but that does not mean that we would not also have common differences or even different commonalities. Most importantly, our beliefs and practices affect each other and the world(s) we inhabit – we are not islands but participants in the construction of social organizational patterns. Language may be the medium for all forms of enquiry into that social world, but it does not follow from that premise that language is all that there is.

So we are left with an acknowledgement that there is no final story – but that stories are still worth telling because that is how we do theory in both practical and academic arenas as our way of organizing and understanding the social world. Truth in the sense I am sketching becomes the attempt to sustain agreement – not the end of enquiry but a temporary consensus on what is important in a particular situation at a particular time. Here we encounter a linguistic problem in that 'truth' is usually seen as a state, and I am arguing it is better seen as a social process. To paraphrase William Thomas, if people define things as true, they are true in their consequences (Jary and Jary, 1991: 660). Or as Richard Bernstein puts it, the aim of philosophy should not be to find the fixed Archimedian point from which we can watch the world rotate around us. Instead we should attempt to develop and sustain a dialogue based on mutual respect and the willingness to have one's views altered (Bernstein, 1983). This version of truth is not a very grand narrative, but it is a narrative nonetheless. It is a story told to convince someone that the world can profitably be seen like this. However, like all convincing stories it needs to sit within what we, as embodied social animals, can do, see and think. The physical, biological and social constraints that I have asserted exist mean that any account will not do, because certain narratives do not, and cannot, correspond with the way that subjects perceive the world acting upon them and their action upon the world. Staffordshire University will not double my wages simply because I define it so, but I can hold a wide variety of views on the salary I do receive. This may be a weak definition of truth but I wish to argue that it is infinitely preferable to giving up on the concept altogether. The abyss of relativism, or the silence of the archive, seems to beckon the analyst who refuses conversation at all.

Ethics and Politics

However, I do not believe it is enough to stop here with a form of qualified realism as if all that is at stake here are the philosophical grounds of enquiry. As I have already suggested, our accounts of the world make a difference to the way that the world develops. Hence, following an epistemological argument with an ethical one, we have a responsibility to be clear about why we wish to tell a particular story in a particular way and that is essentially the arena of politics or Aristotle's 'practical rationality'_ (Bernstein, 1983). If, by writing, we define the world in a particular way which is circumscribed by our idiosyncratic human interests then the intent of the analysis should be clear. As with any critique we must be asking ourselves 'critique in the name of what?' (Bernstein, 1991). Postmodernists have clear difficulties with such a formulation since their stress on avoiding totalization or closure leads to the disavowal of any meta-theoretical ethical or political claims. Ethics and politics are essentially ways of saying 'I think the world would be a better place if such and such were the case.' This necessarily means a disagreement with the ethical/political claims of others, a contest for which postmodernists are ill-equipped and epistemologically unable to engage in. How can you disagree constructively if you can offer nothing but negation?

The presentation of modernism as the precondition of running the trains on time to the death camp has done much to obscure this problem. If modernism is a totalizing attempt to impose rationalized values then its usefulness as political critique is clearly limited. However, I wish to argue that there is a danger of presenting a parody of post-enlightenment thinking that neglects its element of interrogation and critique (Habermas, 1987; Tsoukas, 1992; Reed (Chapter 10) and Thompson (Chapter 11), in this volume). Reflective or critical modernism is as good a term as any to capture this, but the problem is really that postmodernists have themselves totalized at least four centuries of post-enlightenment thought under on pejorative label. Moreover, when convenient it is allowable to further unify this fictive consensus by claiming that certain styles of thought – surrealism, Nietzsche, situationism, late Wittgenstein, Weber – are actually (proto)postmodernist as well. Surely a body of social thought that produced critical thinkers as diverse as Gramsci, Gadamer, Simmel and Bakhtin, and movements as diverse as feminism, anarchism, Marxism and existentialism, can hardly be said to lack its reflective side.

However, I do not believe that it is sufficient to argue that this critique is a central element of the Western cultural tradition and assume that it will always be so – this would be a recipe for dangerous smugness. As Norris (1990), Bernstein (1991) and Linstead (Chapter 3 in this volume) point out, this is the implication of Rorty's liberal irony – that the 'conversation of the West' and liberal democracy are assumed to provide the necessary conditions for any and all critique (1979). It seems to me that comprehensive/systematic modernism has all too often been unquestioned and dominant, and that any body of thought, whether we choose to call it modernism or not, needs continual radicalizing in order that different stories can be told. How else would issues which have been historically marginalized (gender, ethnicity, global inequality, environmental degradation and so on) find their way onto the organizational theorist's agenda which has so far been conducted between white middle-class 'first world' men? What is required is that ethical–political critique be defended against the postmodernist attempt to place all productive disagreement in question *and* the dangers of uncritical modernism. This is a criticism that does not only apply to postmodernism, but to any form of thought that seeks to continually relativize without placing anything in its stead. If the dominant mood of the late 20th century is irony, I would wish this to be replaced with passion and engagement on the grounds that it is difficult to speak clearly when you have your tongue thrust firmly in your cheek.

Going back to my earlier example, and to the central theme of this book, what are the implications of this polemic for me when I consider the University of Staffordshire as an organization? As a, self-titled, critical modernist I must be clear that I believe that this organization is malleable; since the iron cage is made by people it can be unlocked by people. Areas on which I might focus, with the aim of pointing to (what I believe are) oppressions, are the reproduction of inequalities of gender, sexuality, ethnicity, disability, age and socioeconomic class (see Mills, Hearn and Parkin, and Thompson in this volume). This will require that I attend to the distributions of space, status, reward and power and the symbolic and material practices that exclude, include and discipline members and clients. In addition it is necessary that I recognize that the organization has a place in a local, national and global economy of finance and knowledge that acts as a set of structural pressures on the practices of local authorities, potential employers, government departments and trans-national organizations. Before I am misquoted, as I almost certainly will be, I wish to stress that I am not claiming that this must be the agenda for all critical modernists. This is my agenda, and it reflects the problems that I view as important, but I list them here as issues for debate, not as a manifesto for a totalizing modernist project. Mine is not the only story about the organization but, precisely because it is as valid as anyone else's, it is worthy of debate. I put it forward to persuade in the hope that if we can begin to agree on the problems then we can begin to formulate acceptable solutions for the problems we have defined.

So now I have a clearly articulated reason to write about organizations which allows me to borrow from, and critique, both sides of this seemingly unbridgeable divide. I cannot agree with postmodernists that 'anything goes', because I think it is a politically dangerous standpoint as well as having epistemological flaws. Yet neither can I agree with systematic modernists that I, or anyone else for that matter, can ever have the final solution for exactly the same reasons. If truth is seen as temporary consensus then debate about values becomes central and the 'escape route' of postmodernism merely an excuse for leaving the choices to others. If the organization theorist is clear about the intended implications of his/her narratives then they can navigate between the Scylla or relativism and the Charybdis of objectivism (Bernstein, 1983), between saying nothing and saying everything. Where we go from there becomes a matter for moral and political choice. We must not give up on the possibility of progress, but neither must we believe that progress means the same thing to everyone.

Conclusion

This chapter grew out of an enthusiasm for, and fascination with, postmodern ideas. For a while they seemed to me to represent the cutting edge of social theory, and had particularly interesting applications for the study of organizations. However, after writing an article that attempted to outline the choices to be made without making one myself (Parker, 1992a) and seeing it used for purposes I had not intended (Thompson, Chapter 11 in this volume) and critiqued on grounds that I agreed with (Tsoukas, 1992) I felt I had to get off the fence (Parker, 1992b). I may not be able to control the reception of a particular text but I can at least make the message clear for my purposes and hope that others will engage with me on similar terrain. This is clearly an ethical–political line and my meta-narrative is showing but I cannot, in good conscience, write without accepting the implication that organizations can be improved and that my words might help. Only then can we start to discuss the problem of 'who benefits' and how things might be changed. Life after Jean-François Lyotard, or Henry Ford (Hirst, 1989: 321), seems to pose the same problems as life before him, for organizations as much as anything and anyone else.

To summarize, I believe that a 'hard' postmodern epistemology is essentially a way of avoiding responsibility for the implications of organizational analysis. Forms of relativism may be philosophically impenetrable but they are not useful, merely a way of being more 'heteroglossic' than the next theorist. Surely the purpose of any good theory is not only to hypothesize about the world, but to critique it in the hope of changing it. It then becomes incumbent on us to be clear about what aspects of organizations we wish to change, and what our intended outcome might be. In that sense I believe the postmodern periodization and postmodern epistemology to be a distraction from a rigorous analysis of organizational changes within global capitalism. Such things are too important to be left to be concealed by an epistemology that can only lead to extreme ethical–political relativism and an ontology without convincing foundations. Postmodern thinking is undoubtedly challenging and any reflective theorist needs to take account of its influence. Yet, in my (un)final analysis, it is a set of narratives that should be treated as cautionary tales for the unwary and not the death knell of organization theory or its authors.

Bibliography

Abrahamson, E. (1988) 'Fads, Fashions, Adaptions and Imbalances'. Draft paper, New York University.

Abrahamson, E. (1989) 'Organisational Fashion'. Draft paper, New York University.

Adler, P.A. and Adler, P. (1987) 'The Past and the Future of Ethnography', *Journal of Contemporary Ethnography*, 16(1): 4–24.

Agar, M. (1986) *Speaking of Ethnography*. Beverly Hills, CA: Sage.

Ahrne, G. (1990) *Agency and Organisation: Towards an Organizational Theory of Society*. London: Sage.

Alexander, J. (ed.) (1988) *Durkheimian Sociology: Cultural Studies*. Cambridge: Cambridge University Press.

Alexander, J. (1992) 'General Theory in the Post-positivist Mode: The Epistemological Dilemma and the Search for Present Reason', in S. Seidman and D.G. Wagner (eds), *Postmodernism and Social Theory*. Oxford: Blackwell, pp. 322–68.

Allaire, Y. and Firsirotu, M. (1984) 'Theories of Organisational Culture', *Organisation Studies*, 5(3): 193–226.

Allen, V.L. (1975) *Social Analysis*. London: Longman.

Alvarez, J. and Cantos, C. (1989) 'Narrative Fiction as a Way of Knowledge and Application to the Development of Imagination for Action'. Paper presented at the Post Modern Management Conference, Barcelona.

Alvesson, M. (1984) 'On the Idea of Organizational Culture'. Paper presented at Standing Conference on Organisation Studies Conference, Lund.

Alvesson, M. (1987) *Organization Theory and Technocratic Consciousness*. Berlin: de Gruyter.

Alvesson, M. (1990a) 'Organisation: From Substance to Image?', *Organisation Studies*, 11(3): 373–94.

Alvesson, M. (1990b) 'On the Popularity of Organizational Culture', *Acta Sociologica*, 33(1): 31–49.

Alvesson, M. (1993) *Cultural Perspectives on Organisations*. Cambridge: Cambridge University Press.

Alvesson, M. and Berg, P.O. (1992) *Corporate Culture and Organizational Symbolism*. Berlin: de Gruyter.

Alvesson, M. and Willmott, H. (eds) (1992) *Critical Management Studies*. London: Sage.

Arber, S. (1989) 'Class and the Elderly', *Social Studies Review*, 4(3): 90–5.

Argyris, C. (1987) *Personality and Organization*. New York: Garland Publishing.

Armstrong, P. (1984) 'Competition Between the Organisational Professions and the Evolution of Management Control Strategies', in K. Thompson (ed.), *Work, Employment and Unemployment*. Milton Keynes: Open University Press, pp. 97–120.

Armstrong, P. (1991) 'The Influence of Michel Foucault on Historical Research in Accounting: An Assessment'. Paper to the Academy of Accounting Historians Research Methodology Conference.

Arnold, J., Robertson, I.T. and Cooper, C.L. (1991) *Work Psychology*. London: Pitman.

Aronowitz, S. (1987/88) 'Postmodernism and Politics', *Social Text*, 18.

Arrington, C. and Francis, J. (1989) 'Deconstruction, Privilege and Accounting Research', *Accounting, Organisations and Society*, 14(1/2): 1–28.

Asplund, C. (1983) 'The Process of Organisational Liquidation'. Paper presented to the Workshop on Culture and Symbolism in Organisations, Groningen.

Atkinson, P. (1990) *The Ethnographic Imagination*. London: Routledge.

Bakhtin, M. (1981) *The Dialogic Imagination*. Austin: University of Texas Press.

Bakhtin, M. (1984) *Problems of Dostoevsky's Poetics*. Manchester: Manchester University Press.

Baran, B. (1988) 'Office Automation and Women's Work'. In R. Pahl (ed.), *On Work*. Oxford: Blackwell, pp. 684–706.

Barley, S., Meyer, G. and Gash, D. (1988) 'Cultures of Culture', *Administrative Science Quarterly*, 33: 24–60.

Barrett, M. (1987) 'The Concept of Difference', *Feminist Review*, 26: 29–41.

Barthes, R. (1957) *Mythologies*. Paris: Editions du Seuil (translated, New York: Hill & Wang, 1962).

Barthes, R. (1977) 'From Work to Text', in S. Heath (ed.), *Image–Music–Text*. London: Fontana, pp. 155–64.

Barthes, R. (1981) 'The Theory of the Text', in R. Young (ed.), *Untying the Text*. London: Routledge & Kegan Paul, pp. 31–47.

Bartky, S. (1977) 'Towards a Phenomenology of Feminist Consciousness', in M. Vetterling-Braggin, F. Elliston and J. English (eds), *Feminism and Philosophy*. Littlefield, NJ: Adams & Co.

Bartol, K.M. and Martin, D.C. (1991) *Management*. New York: McGraw-Hill.

Baudrillard, J. (1968) *La Systeme des Objects*. Paris: Denoel-Gonthier.

Baudrillard, J. (1970) *La Societe de Consommation*. Paris: Gallimard.

Baudrillard, J. (1972) *Pour une Critique de L'Economie Politique du Signe*. Paris: Gallimard.

Baudrillard, J. (1976) *L'Echange Symbolique et al Mort*. Paris: Gallimard.

Baudrillard, J. (1981) *For a Critique of the Political Economy of the Sign*. St. Louis, MA: Telas.

Baudrillard, J. (1983a) *In the Shadow of the Silent Majority*. New York: Semiotext(e).

Baudrillard, J. (1983b) *Simulations*. New York: Semiotext(e).

Baudrillard, J. (1988a) *An Ecstacy of Communication*. New York: Semiotext(e).

Baudrillard, J. (1988b) *Selected Writings*. Oxford: Polity.

Bauman, Z. (1988a) 'Viewpoint: Sociology and Postmodernity', *Sociological Review*, 36(4): 790–813.

Bauman, Z. (1988b) 'Is There a Postmodern Sociology?', *Theory, Culture and Society*, 5(2/3): 217–37.

Beardsley, M. (1981) *Aesthetics*. Indianapolis: Hackett.

Becker, H. (1982) *Art Worlds*. Los Angeles, CA: University of California Press.

Beckett, S. (1959) *The Beckett Trilogy*. London: Calder.

Bedeian, A. (1989) 'Totems and Taboos', *Academy of Management News*, 19(4): 1–6.

Beetham, D. (1985) *Max Weber and the Theory of Modern Politics*. Cambridge: Cambridge University Press.

Beetham, D. (1987) *Bureaucracy*. Milton Keynes: Open University Press.

Bell, D. (1974) *The Coming of Post-Industrial Society*. Harmondsworth: Penguin.

Bell, E. (1989) 'The Mammy and the Snow Queen'. Paper presented at the Research in Women in Management Conference, Winnipeg.

Bennington, G. (1989) 'Demanding History', in D. Attridge, G. Bennington and R. Young (eds), *Post-Structuralism and the Question of History*. Cambridge: Cambridge University Press, pp. 15–29.

Benson, D. and Hughes, J. (1983) *The Perspective of Ethnomethodology*. Hong Kong: Longman.

Benson, J.K. (1977) 'Innovation and Crisis in Organisational Analysis', in J.K. Benson (ed.), *Organisational Analysis: Critique and Innovation*. Beverly Hills, CA: Sage, pp. 5–17.

Benson, J. (1983) 'Paradigm and Praxis in Organisational Analysis', *Research in Organisational Behaviour*, 5: 33–56.

Berefelt, G. (1977) *Skönt*. Uppsala: Almqvist & Wiksell.

Berg, P.O. (1979) *Emotional Structures in Organisations*. Lund: Studentlitteratur.
Berg, P.O. (1982) '11 Metaphors and Their Theoretical Implications', in P.O. Berg and P. Daudi (eds), *Traditions and Trends in Organisation Theory: Part 2*. Lund; Studentlitteratur.
Berg, P.O. (1985) 'Organisation Change as a Symbolic Transformation Process', in P. Frost et al. (eds), *Organisational Culture*. Beverly Hills, CA: Sage, pp. 281–300.
Berg, P.O. (1989) 'Postmodern Management? From Facts to Fiction in Theory and Practice', *Scandinavian Journal of Management*, 5(3): 201–17.
Berman, M. (1982) *All That is Solid Melts into Air*. New York: Simon & Schuster.
Bernstein, R.J. (1983) *Beyond Objectivism and Relativism*. Oxford: Blackwell.
Bernstein, R.J. (1991) *The New Constellation*. Oxford: Polity.
Best, S. and Kellner, D. (1991) *Postmodern Theory: Critical Interrogations*. London: Macmillan.
Birth, K.K. (1990) 'Reading and the Righting of Writing Ethnographies', *American Ethnologist*, 549–57.
Blackler, F. (1992) 'Formative Contexts and Activity Systems: Postmodern Approaches to the Management of Change', in M. Reed and M. Hughes (eds), *Rethinking Organisation*. London: Sage, pp. 273–300.
Blustein, D.L., Devenis, L.E. and Kidney, B.A. (1989) 'Relationship between the Identity Formation Process and Career Development', *Journal of Counselling Psychology*, 36(2): 196–202.
Boje, D. (1991) 'The Storytelling Organisation', *Administrative Science Quarterly*, 36: 106–26.
Bordo, S. (1991) 'Feminism, Postmodernism and Gender-Scepticism', in L.J. Nicholson (ed.), *Feminism/Postmodernism*. New York: Routledge, pp. 133–56.
Bordwell, D. (1985) *Narration in the Fiction Film*. London: Methuen.
Bordwell, D. and Thompson, K. (1986) *Film Art – an Introduction*. New York: Alfred Knopf.
Borisoff, D. and Merrill, L. (1985) *The Power to Communicate: Gender Differences as Barriers*. IL: Waveland Press.
Bowles, S. and Gintis, H. (1976) *Schooling in Capitalist America*. London: Routledge & Kegan Paul.
Boyne, R. and Rattansi, A. (eds) (1990) *Postmodernism and Society*. London: Macmillan.
Bradbury, M. (1990) 'The World After the Wake', *Guardian*, 20 September.
Brenner, O.C., Tomkiewicz, J. and Schein, V.E. (1989) 'The Relationship Between Sex Role Stereotypes and Requisite Management Characteristics Revisited', *Academy of Management Journal*, 32(3): 662–9.
Brown, R.H. (1976) 'Social Theory as Metaphor', *Theory and Society*, 3: 169–97.
Brown, C. (1992) 'Organisation Studies and Scientific Authority', in M. Reed and M. Hughes (eds), *Rethinking Organisation*. London: Sage, pp. 64–84.
Brundage, J.A. (1987) *Law, Sex and Christian Society in Medieval Europe*. Chicago, IL: University of Chicago Press.
Bruner, J. (1990) *Acts of Meaning*. Cambridge, MA: Harvard University Press.
Brunius, T. (1986) *Estetik förr och nu*. Stockholm: Liber.
Brunnson, N. (1985) *The Irrational Organisation*. Chichester: Wiley.
Brunnson, N. (1989) *The Organisation of Hypocrisy*. Chichester: Wiley.
Bryman, A. (1984) 'Organisation Studies and the Concept of Rationality', *Journal of Management Studies*, 21: 391–404.
Bryman, A. (ed.) (1988) *Doing Research in Organisations*. London: Routledge.
Bryman, A. (1989) *Research Methods and Organisation Studies*. London: Unwin Hyman.
Burchell, S., Clubb, C. and Hopwood, A. (1985) 'Accounting in its Social Context: Towards a History of Value-Added in the United Kingdom', *Accounting, Organisations and Society*, 10(4): 381–413.
Burnham, J. (1942) *The Managerial Revolution*. London: Putnam.
Burns, T. (1970) 'Sociological Explanation', in D. Emmet and A. MacIntyre (eds), *Sociological Theory and Philosophical Analysis*. London: Macmillan, pp. 55–75.

Burrell, G. (1984) 'Sex and Organizational Analysis', *Organization Studies*, 5(2): 97–118.

Burrell, G. (1988) 'Modernism, Postmodernism and Organizational Analysis 2: The Contribution of Michel Foucault', *Organization Studies*. 9(2): 221–35.

Burrell, G. (1989) 'Post Modernism: Threat or Opportunity?', in M.C. Jackson, P. Keys and S.A. Cropper (eds), *Operational Research and the Social Sciences*. New York: Plenum.

Burrell, G. (1990) 'Fragmented Labours', in D. Knights and H. Willmott (eds), *Labour Process Theory*. London: Macmillan.

Burrell, G. (1992a) 'The Organisation of Pleasure', in M. Alvesson and H. Willmott (eds), *Critical Management Studies*. London: Sage, pp. 66–89.

Burrell, G. (1992b) 'Back to the Future', in M. Reed and M. Hughes (eds), *Rethinking Organisation*. London: Sage, pp. 165–83.

Burrell, G. and Hearn, J. (1989) 'The Sexuality of Organization', in J. Hearn et al. (eds), *The Sexuality of Organization*. London: Sage. pp. 1–28.

Burrell, G. and Morgan, G. (1979) *Sociological Paradigms and Organisational Analysis*. London: Heinemann.

Butler, R. (1991) *Designing Organisations: A Decision Making Perspective*. London: Routledge.

Byrne, J. (1990) 'Is research in the Ivory Tower "Fuzzy, Irrelevant, Pretentious"?', *Business Week*, 29 October: 50–2.

Calás, M.B. and Smircich, L. (1991) 'Voicing Seduction to Silence Leadership', *Organisation Studies*, 12(4): 567–601.

Calás, M.B. and Smircich, L. (1992a) 'Re-writing Gender into Organizational Theorizing: Directions from Feminist Perspectives', in M. Reed and M. Hughes (eds), *Rethinking Organisation*. London: Sage, pp. 227–53.

Calás, M.B. and Smircich, L. (1992b) 'Using the "F" word: feminist theories and the social consequences of organizational research', in A. Mills and P. Tancred (eds), *Gendering Organizational Analysis*. Newbury Park, CA: Sage.

Calás, M., Jacobson, S., Jacques, R. and Smircich, L. (1991) 'Is a Women Centred Theory of Management Dangerous?' Paper presented at the National Academy of Management Conference, Miami.

Callinicos, A. (1989) *Against Postmodernism: A Marxist Critique*. Cambridge: Polity.

Canetti, E. (1962) *Crowds and Power*. London: Gollancz.

Carter, P. and Jackson, N. (1989) 'Leadership – A Fantasy of Immaturity?'. Paper presented at Standing Conference on Organisation Studies Conference, INSEAD.

Carter, P. and Jackson, N. (1991) '(Post)Modernism', in F. Vidal (ed.), *Wider Die Regel*. Mossingen-Talheim: Talheimer Verlag.

Cashmore, E. and Troyna, B. (1983) *Introduction to Race Relations*. London: Routledge & Kegan Paul.

Child, J. (1984) *Organisations*. New York: Harper.

Child, J. (1988) 'On Organisations in their Sectors', *Organisation Studies*, 9(1): 13–19.

Clark, P. (1990) 'Chronological Codes and Organisational Analysis', in J. Hassard and D. Pym (eds), *The Theory and Philosophy of Organisations*. London: Routledge, 11: 137–66.

Clark, P. and Starkey, K. (1988) *Organisation Transitions and Innovation Design*. London: Pinter.

Clarke, J. (1988) 'Enter the Cybernauts: Problems in Postmodernism', *Communication*, 10: 383–401.

Clegg, S. (1989) *Frameworks of Power*. London: Sage.

Clegg, S. (1990) *Modern Organizations: Organization Studies in the Postmodern World*. London: Sage.

Clegg, S. and Dunkerley, D. (1977) *Critical Issues in Organisations*. London: Routledge & Kegan Paul.

Clifford, J. (1986) 'Introduction: Partial Truths', in J. Clifford and G. Marcus (eds), *Writing Culture*. London: University of California Press, pp. 1–26.

Clifford, J. (1989) *The Predicament of Culture*. London: Harvard University Press.

Clifford, J. and Marcus, G. (eds) (1986) *Writing Culture*. London: University of California Press.

Cockburn, C. (1985) *Machinery of Dominance*. London: Pluto Press.

Cockburn, C. (1987) *Two-track Training*. London: Macmillan.

Cockburn, C. (1991) *In the Way of Women*. London: Macmillan.

Cohen, P. (1968) *Modern Social Theory*. London: Heinemann.

Cohen, I. (1986) 'The Status of Structuration Theory: A Reply to McLennan', *Theory, Culture and Society*, 3: 123–33.

Collinson, D. (1988) 'Engineering Humour, Masculinity, Joking and Conflict in Shop-floor Relations', *Organization Studies*, 9(2): 181–99.

Collinson, D. (1992) *Managing the Shop Floor: Subjectivity, Masculinity and Workplace Culture*. Berlin: de Gruyter.

Collinson, D. and Hearn, J. (1992) 'Men, Masculinities and Managements: Unities, Differences and their Interrelations, *Academy of Management Review*, 17.

Connerton, P. (1980) *The Tragedy of Enlightenment*. Cambridge: Cambridge University Press.

Connor, S. (1989) *Postmodernist Culture*. Oxford: Blackwell.

Cooper, R.C. (1974) *Job Motivation and Job Design*. London: Institute of Personnel Management.

Cooper, R. (1983) 'The Other: A Model of Human Structuring', in G. Morgan (ed.), *Beyond Method*. London: Sage, pp. 202–18.

Cooper, R. (1987) 'Information, Communication and Organisation: A Post-Structural Revision', *Journal of Mind and Behaviour*, 8(3): 395–416.

Cooper, R. (1989) 'Modernism, Postmodernism and Organisational Analysis 3: The Contribution of Jacques Derrida', *Organisation Studies*, 10(4): 479–502.

Cooper, R. (1990a) 'Organisation/Disorganisation', in J. Hassard and D. Pym (eds), *The Theory and Philosophy of Organisations*. London: Routledge, pp. 167–97.

Cooper, R. (1990b) 'Canetti's Sting', *Notework*, 9(2/3): 91–112.

Cooper, R. (1992) 'Formal Organisation as Representation', in M. Reed and M. Hughes (eds), *Rethinking Organisation*. London: Sage, pp. 254–72.

Cooper, R. and Burrell, G. (1988) 'Modernism, Postmodernism and Organisational Analysis: An Introduction', *Organisation Studies*, 9(1): 91–112.

Cox, D. (1979) Review of G. Burrell and G. Morgan (1979), *Reviewing Sociology*, 1: 3–5.

Cox, M.G. (1986) 'Enter the stranger: unanticipated effects of communication of the success of an organizational newcomer', in L. Thayer (ed.), *Organisation ↔ Communication: Emerging Perspectives*. Norwood, NJ: Ablex.

Crompton, R. (1990) 'Professions in the Current Context', *Work, Employment and Society*, 4: 147–66.

Crook, S. (1990) 'The End of Radical Social Theory', in R. Boyne and A. Rattansi (eds), *Postmodernism and Society*. London: Macmillan, 11: 46–75.

Crook, S., Pakulski, J. and Waters, M. (1992) *Postmodernisation: Change in Advanced Society*. London: Sage.

Crozier, M. (1964) *The Bureaucratic Phenomenon*. London: Tavistock.

Crozier, M. (1985) 'Comparing Structures and Comparing Games', in D.S. Pugh (ed.), *Organisation Theory*. Harmondsworth: Penguin, pp. 106–19.

Crozier, M. and Friedberg, E. (1980) *Actors and Systems*. Chicago, IL: University of Chicago Press.

Culler, J. (1975) *Structuralist Poetics*. London: Routledge.

Cummings, L. and Frost, P. (1985) *Publishing in the Organisational Sciences*. Homewood, IL: Irwin.

Czarniawska-Joerges, B. (1988) *To Coin a Phrase*. Stockholm: Study of Power and Democracy in Sweden.

Czarniawska-Joerges, B. (1989) 'Don Quijote and Capitalism in Poland', *Studies in Action and Enterprise*. Stockholm University: Företagsekonomiska Institutionen.

Czarniawska-Joerges, B. (1990) *In the Eyes of the Innocent: Students on Organisational Power*. Stockholm: Regeringskansliets Offsetcentral.

Czarniawska-Joerges, B. (1991) 'Gender, Power, Organisations: An Interruptive Intervention'. Paper presented at Towards a New Theory of Organisations Conference, University of Keele.

Czarniawska-Joerges, B., Gustaffson, C. and Björkegren, D. (1990) 'Purists versus Pragmatists'. Paper presented at Academy of Management Meeting, San Francisco.

Dandeker, C. (1990) *Surveillance, Power and Modernity.* Cambridge: Polity.

Daudi, P. (1990) 'Con-Versing in Management's Public Place', *Scandinavian Journal of Management,* 6: 285–307.

Deal, T. and Kennedy, A. (1982) *Corporate Cultures.* Reading, MA: Addison-Wesley.

De Certeau, M. (1984) *The Practice of Everyday Life.* Berkeley, CA: University of California Press.

Debord, G. (1970) *The Society of the Spectacle.* Detroit, MI: Black & Red.

Deetz, S. (1985) 'Culture-critical Research: New Sensibilities and Old Realities', *Journal of Management,* 11(2): 121–36.

Deleuze, G. and Guattari, F. (1984) *Anti-Oedipus.* London: Athlone.

De Man, P. (1984) 'Phenomenality and Materiality in Kant', in G. Shapiro and A. Sica (eds), *Hermeneutics: Questions and Prospects.* Amherst, MA: University of Massachusetts Press, pp. 121–44.

Denzin, N. (1990) 'Writing the Interpretive Post-Modern Ethnography', *Journal of Contemporary Ethnography,* 19(2): 231–6.

Denzin, N. (1991) *Images of Postmodern Society.* London: Sage.

Derrida, J. (1973) *Speech and Phenomena.* Evanston, IL: Northwestern University Press.

Derrida, J. (1976) *Of Grammatology.* Baltimore, MD: Johns Hopkins University Press.

Derrida, J. (1978) *Writing and Difference.* London: Routledge & Kegan Paul.

Derrida, J. (1981) *Positions.* Chicago, IL: Chicago University Press.

Derrida, J. (1982) *Margins of Philosophy.* London: Harvester.

Devereux, G. (1979) 'Fantasy and Symbol as Dimensions of Reality', in R. Hook (ed.), *Fantasy and Symbol.* London: Academic Press.

Dews, P. (1986) 'The Nouvelle Philosophie and Foucault', in M. Gane (ed.), *Towards a Critique of Foucault.* London: Routledge & Kegan Paul, pp. 65–105.

DiTomasio, N. (1989) 'Sexuality in the Workplace: Discrimination and Harassment', in J. Hearn et al. (eds), *The Sexuality of Organization.* London: Sage, pp. 71–90.

Donaldson, L. (1985) *In Defence of Organisation Theory.* Cambridge: Cambridge University Press.

Doray, B. (1988) *From Taylorism to Fordism.* London: Free Association Books.

Dore, R. (1989) 'Where are we Now: Musings of an Evolutionist', *Work, Employment and Society,* 3(4): 425–46.

Drazin, R. and Sandelands, L. (1989) 'Autogenesis and the Process of Organising'. Draft paper, Emory and Columbia Universities.

Dreyfus, H.L. and Rabinow, P. (1982) *Michel Foucault. Beyond Structuralism and Hermeneutics.* Brighton: Harvester Press.

Duveen, G. and Lloyd, B. (1986) 'The Significance of Social Identities', *British Journal of Social Psychology,* 25: 219–30.

Dwyer, K. (1977) 'On the Dialogic of Fieldwork', *Dialectical Anthropology,* 2: 143–51.

Dwyer, K. (1979) 'The Dialectic of Ethnology', *Dialectical Anthropology,* 4: 205–24.

Dyer, W. (1985) 'The Cycle of Cultural Evolution in Organisations', in R. Kilmann et al. (eds), *Gaining Control of the Corporate Culture.* San Francisco, CA: Jossey-Bass, pp. 200–29.

Eagleton, T. (1990) *The Ideology of the Aesthetic.* Oxford: Blackwell.

Ebers, M. (1985) 'Understanding Organisations: The Poetic Mode', *Journal of Management,* 7(2): 51–62.

Eco, U. (1987) *Travels in Hyperreality,* New York: Basic Books.

Eco, U. (1990) *The Limits of Interpretation.* Bloomington, IN: Indiana University Press.

Egri, C. and Frost, P.J. (1989) 'Threats to Innovation; Roadblocks to Implementation: The

Politics of the Productive Process', in M. Jackson et al. (eds), *Operational Research and the Social Sciences*. New York: Plenum.

Elias, N. (1982) *The Civilising Process: State Formation and Civilisation*. Oxford: Blackwell.

Emery, R. (ed.) (1969) *Systems Thinking: Selected Readings*. Harmondsworth: Penguin.

Enrenreich, B. and English, D. (1973) *Witches, Midwives and Nurses: a History of Women Healers*. New York: Feminist Press.

Eribon, D. (1991) *Michel Foucault*. Cambridge, MA: Harvard University Press.

Ericson, D. (1988) *In the Stockholm Art World*. Stockholm: Studies in Social Anthropology.

Evans, T. (1988) *A Gender Agenda*. Sydney: Allen & Unwin Australia.

Faulk, J. and Steinfield, C. (eds) (1990) *Organisations and Communication Technology*. London: Sage.

Featherstone, M. (ed.) (1988) *Theory, Culture and Society*, Special Issue, 5(2/3).

Featherstone, M. (1991) *Consumer Culture and Postmodernism*. London: Sage.

Feldman, S. (1986) 'Management in Context', *Journal of Management Studies*, 23(6): 587–607.

Felski, R. (1988) 'Feminism and Postmodernism'. Paper presented to the School of Humanities Postmodernism Seminar Series, Murdoch University.

Felski, R. (1989) 'Feminist Theory and Social Change', *Theory, Culture and Society*, 6(2): 219–40.

Felstead, A. (1991) 'The Social Organisation of the Franchise: A Case of Controlled Self Employment', *Work, Employment and Society*, 5(1): 37–57.

Fennell, G., Phillipson, C. and Evers, H. (1988) *The Sociology of Old Age*. Milton Keynes: Open University Press.

Ferguson, K.E. (1984) *The Feminist Case Against Bureaucracy*. Philadelphia, PA: Temple University Press.

Ferguson, K.E. (1987) 'Work, Text and Act in Discourses of Organisation', *Women and Politics*, 7(2): 1–21.

Flax, J. (1987) 'Postmodernism and Gender Relations in Feminist Theory', *Signs*, 12(4): 621–43.

Flax, J. (1990) *Thinking Fragments: Psychoanalysis, Feminism and Postmodernism in the Contemporary West*. Berkeley, CA: University of California Press.

Foreman, A. (1977) *Femininity as Alienation: Women and the Family in Marxism and Psychoanalysis*. London: Pluto.

Foster, H. (1985) 'Postmodernism: A Preface', in H. Foster (ed.), *Postmodern Culture*. London: Pluto.

Foucault, M. (1970) *The Order of Things*. London: Tavistock.

Foucault, M. (1971) 'Orders of Discourse', *Social Science Information*, 10(2): 7–30.

Foucault, M. (1974) *The Archeology of Knowledge*. London: Tavistock.

Foucault, M. (1976) *The History of Sexuality, Volume One*. New York: Vintage Books.

Foucault, M. (1979) *Discipline and Punish*. Harmondsworth: Penguin.

Foucault, M. (1980) *Power/Knowledge*. Brighton: Harvester.

Fox, S. (1990) 'Strategic Human Resource Management: Postmodern Conditioning for the Corporate Culture', *Management Education and Development*, 21(3): 192–206.

Freire, P. (1972) *The Pedagogy of the Oppressed*. Harmondsworth: Penguin.

Freire, P. (1985) *The Politics of Education*. Basingstoke: Macmillan.

French, M. (1985) *Beyond Power*. New York: Summit Books.

Friedmann, J. (1988) 'Cultural Logics of the Global System: A Sketch', *Theory, Culture and Society*, 5(2/3): 447–60.

Frost, P.J. (1987) 'Power, Politics and Influence', in F. Jablin et al. (eds), *Handbook of Organisational Communication*. Newbury Park, CA: Sage.

Frost, P.J., Moore, L., Louis, M., Lundberg, C. and Martin, J. (eds) (1985) *Organisational Culture*. Beverly Hills, CA: Sage.

Frost, P., Moore, L., Louis, M., Lundberg, C. and Martin, J. (eds) (1991) *Reframing Organizational Culture*. Beverley Hills, CA: Sage.

Fukuyama, F. (1992) *The End of History and the Last Man*. London: Hamish Hamilton.

Gagliardi, P. (1986) 'The Creation and Change of Organisational Cultures', *Organisation Studies*, 7(2): 117–34.

Gagliardi, P. (ed.) (1990) *Symbols and Artefacts: Views of the Corporate Landscape*. Berlin: de Gruyter.

Game, A. (1989) 'Research and Writing: Secretaries and Bosses', *Journal of Pragmatics*, 13: 343–61.

Gans, H.J. (1974) *Popular Culture and High Culture*. New York: Basic Books.

Garfield, C. (1986) *Peak Performers: The New Heroes in Business*. London: Hutchinson.

Garfinkel, H. (1987) *Studies in Ethnomethodology*. Cambridge: Polity.

Garland, D. (1991) *Punishment and Modern Society*. Oxford: Clarendon.

Geertz, C. (1973) *The Interpretation of Cultures*. New York: Basic Books.

Geertz, C. (1983) *Local Knowledge*. New York: Basic Books.

Geertz, C. (1988) *Works and Lives: the anthropologist as author*. Stanford, CA: Stanford University Press.

Gergen, K. (1989) 'Organisation Theory in the Postmodern Era'. Paper presented at Rethinking Organisation Conference, University of Lancaster.

Gergen, K. (1992) 'Organization Theory in the Postmodern Era', in M. Reed and M. Hughes (eds), *Rethinking Organization*. London: Sage, pp. 207–26.

Gheradi, S. and Turner, B. (1987) 'Real Men Don't Collect Soft Data', Quaderno 13, University of Trento.

Gibson, J.L., Ivancevich, J.M. and Donnelly, J.H. (1991) *Organisations: Behaviour, Structure, Processes*. Homewood, IL: Irwin.

Giddens, A. (1984) *The Constitution of Society*, Cambridge: Polity.

Giddens, A. (1985) *The Nation State and Violence*. Cambridge: Polity.

Giddens, A. (1987a) *Social Theory and Modern Sociology*. Cambridge: Polity.

Giddens, A. (1987b) 'Structuralism, Post-structuralism and the Production of Culture', in A. Giddens and J. Turner (eds), *Social Theory Today*. Cambridge: Polity, pp. 195–223.

Giddens, A. (1989) 'A Reply to My Critics', in D. Held and B. Thompson (eds), *Social Theory and Modern Societies*. Cambridge: Cambridge University Press.

Giddens, A. (1990) *The Consequences of Modernity*. Cambridge: Polity.

Giddens, A. (1991) *Modernity and Self-identity*. Cambridge: Polity.

Gies, F. and Gies, J. (1980) *Women in the Middle Ages*. New York: Harper & Row.

Gioia, D.A. and Pitre, E. (1989) 'Multi-paradigm Perspectives on Theory Building', *Academy of Management Review*, 5(4): 584–602.

Giordano, L. (1988) 'Beyond Taylorism', in D. Knights and H. Willmott (eds), *New Technology and the Labour Process*. London: Macmillan.

Gitlin, T. (1985) *Inside Prime Time*. New York: Pantheon.

Gouldner, A. (1971) *The Coming Crisis in Western Sociology*. London: Heinemann.

Gregory, K. (1983) 'Native View Paradigms: Multiple Cultures and Culture Conflicts in Organisations', *Administrative Science Quarterly*, 28(3): 359–76.

Griffin, C. (1985) *Typical Girls*. London: Routledge & Kegan Paul.

Griffin, S. (1982) 'The Way of All Ideology', in N.O. Keohane, M.Z. Rosaldo and B.C. Gelpi (eds), *Feminist Theory: A Critique of Ideology*. Brighton: Harvester, pp. 273–92.

Grosz, E. (1987) 'Feminist Theory and the Challenge to Knowledges', *Women's Studies International Forum*, 10: 475–80.

Gudykunst, W., Stewart, L. and Ting-Toomey, S. (eds) (1985) *Communication, Culture and Organisational Process*. Beverly Hills, CA: Sage.

Guillet de Monthoux, P. (1988) 'Doctor Clerambault in Zola's Paradise', *Studies in Action and Enterprise*. Stockholm University: Foretagsekonomiska Institutionen.

Habermas, J. (1972) *Knowledge and Human Interests*. London: Heinemann.

Habermas, J. (1974) *Theory and Practice*. London: Heinemann.

Habermas, J. (1979) *Communication and the Evolution of Society*. London: Heinemann.

Habermas, J. (1981) 'Modernity versus Postmodernity', *New German Critique*, 22: 3–14.

Habermas, J. (1985) 'Modernity: An Incomplete Project', in H. Foster (ed.), *Postmodern Culture*. London: Pluto.

Habermas, J. (1987) *Lectures on the Philosophical Discourse of Modernity*. Cambridge, MA: MIT Press.

Hacker, B.C. (1988) 'From Military Revolution to Industrial Revolution: Armies, Women and Political Economy in Early Modern Europe', in E. Isaksson (ed.), *Women and the Military System*. New York: St Martin's Press.

Hackman, J.R. and Porter, L.W. (1968) 'Expectancy Theory Predictions of Work Effectiveness', *Organisational Behaviour and Human Performance*, 3: 417–26.

Hahn, H. (1988) 'Can Disability be Beautiful?, *Social Policy*, 18(3): 26–32.

Halbert, M. (1989) 'Feminist Epistemology: An Impossible Project?', *Radical Philosophy*, 53: 3–7.

Hall, M. (1989) 'Private Experiences in the Public Domain: Lesbians in Organizations' in J. Hearn et al. (eds), *The Sexuality of Organization*. London: Sage, pp. 125–38.

Hall, S. and Jacques, M. (eds), (1989) *New Times*. London: Lawrence & Wishart.

Hallet, S. (1988) 'Privatisation and the Restructuring of a Public Utility'. Paper to Employment Research Unit Conference, Cardiff Business School.

Hammersley, M. (1990) 'What's Wrong with Ethnography? The Myth of Theoretical Description', *Sociology*, 24(4): 597–615.

Handy, C. (1987) *The Future of Work*. Oxford: Blackwell.

Handy, C. (1989) *The Age of Unreason*. London: Business Books.

Harding, S. (1986) *The Science Question in Feminism*. Milton Keynes: Open University Press.

Harland, R. (1987) *Superstructuralism: The Philosophy of Structuralism and Post-Structuralism*. London: Methuen.

Harriman, A. (1985) *Women/Men, Management*. New York: Praeger.

Harvey, D. (1989) *The Condition of Postmodernity*. Oxford: Blackwell.

Harvey, L. (1982) 'The Use and Abuse of Kuhnian Paradigms in the Sociology of Knowledge', *Sociology*, 16(1): 85–101.

Hassard, J. and Pym, D. (eds) (1990) *The Theory and Philosophy of Organisations*. London: Routledge.

Hatton, M.J. (1990) *Corporations and Directors*. Toronto: Thompson.

Hearn, J. (1987) *The Gender of Oppression: Men, Masculinity and the Critique of Marxism*. Brighton: Wheatsheaf.

Hearn, J. (1991) 'Men and Gender Divided Organisations – or Patriarchies, Sexualities, Masculinities and Managements'. Paper presented at Men and Work Life Seminar, University of Tampere.

Hearn, J. (1992) *Men in the Public Eye. The Construction and Deconstruction of Public Men and Public Patriarchies*. London: Routledge.

Hearn, J. and Parkin, W. (1983) 'Gender and Organisations: A Selected Review and Critique of a Neglected Area', *Organisation Studies*, 4(3): 219–42. Reprinted in A. Mills and P. Tancred (eds), *Gendering Organizational Analysis*. Newbury Park, CA: Sage.

Hearn, J. and Parkin, W. (1987) *'Sex' and 'Work'. The Power and Paradox of Organizational Sexuality*. Brighton: Wheatsheaf.

Hearn, J., Sheppard, D.L. Tancred-Sheriff, P. and Burrell, G. (eds) (1989) *The Sexuality of Organization*. London: Sage.

Hebdige, D. (1979) *Subculture: The Meaning of Style*. London: Methuen.

Hebdige, D. (1989) 'After the Masses', *Marxism Today*, January: 48–53.

Hekman, S. (1990) 'Hermeneutics and the Crisis of Social Theory', in J. Clark, C. Modgil and F. Modgil (eds), *Anthony Giddens: Consensus and Controversy*. London: Falmer.

Held, D. (1976) *Introduction to Critical Theory: Horkheimer to Habermas*. London: Hutchinson.

Henriques, J., Hollway, W., Urwin, C., Venn, C. and Walkerdine, V. (1984) *Changing the Subject*. London: Methuen.

Herzberg, F. (1966) *Work and the Nature of Man*. New York: Staples Press.

Hickman, C. and Silva, M. (1985) *Creating Excellence*. London: Allen & Unwin.

Hickson, D.J., Hinings, C.R., Lee, C.A., Schneck, R.E. and Pennings, J.M. (1971) 'A

Strategic Contingencies Theory of Intraorganisational Power', *Administrative Science Quarterly*, 16(2): 216–29.

Hinings, R. (1988) 'Defending Organisation Theory: A British View from North America', *Organisation Studies*, 9(7): 2–7.

Hirst, P. (1989) 'After Henry', in S. Hall and M. Jacques (eds), *New Times*. London: Lawrence & Wishart, pp. 321–9.

Hirst, P. and Zeitlin, J. (1991) 'Flexible Specialisation Versus Post-Fordism', *Economy and Society*, 20(1): 1–56.

Hopfl, H. (1991) 'The Making of the Corporate Acolyte', *Journal of Management Studies*, 29(1): 23–33.

Hopwood, A. (1987) 'The Archeology of Accounting Systems', *Accounting, Organisations and Society*, 13(3): 207–35.

Hoskin, K. and Macve, R. (1988) 'The Genesis of Accountability', *Accounting, Organisations and Society*, 13(1): 37–73.

Hospers, J. (1967) *An Introduction to Philosophical Analysis*. London: Routledge & Kegan Paul.

Hyman, R. (1988) 'Flexible Specialisation: Miracle or Myth', in R. Hyman and W. Streek (eds), *Trade Unions, Technology and Industrial Democracy*. Oxford: Blackwell.

Iacocca, L. with Novak, W. (1984) *Iacocca – an Autobiography*. New York: Bantam.

Ilgen, D. and Klein, H. (1989) 'Organisational Behaviour', in M. Rosenweig and L. Porter (eds), *Annual Review of Psychology*, 40: 327–52.

International Labour Reports (1986) 'General Motors Brave New World'. May–June.

Irigaray, L. (1985) *This Sex Which Is Not One*. Ithaca, NY: Cornell University Press.

Jablin, F., Putnam, L., Roberts, K. and Porter, L. (eds) (1987) *Handbook of Organisational Communication*. Newbury Park, CA: Sage.

Jackall, R. (1988) *Moral Mazes: the World of Corporate Managers*. New York: Oxford University Press.

Jackson, N. (1986) 'Motivation and the Gift Relationship'. Unpublished doctoral thesis: University of Aston.

Jackson, N. and Carter, P. (1984) 'The Attenuating Function of Myth in Human Understanding, *Human Relations*, 37(7): 515–33.

Jackson, N. and Carter, P. (1986) 'Desire versus Interest', *Dragon*, 1(3): 48–60.

Jackson, N. and Carter, P. (1991) 'In Defence of Paradigm Incommensurability', *Organisation Studies*, 12(1): 109–28.

Jackson, N. and Willmott, H. (1987) 'Beyond Epistemology and Reflective Conversation: Towards Human Relations', *Human Relations*, 40(6): 361–80.

Jacobson, S.W. and Jacques, R. (1990) 'Of Knowers, Knowing and the Known: A Gender Framework for Revisioning Organisational and Management Scholarship'. Paper presented at Annual Meeting of the Academy of Management, San Francisco.

Jacoby, H. (1973) *The Bureaucratisation of the World*. Berkeley, CA: University of California Press.

Jameson, F. (1984) 'Postmodernism, or the Cultural Logic of Late Capitalism', *New Left Review*, 146: 83–93.

Jameson, F. (1985) 'Postmodernism and Consumer Society', in H. Foster (ed.), *Postmodern Culture*. London: Pluto, pp. 111–25.

Jameson, F. (1991) *Postmodernism, Or, The Cultural Logic of Late Capitalism*. London: Verso.

Jary, D. and Jary, J. (1991) *Dictionary of Sociology*. London: HarperCollins.

Jeffcutt, P.S. (1983) 'Thought in Organisations', *International Studies of Management and Organisation*, 13(2): 35–42.

Jeffcutt, P.S. (1984) 'Metaphors of the Organisation'. Paper presented to Standing Conference on Organisational Symbolism Conference, University of Lund.

Jeffcutt, P.S. (1986) 'Organisation Discourse', *CEBES Journal*, 1: 34–44.

Jeffcutt, P.C. (1988) 'Verbal Imagery and Organisation', *Dragon*, 2(3): 77–91.

Jeffcutt, P.S. (1989) 'Persistence and Change in an Organisation Culture'. Unpublished PhD thesis, University of Manchester.

Jeffcutt, P.S. (1990a) 'Transitions in a Transient Organisation', in J. Corbett (ed.), *Uneasy Traditions*. Basingstoke: Falmer.

Jeffcutt, P.S. (1990b) 'The Structures of Transition and the Transitions of Structures in Organisational Settings'. Paper presented to the Standing Conference on Organisational Symbolism Conference, University of Saarland.

Jeffcutt, P.S. (1991) 'Styles of Representation in the Analysis of Organisational Symbolism'. Paper presented to the Standing Conference on Organisational Symbolism Conference, University of Copenhagen.

Jeffcutt, P.S. (1993a) 'From Interpretation to Representation', in J. Hassard and M. Parker (eds) *Postmodernism and Organizations*. London: Sage.

Jeffcutt, P.S. (1993b) 'From Interpretation to Representation in Organisational Analysis: Postmodernism, Ethnography and Organisational Symbolism', *Organisational Studies* (in press).

Jeffcutt, P.S. (1993c) 'The Interpretation of Organisation: A Contemporary Analysis and Critique', *The Journal of Management Studies* (in press).

Jeffcutt, P.S. (forthcoming) *The Culture of Organization*. London: Sage.

Johnson, B. (1980) *The Critical Difference*. Baltimore, MD: Johns Hopkins University Press.

Jones, M., Moore, M. and Snyder, R. (eds) (1988) *Inside Organisations*. Beverly Hills, CA: Sage.

Kafka, F. (1961) *Parables and Paradoxes*. New York: Secker & Warburg.

Kanter, R.M. (1979) 'Power Failure in Management Circuits', *Harvard Business Review*. 57(4): 65–75.

Kanter, R. (1983) *The Change Masters*. London: Allen & Unwin.

Kaplan, D. and Zeigler, C. (1985) 'Class Hierarchies and Social Control', *Human Organisation*, 44(1): 83–8.

Kellner, D. (1987) 'Baudrillard, Semiurgy and Death', *Theory, Culture and Society*, 4(1): 125–46.

Kellner, D. (1988a) 'Postmodernism as Social Theory: Some Challenges and Problems', *Theory, Culture and Society*, 5(2/3): 239–70.

Kellner, D. (1988b) *Jean Baudrillard: From Marxism to Postmodernism and Beyond*. Cambridge: Polity.

Kellner, D. (1989) *Critical Theory, Marxism and Modernity*. Cambridge: Polity.

Kerr, C., Dunlop, T., Harbison, F. and Myers, C. (1963) *Industrialism and Industrial Man*. London: Heinemann.

Kets de Vries, M.F.R. (ed.) (1984) *The Irrational Executive*. New York: International Universities Press.

Kets de Vries, M.F.R. (1989a) 'The Leader as Mirror: Clinical Reflections', *Human Relations*, 42(7): 607–23.

Kets de Vries, M.F.R. (1989b) 'Leaders who Self-destruct: the Causes and Cures', *Organizational Dynamics*, 18: 5–17.

Kets de Vries, M.F.R. (1989c) 'Alexithymia in Organizational Life: the Organization Man Revisited', *Human Relations*. 42(12): 1079–93.

Kets de Vries, M.F.R. (1990) 'Leaders on the Couch: the Case of Roberto Calvi'. Paper presented at the symposium of the Clinical Approaches to the Study of Managerial and Organizational Dynamics, Montreal.

Kets de Vries, M.F.R. and Miller, D. (1984) *The Neurotic Organization*. San Francisco, CA: Jossey-Bass.

Kilmann, R., Saxon, M. and Serpa, R. (eds) (1985) *Gaining Control of the Corporate Culture*. San Francisco, CA: Jossey-Bass.

Knights, D. and Morgan, G. (1991) 'Strategic Discourse and Subjectivity: Towards a Critical Analysis of Corporate Strategy in Organisations', *Organisation Studies*, 12(2): 251–74.

Knights, D. and Willmott, H. (eds) (1990) *Labour Process Theory*. London: Macmillan.

Kohut, H. (1971) *The Analysis of the Self*. New York: International Universities Press.

Kreiner, K. (1989) 'The Postmodern Epoch of Organisation Theory'. Paper presented at the Post Modern Management Conference, Barcelona.

Kristeva, J. (1980a) *Desire in Language. A Semiotic Approach to Literature and Art*. Oxford: Blackwell.

Kristeva, J. (1980b) 'Postmodernism', *Bucknell Review*, 25: 136–41.

Kuhn, T. (1962) *The Structure of Scientific Revolutions*. Chicago, IL: Chicago University Press.

Kuhn, T. (1970) *The Structure of Scientific Revolutions*. Chicago, IL: Chicago University Press (second edition with postscript).

Kuhn, T. (1974) 'Reflection on My Critics', in I. Lakatos and A. Musgrave (eds), *Criticism and the Growth of Knowledge*. Cambridge: Cambridge University Press, pp. 231–78.

Kumazawa, M. and Yamada, J. (1988) 'Job and Skill under the Lifelong Nenko Employment Practice', in S. Wood (ed.), *The Transformation of Work*. London: Hutchinson.

Kunda, G. (1986) 'Ideology as a System of Meaning', *International Studies of Management and Organisation*, 16(1) 54–79.

Lacoue-Labarthe, P. (1986) 'On the Sublime', *ICA Documents*, 4.

Lakoff, G. and Johnson, M. (1980) *Metaphors We Live By*. Chicago, IL: Chicago University Press.

Lammers, C. and Szell, G. (eds) (1989) *International Handbook of Participation in Organisations, Volume 1*. Oxford: Oxford University Press.

Lasch, C. (1983) *The Culture of Narcissism*. New York: Warner Books.

Lash, S. (1988) 'Discourse or Figure? Postmodernism as a Regime of Signification', *Theory, Culture and Society*, 5(2/3): 311–36.

Lash, S. (1990) *Sociology of Postmodernism*. London: Routledge.

Lash, S. and Urry, J. (1987) *The End of Organised Capitalism*. Oxford: Polity.

Latour, B. (1990) *Science in Action*. Milton Keynes: Open University Press.

Lawler, E.E. and Suttle, J.L. (1973) 'Expectancy Theory and Job Behaviour', *Organisational Behaviour and Human Performance*, 9: 482–503.

Lawson, H. (1985) *Reflexivity: The Post Modern Predicament*. London: Hutchinson.

Lecercle, J.J. (1985) *Philosophy Through the Looking Glass*. London: Hutchinson.

Lefebvre, H. (1971) *Everyday Life in the Modern World*. New York: Harper & Row.

Leiss, W., Kline, S. and Jhally, S. (1986) *Social Communication in Advertising*. Toronto: Methuen.

Letiche, H. (1990) 'Five Post-modern Aphorisms for Trainers', *Management Education and Development*, 21(3): 207–18.

Linstead, S. (1984) 'Symbolism and Ambiguity in Organisations'. Paper presented to the Standing Conference on Organisational Symbolism Conference, University of Lund.

Linstead, S. (1985a) 'Organisational Induction: The Re-creation of Order and the Re-reading of Discourse', *Personnel Review*, 14(1).

Linstead, S. (1985b) 'Breaking the Purity Rule: Industrial Sabotage and the Symbolic Process', *Personnel Review*, 14(3): 12–19.

Linstead, S. and Grafton-Small, R. (1989) 'Organisational Bricolage', in B. Turner (ed.), *Organisational Symbolism*. Berlin: de Gruyter, pp. 291–309.

Linstead, S. and Grafton-Small, R. (1990a) 'Theory as Artifact: Artifact as Theory', in P. Gagliardi (ed.), *Symbols and Artefacts*. Berlin: de Gruyter, pp. 387–419.

Linstead, S. and Grafton-Small, R. (1990b) 'Corporate Culture: the Reading and the Text'. Paper presented to the British Academy of Management Conference, University of Glasgow.

Linstead, S. and Grafton-Small, R. (1991) 'On Reading Organisational Culture'. Working paper, School of Management, University of Lancaster.

Linstead, S. and Grafton-Small, R. (1992) 'On Reading Organisational Culture', *Organisation Studies*, 13(3): 331–56.

Littler, C. (1990) 'The Labour Process Debate: A Theoretical Review', in D. Knights and H. Willmott (eds), *Labour Process Theory*. London: Macmillan, pp. 46–94.

Livingstone, D.W. and Luxton, M. (1989) 'Gender Consciousness at Work: Modifications of the Male Breadwinner Norm among Steelworkers and their Spouses', *Canadian Review of Sociology and Anthropology*, 26(2): 240–75.

Lodge, D. (1990) *After Bakhtin: Essays on Fiction and Criticism*. London: Routledge.

Lundberg, C. (1985) 'On the Feasibility of Cultural Intervention in Organisations', in P. Frost et al. (eds), *Organisational Culture*. Beverly Hills, CA: Sage, pp. 169–86.

Luthans, F. (1985) *Organisational Behaviour*. New York: McGraw-Hill.

Lyotard, J-F. (1984) *The Postmodern Condition: A Report on Knowledge*. Manchester: Manchester University Press.

Lyotard, J-F. and Thébaud, J-L. (1985) *Just Gaming*. Manchester: Manchester University Press.

MacDonald, B. and Rich, C. (1983) *Look me in the Eye: Old Age, Aging and Ageism*. London: Women's Press.

Mackie, M. (1987) *Constructing Men and Women*. Toronto: Holt, Rinehart & Winston of Canada.

MacIntyre, A. (1981) *After Virtue: A Study in Moral Theory*. London: Duckworth.

Mangham, I. and Overington, M. (1987) *Organisations as Theatre*. Chichester: Wiley.

Marcus, G. and Cushman, D. (1982) 'Ethnographies as Texts', *Annual Review of Anthropology*, 11: 25–69.

Marcus, G. and Fischer, M. (1986) *Anthropology as Cultural Critique*. London: University of Chicago Press.

Marcuse, H. (1964) *One Dimensional Man*. Boston, MA: Beacon Press.

Marglin, S. (1980) 'The Origins and Function of Hierarchy in Capitalist Production', in T. Nichols (ed.), *Capital and Labour*. Glasgow: Fontana.

Marshall, H. and Wetherell, M. (1989) 'Talking about Career and Gender Identities: a Discourse Analysis Perspective', in S. Skevington and D. Baker (eds), *The Social Identity of Women*. London: Sage, pp. 106–29.

Martin, J. (1990a) 'Re-reading Weber: Searching for Feminist Alternatives to Bureaucracy'. Paper presented at the annual meeting of the Academy of Management in San Francisco.

Martin, J. (1990b) 'Deconstructing Organisational Taboos: The Suppression of Gender Conflict in Organisations', *Organisational Science*, 1(4): 339–59.

Martin, J. and Siehl, C. (1983) 'Organisational Culture and Counter Culture', *Organisational Dynamics*, 12(2): 52–64.

Martin, P.Y. (1981) 'Women, Labour Market and Employment Organisations: A Critical Analysis' in D. Dunkerley and G. Salaman (eds), *The International Yearbook of Organisation Studies, 1981*. London: Routledge & Kegan Paul, pp. 128–50.

Maslow, A. (1943) 'A Theory of Human Motivation', *Psychological Review*, 50: 370–96.

Maslow, A. (1954) *Motivation and Personality*. New York: Harper.

Mayntz, R. (1964) 'The Study of Organisations', *Current Sociology*, 13(3): 95–156.

McArthur, T. (1986) *Worlds of Reference*. Cambridge: Cambridge University Press.

McCloskey, D. (1985) *The Rhetoric of Economics*. Brighton: Harvester.

McGregor, D. (1960) *The Human Side of Enterprise*. New York: McGraw-Hill.

McNeil, K. (1978) 'Understanding Organisational Power: Building on the Weberian Legacy', *Administrative Science Quarterly*, 23(1): 65–90.

Meegan, R. (1988) 'A Crisis in Mass Production', in J. Allen and D. Massey (eds), *The Economy in Question*. London: Sage.

Meek, V. (1988) 'Organisational Culture: Origins and Weaknesses', *Organisation Studies*, 9(4): 453–73.

Meissner, M. (1986) 'The Reproduction of Women's Domination', in L. Thayer (ed.), *Organization ↔ Communication: Emerging Perspectives*. Norwood, NJ: Ablex, pp. 51–67.

Meyerson, D. and Martin, J. (1987) 'Culture Change', *Journal of Management Studies*, 24(6): 623–47.

Michels, R. (1968) *Political Parties*. London: Collier Macmillan.

Middleton, P. (1989) 'Socialism, Feminism and Men', *Radical Philosophy*, 53: 8–19.

Miller, P. and O'Leary, T. (1987) 'Accounting and the Estimation of the Governable Person', *Accounting, Organisations and Society*, 12(3): 235–66.

Mills, A.J. and Chiaramonte, P. (1991) 'Organisation as Gendered Communication', *Canadian Journal of Communication*, 16(4).

Mills, A.J. and Murgatroyd, S.J. (1991) *Organizational Rules: a Framework for Understanding Organizations*. Milton Keynes: Open University Press.

Mills, A.J. and Tancred, P. (eds) (1992) *Gendering Organizational Analysis*. Newbury Park, CA: Sage.

Mills, C.W. (1959) *The Sociological Imagination*. Harmondsworth: Penguin.

Mintzberg, H. (1983) *Structure in Fives: Designing Effective Organisations*. Englewood Cliffs, NJ: Prentice Hall.

Mitroff, I. and Kilmann, R. (1985) 'Corporate Taboos as the Key to Unlocking Culture', in R. Kilmann et al. (eds), *Gaining Control of the Corporate Culture*. San Francisco, CA: Jossey-Bass, pp. 184–9.

Mitter, S. (1985) 'Industrial Restructuring and Manufacturing Homework: Immigrant Women in the UK Clothing Industry', *Capital and Class*, 27.

Moi, T. (1985) *Sexual/Textual Politics. Feminist Literary Theory*. London: Routledge.

Morgan, G. (1980) 'Paradigms, Metaphors and Puzzle Solving in Organization Theory', *Administrative Science Quarterly*, 25: 605–22.

Morgan, G. (1983a) 'More on Metaphor: Why We Cannot Control Tropes in Administrative Science', *Administrative Science Quarterly*, 28: 601–8.

Morgan, G. (ed.) (1983b) *Beyond Method*. London: Sage.

Morgan, G. (1986) *Images of Organisation*. London: Sage.

Morgan, G. (1988) *Riding the Waves of Change*. San Francisco, CA: Jossey-Bass.

Morgan, G. (1990) *Organisations in Society*. London: Macmillan.

Morgan, G., Frost, P. and Pondy, L. (1983) 'Organisational Symbolism', in L. Pondy et al. (eds), *Organisational Symbolism*. Greenwich, CT: JAI Press, pp. 3–35.

Morris, J. (ed.) (1989) *Able Lives: Women's Experience of Paralysis*. London: Women's Press.

Morris, J. (1991) *Pride Against Prejudice, Transforming Attitudes to Disability*. London: Women's Press.

Morris, M. (1988) *The Pirate's Fiancee: Feminism, Reading, Postmodernism*. London: Verso.

Mulgan, G. (1989) 'The Power of the Weak' in S. Hall and M. Jacques (eds), *New Times*. London: Lawrence and Wishart, pp. 347–63.

Mulkay, M. (1990) *Sociology of Science: A Sociological Pilgrimage*. Milton Keynes: Open University Press.

Mumby, D.K. and Putnam, L.L. (1992) 'Bounded Rationality as an Organisational Construct: A Feminist Critique', *Academy of Management Review*, 17.

Murphy, J.W. (1988) 'Making Sense of Postmodern Sociology', *British Journal of Sociology*, 39(4): 600–14.

Murray, F. (1987) 'Flexible Specialisation and the Third Italy', *Capital and Class*, 33: 84–95.

Naisbett, J. (1982) *Megatrends*. New York: Warren Books.

Nelson, A. (1990) 'Equal Opportunities: Dilemmas, Contradictions, White Men and Class', *Critical Social Policy*, 28: 25–42.

Nicholson, L.J. (ed.) (1990) *Feminism/Postmodernism*. London: Routledge.

Norris, C. (1985) *The Contest of Faculties: Philosophy and Theory after Deconstruction*. London: Methuen.

Norris, C. (1987) *Derrida*. Cambridge, MA: Harvard University Press.

Norris, C. (1990) *What's Wrong with Postmodernism: Critical Theory and the Ends of Philosophy*. London: Harvester Wheatsheaf.

O'Brien, M. (1981) *The Politics of Reproduction*. London: Routledge & Kegan Paul.

O'Brien, M. (1984) 'The Commatization of Women', *Interchange: A Quarterly Review of Education*, 15(2): 43–60.

Ödeen, M. (1988) *Dramatiskt Berattande*. Köthen, Germany: Carlsson.

Oliver, M. (1990) *The Politics of Disability*. London: Macmillan.

Olson, C. (1970) *The Special View of History*. Berkeley, CA: Oyez.

O'Neill, J. (1986) 'The Disciplinary Society', *British Journal of Sociology*, 31(1): 42–60.

O'Neill, J. (1988) 'Religion and Postmodernism: The Durkheimian Bond in Bell and Jameson', in M. Featherstone (ed.), *Theory, Culture and Society*, special issue 5(2/3): 225–39.

Oseen, C. (1991) 'A Feminist Poststructuralist Reconceptualization of Organizational Theory as it Pertains to the Organizational Newcomer'. Paper presented at the Critical Approaches to Organizations session of the annual meeting of the Canadian Sociology and Anthropology Association, Queens University, Ontario.

Ouchi, W. and Jaeger, A. (1978) 'Type Z Organisation: Stability in the Midst of Mobility', *Academy of Management Review*, 3: 293–317.

Ouchi, W. and Wilkins, A. (1985) 'Organisational Culture', *Annual Review of Sociology*, 11: 457–83.

Parker, I. (1989) 'Discourse and Power', in J. Shotter and K. Gergen (eds), *Texts of Identity*. London: Sage, 56–89.

Parker, M. (1992a) 'Postmodern Organisations or Postmodern Organisation Theory?', *Organisation Studies*, 13(1): 1–17.

Parker, M. (1992b) 'Getting Down from the Fence: A Reply to Tsoukas', *Organisation Studies*, 13(4): 651–3.

Parkin, W. (1989) 'Private Experiences in the Public Domain: Sexuality and Residential Care Organisations', in J. Hearn et al. (eds), *The Sexuality of Organization*. London: Sage, pp. 110–24.

Pearce, W.B. and Chen, V. (1989) 'Ethnography as Sermonic: The Rhetorics of Clifford Geertz and James Clifford', in H.W. Simons (ed.), *Rhetoric in the Human Sciences*. London: Sage, pp. 119–32.

Peitchinis, S.G. (1989) *Women at work.* Toronto: McClelland & Stewart.

Pepper, S. (1972) *World Hypotheses*. Berkeley, CA: University of California Press.

Perry, N. (1992) 'Putting Theory in its Place: The Social Organisation of Organisational Theorising', in M. Reed and M. Hughes (eds), *Rethinking Organisation*. London: Sage, pp. 85–101.

Peters, T. (1987) *Thriving on Chaos*. London: Macmillan.

Peters, T. and Waterman, R. (1982) *In Search of Excellence*. New York: Harper & Row.

Pettigrew, A. (1979) 'On Studying Organisational Cultures', *Administrative Science Quarterly*, 24(4): 570–81.

Pettigrew, A. (1985) *The Awakening Giant: Continuity and Change in ICI*. Oxford: Blackwell.

Pheby, K. (1988) *Interventions: Displacing the Metaphysical Subject*. Washington, DC: Maissoneuve.

Pinder, C. and Bourgeois, V. (1982) 'Controlling Tropes in Administrative Science', *Administrative Science Quarterly*, 27: 601–8.

Piore, M. and Sabel, C. (1984) *The Second Industrial Divide*. New York: Basic Books.

Plato (1976) *The Republic*. Harmondsworth: Penguin.

Platt, R. (1989) 'Reflexivity, Recursion and Social Life: Elements for a Postmodern Sociology', *Sociological Review*, 37(4): 636–67.

Pollert, A. (1988) 'Dismantling Flexibility', *Capital and Class*, 34: 42–75.

Pondy, L.R., Frost, P.J., Morgan, G. and Danridge, T.C. (eds) (1983) *Organizational Symbolism*. Greenwich, CT: JAI Press.

Poole, R. (1991) *Morality and Modernity*. London: Routledge.

Popper, K. (1986) *Unended Quest*. Glasgow: Flamingo.

Porter, L.W. and Lawler, E.E. (1968) *Managerial Attitudes and Performance*. Homewood, IL: Irwin.

Poster, M. (1984) *Foucault, Marxism and History*. Cambridge: Polity.

Poster, M. (1990) *The Mode of Information: Poststructuralism and Social Context*. Oxford: Polity.

Power, M. (1990) 'Modernism, Postmodernism and Organisation', in J. Hassard and D. Pym (eds), *The Theory and Philosophy of Organisations*. London: Routledge, pp. 109–24.

Pringle, R. (1989a) 'Bureaucracy, Rationality and Sexuality: The Case of Secretaries', in J. Hearn et al. (eds), *The Sexuality of Organization*. London: Sage, pp. 158–77.

Pringle, R. (1989b) *Secretaries Talk*. London: Verso.

Quinn, R. and Cameron, K. (eds) (1988) *Paradox as Transformation; Towards a Theory of Change in Organisation and Management*. Cambridge, MA: Ballinger.

Rabinow, P. (1986a) 'Representations are Social Facts: Modernity and Post Modernity in Anthropology', in J. Clifford and G. Marcus (eds), *Writing Culture*. London: University of California Press, pp. 234–61.

Rabinow, P. (1986b) *The Foucault Reader*. London: Penguin.

Rainnie, A. (1988) *Employment Relations in the Small Firm*. London: Routledge & Kegan Paul.

Rakow, L.F. (1986) 'Rethinking Gender Research in Communication', *Journal of Communication*, 36(4): 11–24.

Ravetz, J. (1971) *Scientific Knowledge and its Social Problems*. London: Routledge.

Ray, C. (1986) 'Corporate Culture: The Last Frontier of Control', *Journal of Management Studies*, 23(3): 287–97.

Reed, M. (1985) *Redirections in Organisational Analysis*. London: Tavistock.

Reed, M. (1989) 'The End of Organised Society: A Theme in Search of a Theory', paper presented to Rethinking Organization Conference, University of Lancaster.

Reed, M. (1990a) 'The Labour Process Perspective on Management Organisation: A Critique and Reformulation', in J. Hassard and D. Pym (eds), *The Theory and Philosophy of Organisations*. London: Routledge, pp. 63–82.

Reed, M. (1990b) 'From Paradigms to Images: The Paradigm Warrior Turns Postmodernist Guru', *Personnel Review*, 19(3): 35–40.

Reed, M. (1991a) 'The Disorganised Society: A Theme in Search of a Theory?', in P. Blyton and I. Morris (eds), *A Flexible Future? Prospects for Employment and Organisation*. Berlin: de Gruyter, pp. 23–42.

Reed, M. (1991b) 'Scripting Scenarios for a New Organisation: Theory and Practice', *Work, Employment and Society*, 5(1): 119–32.

Reed, M. (1991c) 'A Revolution in the Study of Work?', *British Journal of Industrial Relations*, 29(3): 507–12.

Reed, M. (1992) *The Sociology of Organisations*. London: Harvester.

Reed, M. and Anthony, P. (1992) 'Professionalising Management and Managing Professionalisation: British Management in the 1980s', *Journal of Management Studies*, June.

Reed, M.I. and Hughes, M.D. (eds) (1992) *Rethinking Organization: New Directions in Organizational Research and Analysis*. London: Sage.

Reich R.B. (1991) *The Work of Nations*. London: Simon & Schuster.

Ricoeur, P. (1978) 'Metaphor and the Main Problem of Hermeneutics', in *The Philosophy of Paul Ricoeur*. Boston, MA: Beacon Press.

Riley, D. (1988) *'Am I That Name?' Feminism and the Category of Women in History*. London: Macmillan.

Robbe-Grillet, A. (1977) 'Order and Disorder in Film and Fiction', *Critical Enquiry*, 4: 1–20.

Robbins, S.P. (1991) *Organisational Behaviour*. Englewood Cliffs, NJ: Prentice Hall.

Roethlisberger, F. (1977) *The Elusive Phenomena*. Boston, MA: Harvard University Press.

Rogers, R. (1990) *Architecture: a Modern View*. London: Thames & Hudson.

Rorty, R. (1979) *Philosophy and the Mirror of Nature*. Princeton, NJ: Princeton University Press.

Rorty, R. (1982) *Consequences of Pragmatism*. Minneapolis, MN: University of Minnesota Press.

Rosaldo, M.Z. (1974) 'Women, Culture and Society: a Theoretical Overview', in M.Z. Rosaldo and L. Lamphere (eds), *Women, Culture and Society*. Stanford, CA: Stanford University Press, pp. 17–42.

Rosaldo, R. (1989) *Culture and Truth*. Boston, MA: Beacon Press.

Rose, G. (1988) 'Architecture to Philosophy – the Postmodern Complicity', in M. Featherstone (ed.), *Theory, Culture and Society*, special issue, 5(2/3): 357–71.

Rose, M. (1988) *Industrial Behaviour*. London: Penguin.

Rose, N. (1989) *Governing the Soul: The Shaping of the Private Self*. London: Routledge.

Rosen, M. (1985) 'Breakfast at Spiro's: Dramaturgy and Dominance', *Journal of Management*. 11(2): 31–48.

Rosen, M. (1986) 'Some Notes from the Field', *Dragon*, 1(6): 57–77.

Rosen, M. (1988) 'You Asked for It: Christmas at the Bosses' Expense', *Journal of Management Studies*, 25(5): 463–81.

Rosen, M. (1990) 'Crashing in '87: Power and Symbolism in the Dow', in P. Gagliardi (ed.), *Symbols and Artefacts*. Berlin: de Gruyter, pp. 115–35.

Rosen, M. (1991) 'Coming to Terms with the Field: Understanding and Doing Organisational Ethnography', *Journal of Management Studies*, 28(1): 1–24.

Ryan, M. (1982) *Marxism and Deconstruction: A Critical Articulation*. Baltimore, MD: Johns Hopkins University Press.

Ryan, M. (1988) 'Postmodern Politics', in M. Featherstone (ed.), *Theory, Culture and Society*, special issue, 5(2/3): 559–76.

Sahlins, M. (1985) *Islands of History*. Chicago, IL: University of Chicago Press.

Said, E. (1978) *Orientalism*. London: Routledge.

Sampson, E. (1989) 'The Deconstruction of the Self', in J. Shotter and K. Gergen (eds), *Texts of Identity*. London: Sage, pp. 1–19.

Sandelands, L. and Buckner, G. (1989) 'Of Art and Work: Aesthetic Experience and the Psychology of Work Feelings', *Research in Organisational Behaviour*, 2: 105–31.

Sandelands, L. and Drazin, R. (1989) 'On the Language of Organisation Theory', *Organisation Studies*, 10(4): 457–77.

Sandelands, L. and Strivatsan, V. (1989) 'Experience and Organisation Studies'. Draft paper, University of Michigan.

Sangren, P.S. (1988) 'Rhetoric and the Authority of Ethnography', *Current Anthropology*, 29(3): 405–24.

Saussure, F. de (1974) *Course in General Linguistics*. London: Fontana.

Sayer, D. (1991) *Capitalism and Modernity*. London: Routledge.

Schein, E. (1980) *Organisational Psychology*. Englewood Cliffs, NJ: Prentice Hall.

Schein, E. (1985) 'How Culture Forms, Develops and Changes', in R. Kilmann et al. (eds), *Gaining Control of the Corporate Culture*. San Francisco, CA: Jossey-Bass, pp. 17–43.

Schattschneider, E.E. (1960) *The Semi-Sovereign People: A Realist View of Democracy in America*. New York: Holt, Rinehart & Winston.

Schneider, S. and Shrivastava, P. (1984) 'The Content of Basic Assumptions'. Paper presented to the Standing Conference on Organisational Symbolism Conference, University of Lund.

Schön, D. (1979) 'Generative Metaphor', in A. Ortony (ed.), *Metaphor*. Cambridge: Cambridge University Press.

Schultz, M. (1989) 'Postmodern Pictures of Corporate Culture'. Paper presented at the Post Modern Management Conference, Barcelona.

Schwab, D.P., Olan-Gottleib, J.D. and Heneman, H.G. (1979) 'Between-subjects Expectancy Theory Research', *Psychological Bulletin*, 86(1): 139–47.

Schwartz, H. (1990) 'The Symbol of the Space Shuttle and the Degeneration of the American Dream', in P. Gagliardi (ed.), *Symbols and Artefacts*. Berlin: de Gruyter, pp. 301–24.

Seabrook, J. (1990) *The Myth of the Market: Promises and Illusions*. Hartland: Green Books.

Seidman, S. (1992) 'Postmodern Social Theory as Narrative with a Moral Intent', in S. Seidman and D. Wagner (eds), *Postmodernism and Social Theory*. Oxford: Blackwell, pp. 47–81.

Seidman, S. and Wagner, D.G. (eds) (1992) *Postmodernism and Social Theory*. Oxford: Blackwell.

Shotter, J. and Gergen, K. (eds) (1989) *Texts of Identity*. London: Sage.

Shusterman, R. (1988) 'Postmodernist Aestheticism: A New Moral Philosophy', in M. Featherstone (ed.), *Theory, Culture and Society*, special issue, 5(2/3): 337–56.

Sievers, B. (1987) 'Work, Death and Life Itself'. Working Paper 98, Bergische University.

Silver, J. (1987) 'The Ideology of Excellence: Management and Neo-Conservatism', *Studies in Political Economy*, 24: 105–29.

Silverman, D. (1970) *The Theory of Organisations*. London: Heinemann.

Silverman, D. (1975) *Reading Castaneda: A Prologue to the Social Sciences*. London: Routledge.

Silverman, D. (1985) *Qualitative Methodology and Sociology*. London: Gower.

Silverman, D. (1991) 'On Throwing Away Ladders: Re-writing the Theory of Organisations'. Paper presented to the New Theory of Organisations Conference, University of Keele.

Silverman, D. and Jones, J. (1976) *Organisational Work*. London: Collier Macmillan.

Slatter, S. (1984) *Corporate Recovery*. Harmondsworth: Penguin.

Smart, B. (1990) 'Modernity, Postmodernity and the Present', in B.S. Turner (ed.), *Theories of Modernity and Postmodernity*. London: Sage, pp. 14–30.

Smart, B. (1992) *Modern Conditions, Postmodern Controversies*. London: Routledge.

Smircich, L. (1983a) 'Concepts of Culture and Organisational Analysis', *Administrative Science Quarterly*, 28: 339–58.

Smircich, L. (1983b) 'Organisations as Shared Meanings', in L. Pondy et al. (eds), *Organisational Symbolism*. Greenwich, CT: JAI Press, pp. 55–68.

Smircich, L. (1985) 'Is Organisational Culture a Paradigm for Understanding Organisations and Ourselves?', in P. Frost et al. (eds), *Organisational Culture*. Beverly Hills, CA: Sage, pp. 55–72.

Smircich, L. and Calás, M. (1987) 'Organisational Culture: A Critical Assessment', in F. Jablin et al. (eds), *Handbook of Organisational Communication*. Newbury Park, CA: Sage.

Smith, C. (1989) 'Flexible Specialisation, Automation and Mass Production', *Work, Employment and Society*, 3(2): 203–20.

Smith, C., Child, J. and Rowlinson, M. (1990) *Reshaping Work: The Cadbury Experience*. Cambridge: Cambridge University Press.

Smith, K. and Simmons, V. (1983) 'A Rumplestiltskin Organisation: Metaphors on Metaphors in Field Research, *Administrative Science Quarterly*, 28(3): 377–92.

Sontag, S. (1966) *Against Interpretation*. New York: Farrar Strauss Giroux.

Spencer, J. (1989) 'Anthropology as a Kind of Writing', *Man*, 24(1): 145–64.

Spender, D. and Sarah, E. (1980) *Learning to Lose, Sexism and Education*. London: Women's Press.

Sperber, D. (1975) *Rethinking Symbolism*. Cambridge: Cambridge University Press.

Stablein, R. (1989) 'Structure of Debate in Organisation Studies'. Paper presented at Academy of Management meeting, Washington DC.

Stallybrass, P. and White, A. (1986) *The Politics and Poetics of Transgression*. London: Methuen.

Stanley, L. (1990) 'Doing Ethnography: Writing Ethnography – A Comment on Hammersley', *Sociology*, 24(4): 617–27.

Starkey, K., Wright, M. and Thompson, S. (1991) 'Flexibility, Heirarchy, Markets', *British Journal of Management*, 2(3): 165–76.

Strumingher, L.S. (1979) *Women and the Making of the Working Class of Lyon, 1830–1870*. Vermont: Eden Press.

Stuart-Hughes, H. (1958) *Consciousness and Society: The Re-orientation of European Social Thought*. New York: Vintage Books.

Sutton, R. (1987) 'The Process of Organisational Death', *Administrative Science Quarterly*, 32: 542–69.

Sypher, B., Applegate, J. and Sypher, H. (1985) 'Culture and Communication in Organisational Contexts', in W. Gudykunst et al. (eds), *Communication, Culture and Organisational Process*. Beverly Hills, CA: Sage.

Taylor, F. (1947) *Scientific Management*. New York: Harper & Row.

Taylor, N. (ed.) (1986) *All in a Day's Work. A Report on Anti-Lesbian Discrimination in Employment and Unemployment in London*. London: Lesbian Employment Rights.

Tester, K. (1990) 'The Uses of Error: The Collapse of "Really Existing Socialism"', *Telos*, 83: 151–61.

Thayer, L. (ed.) (1986) *Organization* ↔ *Communication: Emerging Perspectives*. Norwood, NJ: Ablex.

Thomas, A. (1989) 'One Minute Management Education', *Management Education and Development*, 20(1): 23–38.

Thompson, E. (1978) *The Poverty of Theory and Other Essays*. London: Merlin.

Thompson, J. (1983) *Learning Liberation*. Beckenham: Croom Helm.

Thompson, P. (1989) *The Nature of Work*. London: Macmillan.

Thompson, P. and Bannon, E. (1985) *Working the System*. London: Pluto.

Thompson, P. and McHugh, D. (1990) *Work Organisations: A Critical Introduction*. London: Macmillan.

Thompson, P., Wallace, T. and Flecker, J. (1991) 'Taking Control: An Analysis of the Organisational Consequences of Mergers and Acquisitions in Britain and Austria'. Paper presented at the EGOS Conference, Vienna.

Tinker, T. (1986) 'Metaphor or Reification: Are Radical Humanists Really Libertarian Anarchists?', *Journal of Management Studies*, 25: 363–84.

Toulmin, S. (1972) *Human Understanding, Volume 1*. Princeton, NJ: Princeton University Press.

Townley, B. (1990) 'Foucault, Power/Knowledge and its Relevance for HRM', Paper presented at Employment Research Unit Conference at Cardiff Business School.

Travers, A. (1989) 'Symbolic Life and Organisation Research in a Postmodern Frame', in B. Turner (ed.), *Organisational Symbolism*. Berlin: de Gruyter, pp. 271–90.

Trice, H. (1985) 'Rites and Ceremonials in Organisational Cultures', *Research in the Sociology of Organisations*, 4: 221–70.

Tsoukas, H. (1991a) 'The Missing Link: A Transformational View of Metaphors in Organisational Science', *Academy of Management Review*, 16: 566–85.

Tsoukas, H. (1991b) 'Analogies and Metaphors in Organisational Theory: A Critical Review'. Paper presented at Towards a New Theory of Organisations Conference, University of Keele.

Tsoukas, H. (1992) 'Postmodernism, Reflective Rationalism and Organizational Studies: A Reply to Martin Parker', *Organisation Studies*, 13(4): 641–9.

Turner, B. (1978) *Man Made Disasters*. London: Wykeham Press.

Turner, B. (1986) 'Sociological Aspects of Organisational Symbolism', *Organisation Studies*, 7(2): 101–15.

Turner, B. (1988) 'Connoisseurship in the Study of Organisational Cultures', in A. Bryman (ed.), *Doing Research in Organizations*. London: Routledge, pp. 108–22.

Turner, B. (ed.) (1989) *Organisational Symbolism*. Berlin: de Gruyter.

Turner, B. (1990) 'The Rise of Organisational Symbolism', in J. Hassard and D. Pym (eds), *The Theory and Philosophy of Organisations*. London: Routledge, pp. 83–96.

Turner, B.S. (ed.) (1990) *Theories of Modernity and Postmodernity*. London: Sage.

Turner, C. (1990) 'Lyotard and Weber: Postmodern Rules and Neo-Kantian Values', in B.S. Turner (ed.), *Theories of Modernity and Postmodernity*. London: Sage, pp. 108–16.

Turner, E. (ed.) (1986) *On the Edge of the Bush: Anthropology as Experience*. Tucson, AZ: University of Arizona Press.

Turner, S. (1977) 'Complex Organisations as Savage Tribes', *Journal for the Theory of Social Behaviour*, 7: 99–125.

Turner, S. (1983) 'Studying Organisation Through Levi-Strauss's Structuralism', in G. Morgan (ed.), *Beyond Method*. London: Sage, pp. 189–201.

Turner, V. (1974) *Dramas, Fields and Metaphors*. Ithaca, NY: Cornell University Press.

Turner, V. (1986) *Anthropology of Performance*. New York: Performing Arts Journal Publications.

Tyler, S. (1986) 'Post Modern Ethnography', in J. Clifford and G. Marcus (eds), *Writing Culture*. London: University of California Press, pp. 122–40.

Ure, A. (1965) *The Philosophy of Manufactures* (first published, 1835). New York: Harper & Row.

Ussher, J. (1991) *Women's Madness: Misogyny or Mental Illness.* Hemel Hempstead: Harvester Wheatsheaf.

Van de Ven, A. and Poole, M. (1988) 'Paradoxical Requirements for a Theory of Change', in R. Quinn and K. Cameron (eds), *Paradox as Transformation.* Cambridge, MA: Ballinger.

Van Maanen, J. (ed.) (1983) *Qualitative Methodology.* Beverly Hills, CA: Sage.

Van Maanen, J. (1988) *Tales of the Field.* Chicago, IL: Chicago University Press.

Van Maanen, J. and Kolb, D. (1985) 'The Professional Apprentice', *Research in the Sociology of Organisations,* 4: 1–33.

Velikovsky, I. (1971) *Worlds in Collision.* London: Macmillan.

Venn, D. (1984) 'The Subject of Psychology', in J. Henriques et al. (eds), *Changing the Subject.* London: Methuen, pp. 119–52.

Von Vucht Tijssen, L. (1990) 'Women Between Modernity and Postmodernity', in B. Turner (ed.), *Theories of Modernity and Postmodernity.* London: Sage, pp. 147–63.

Vroom, V.H. (1964) *Work and Motivation.* New York: Wiley.

Wakefield, N. (1990) *Postmodernism.* London: Pluto.

Waldo, D. (1968) *The Novelist on Organisation and Administration: an Enquiry into the Relationship Between Two Worlds.* University of California, Berkeley, CA: Institute of Governmental Studies.

Walkerdine, V. (1990) *School Girl Fictions.* London: Virago.

Walter, G.A. (1983) 'Psyche and Symbol', in Pondy et al. (eds), *Organizational Symbolism.* Greenwich, CT: JAI Press, pp. 257–71.

Weber, M. (1967) *The Protestant Ethic and the Spirit of Capitalism.* London: Unwin.

Weber, S. (1990) 'The Vaulted Eye; Remarks on Knowledge and Professionalism', *Yale French Studies,* 77: 44–60.

Webster, J. and Starbuck, W.H. (1988) 'Theory Building in Industrial and Organisational Psychology', in C.L. Cooper and I. Robertson (eds), *International Review of Industrial and Organisational Psychology.* Chichester: Wiley, pp. 93–138.

Webster, S. (1982) 'Dialogue and Fiction in Ethnographic Truth', *Dialectical Anthropology,* 8: 91–114.

Webster, S. (1983) 'Ethnography as Storytelling', *Dialectical Anthropology,* 8: 185–205.

Weick, K. (1985) 'The Significance of Corporate Culture', in P. Frost et al. (eds), *Organisational Culture.* Beverly Hills, CA: Sage, pp. 381–90.

Weinstein, D. and Weinstein, M.A. (1990) 'Simmel and the Theory of Postmodern Society', in B.S. Turner (ed.), *Theories of Modernity and Postmodernity.* London: Sage, pp. 75–87.

Welleck, R. and Warren, A. (1967) *Litteraturteori.* Malmö: Aldus/Bonniers.

Wetherell, M., Stiven, H. and Potter, J. (1987) 'Unequal Egalitarianism: a Preliminary Study of Discourses Concerning Gender and Employment Opportunities', *British Journal of Social Psychology.* 26: 59–71.

Whitaker, A. (1992) 'The Transformation in Work', in M. Reed and M. Hughes (eds), *Rethinking Organisation.* London: Sage, pp. 184–206.

White, H. (1987) *The Content of the Form.* Baltimore, MD: Johns Hopkins University Press.

White, S.K. (1987/88) 'Justice and the Postmodern Problematic', *Praxis International,* 7(3/4): 306–19.

Whitley, R. (1984) 'The Fragmented State of Management Studies: Reasons and Consequences', *Journal of Management Studies,* 21(1): 331–48.

Whittington, R. (1989) *Corporate Strategies in Recession and Recovery.* London: Unwin Hyman.

Whyte, W.H. (1956) *The Organization Man.* New York: Simon & Schuster.

Wickham, G. (1987) 'Turning the Law into Laws for Political Analysis', in G. Wickham (ed.), *Social Theory and Legal Politics.* Sydney: Local Consumption Publications, pp. 40–54.

Wickham, G. (1990) 'The Political Possibilities of Postmodernism', *Economy and Society,* 19(1): 121–49.

Wilkins, A. and Ouchi, W. (1983) 'Efficient Cultures', *Administrative Science Quarterly*, 28(3): 468–81.

Williams, K. et al. (1987) 'The End of Mass Production', *Economy and Society*, 16(3): 405–39.

Willis, P. (1977) *Learning to Labour*. Farnborough: Saxon House.

Willis, P. (1983) 'Cultural Production and Reproduction', in L. Barton and S. Walker (eds), *Race, Class and Education*. London: Croom Helm.

Willis, P. (1990) *Common Culture*. Milton Keynes: Open University Press.

Willmott, H. (1990) 'Beyond Paradigmatic Closure in Organisational Enquiry', in J. Hassard and D. Pym (eds), *The Theory and Philosophy of Organisation*. London: Routledge, pp. 44–62.

Willmott, H. (1991) 'Theorising Agency: Power and Subjectivity in Organisation Studies'. Paper presented to New Theory of Organisations Conference, University of Keele.

Wittgenstein, L. (1953) *Philosophical Investigations*. London: Blackwell.

Wittgenstein, L. (1958) *The Blue and Brown Books*. London: Blackwell.

Wolff, J. (1987) *The Social Production of Art*. Hong Kong: Macmillan.

Wolin, S. (1988) 'On the Theory and Practice of Power', in J. Arac (ed.), *After Foucault: Humanistic Knowledge, Postmodern Challenges*. New Brunswick, NJ: Rutgers University Press, pp. 179–201.

Worton, M. and Still, J. (eds) (1990) *Intertextuality*. Manchester: Manchester University Press.

Wright, P. (1987) 'Excellence', *London Review of Books*, 21 May: 8–11.

Wuthnow, R. (1987) *Meaning and Moral Order – Explorations in Cultural Analysis*. Berkeley, CA: University of California Press.

Wyndham, J. (1954) *The Day of the Triffids*. Harmondsworth: Penguin.

Young, E. (1989) 'On the Naming of the Rose: Interests and Multiple Meanings as Elements of Organisational Culture', *Organisation Studies*, 10(2): 187–206.

Zaleznik, A. and Kets de Vries, M. (1984) *Leadership as a Text. An Essay on Interpretation*. Research Report, Harvard Business School.

Zuboff, S. (1988) *In the Age of the Smart Machine*. London: Heinemann.

Index